VISIONS OF PERSIA

HARVARD STUDIES IN COMPARATIVE LITERATURE
FOUNDED BY WILLIAM HENRY SCHOFIELD
48

VISIONS OF PERSIA

MAPPING THE TRAVELS OF ADAM OLEARIUS

ELIO CHRISTOPH BRANCAFORTE

HARVARD UNIVERSITY DEPARTMENT OF COMPARATIVE LITERATURE

DISTRIBUTED BY HARVARD UNIVERSITY PRESS

CAMBRIDGE, MASSACHUSETTS, AND LONDON, ENGLAND

2003

PRINTED IN THE UNITED STATES OF AMERICA

FIRST PRINTING

ISBN 0-674-01221-6 (cl.)
ISBN 0-674-01254-2 (pa.)
Library of Congress Control Number: 2003112568

This book is printed on acid-free paper, and its binding materials have been chosen for strength and durability.

To my parents,
BB and CB,
for many an idea . . .
and for aid
in all its (DIS)guises

We can distinguish five grades of travelers: those of the first and lowest grade are those who travel and, instead of seeing, are themselves seen — they actually become traveled and are as though blind; next come those who actually see the world; the third experience something as a consequence of what they have seen; the fourth absorb into themselves what they have experienced and bear it away with them; lastly there are a few men of highest energy who, after they have experienced and absorbed all they have seen, necessarily have to body it forth again out of themselves in works and actions as soon as they have returned home. It is like these five species of traveler that all men travel through the whole journey of life, the lowest purely passive, the highest those who transform into action and exhaust everything they experience.

— Friedrich Nietzsche, *Human All Too Human*

Contents

Illustrations

Acknowledgments

It has been a long journey of discovery, made all the more pleasurable because of the help and support I have received from many individuals along the way.

First, and foremost, I would like to express my gratitude to Peter Burgard, and to David Roxburgh, and Judith Ryan for their insightful reading of this work during the various stages of its development.

This study was born in Germany, and I would like to thank Wilfried Barner, Hannah Weischedel, as well as Jill Bepler, Martin Bircher, Christian Hogrefe, and Mara Wade for their advice; and Dieter Lohmeier, for his insights on the Gottorf court. I am grateful to Günther Findel for awarding me a fellowship to the Herzog August Bibliothek in Wolfenbüttel; and the American-Scandinavian Foundation, as well as the Lois Roth Endowment for allowing me to conduct research at the Danish Royal Library in Copenhagen.

At Harvard University I was able to develop my topic with the help of many teachers, colleagues and friends: Christopher Braider, Sandra Naddaff, Marc Shell, and Jan Ziolkowski; as well as Begoña Aretxaga, Tom Conley, and Roy Mottahedeh. For their comments on different sections of the book I am grateful to Alix Cooper and Barbard Keys; Jaime Javier Rodríguez, Markus Schmidt, and Ramyar Rossoukh; and especially Jülide Aker, Charles Cabell, and Glenn Magid.

In the Department of Comparative Literature, I should like to thank Bette Anne Farmer, who was there at the beginning, and Kathy George, who was there at the end.

At Dudley House, Susan Zawalich's kindness and energy were an inspiration. Thanks are due also to David Woodberry and Chad Conlan for their help.

At the Harvard Map Library, I was fortunate to have Joseph Garver introduce me to the world of cartography. I should also like to thank David Cobb, Martin von Wyss, and Bonnie Burns for their advice with cartographic matters.

I am indebted to the staff at the Houghton and Widener Libraries, in particular John Emerson, Thomas Ford, and Susan Halpert.

I would also like to thank a number of friends for their help over the years: Michele Jaffe, Charitini Douvaldzi, Geraldine Grimm, Erdem Cipa, Andrew Cohen, and Jack Cheng; as well as Juyun and Namwon Song. For their long-distance advice, I am grateful to Antoine Gourdon, Rob Voynow, Sajeel Khan, Jerry Hunter, and Kenneth Marty.

For matters concerning the world of Safavid Persia, I would like to thank Farhad Hakimzadeh, Willem Floor, Houchang Chehabi, and Rudi Matthee, as well as Bruce Fudge and Nagmeh Sohrabi. Sonja Brentjes gave valuable advice on Islamic cartography, and Guive Mirfendereski shared his knowledge of Persian geography with me. I am also grateful to the Hafezi family, who made me feel at home in Iran.

At Tulane University I benefited from the advice of William Craft Brumfield, George Cummins, and Jaimey Fisher, as well as the assistance of Clay McGovern, Sean Russell, and Cheryl Catron. Olga Tapperwijn assisted me with Dutch translations; Kheireddine Bekkai with Arabic, and Hanneke Grootenboer with Dutch Baroque art.

I would like to thank Susan Hayes for her expert editorial assistance, and for seeing the manuscript through its final stages.

I am grateful to the Herzog August Bibliothek Wolfenbüttel, the Sächsische Landesbibliothek- Staats- und Universitätsbibliothek Dresden, the Houghton Library at Harvard College, the Harvard Map Library, the Burndy Library (Dibner Institute for the History of Science and Technology, Cambridge, Massachusetts), and the Rare Books Division of the Princeton University Library for having granted me permission to reproduce material from their collections.

Finally, from the "inner circle," I am grateful to Irina Shingiray for her support and for sharing her expertise on the Volga, the Caspian Sea, and Tatar ethnography. I should also like to thank my sisters, Daniela and Stephanie for their help and encouragement, and for many conversations on literature and anthropology. And all this would not have been possible without my parents, Charlotte Lang and Benito Brancaforte, who not only introduced me to the Baroque, but who also took me along on their own travels.

Introduction

In the following study I shall examine how aspects of Safavid Persia are portrayed in Adam Olearius's visual and narrative work and how he creates a representation of the land for a Western audience. I will analyze two specific works that belong to genres that combine word and image, as well as art and science: the frontispiece and the map. While some scholars have considered the engravings produced at the Gottorf court, the works I have chosen to analyze have not yet been examined in light of the visual and discursive nexus in Olearius's depiction of the "other," namely how word and image interact in order to create a more complete understanding of the country visited. The author follows a specific strategy in bringing both the visual and the discursive into play, and underlines the fact that both are necessary in order to represent the reality that he has experienced. This strategy also raises questions concerning the role of the reader/viewer, who constantly has to switch back and forth from the text to the image in order to understand what is happening in the account. As Tom Conley, in discussing the word/image dichotomy in Early-Modern French cartography, observes: "The mass of textual material that accompanies single-sheet or atlas maps tends to reveal its ideological perspective in the gaps between a silent, spatial, schematic rendering of an area (in visual form) and a voluble, copious, emphatic, printed discourse that strives to tell of the invisible history that the image cannot put into words." This notion of a gap, or area in between, which contains information that cannot be fully expressed in either verbal or visual form can be applied to my analysis of Adam Olearius's work as well. I will argue that the German author also "hides" information in the spaces between the frontispiece and the text, or the travel account and the cartographic text, information that relates to questions of authorship, political power, and intellectual influence (such as the Islamic sources that are silenced in Olearius's text).

In general, my analysis addresses the question of representation, namely how the object of this study, Persia and its peoples, is depicted in a text. Or, as the critic Mary Louise Pratt asks in the introduction to her work, *Imperial Eyes,* "How has travel and exploration writing *produced* 'the rest of the world' for European readerships at particular points in Europe's expansionist trajectory?" This study offers a reading of a select few visual documents (maps and frontispieces) in conjunction with the texts to which they refer. I hope to demonstrate the interdependence of the two, the visual and the verbal, and show how they complement each other and work together in order to produce a vision of a world that was only vaguely known to seventeenth–century Europeans.

Abbreviations

Behzad
: Behzad, Faramarz. *Adam Olearius' "Persianischer Rosenthal." Untersuchungen zur Übersetzung von Saadis "Golestan" im 17. Jahrhundert.* Göttingen: Vandenhoeck & Ruprecht, 1970.

Bishr
: Bishr, Naime Omar. "Das *Persianische Rosenthal* von Adam Olearius und Sa'dis *Gulestan:* Eine geistesgeschichtliche Untersuchung." Dissertation. Rutgers University, 1974.

CF
: Corbett, Margery, and Ronald Lightbown. *The Comely Frontispiece: The Emblematic Title-Page in England, 1550–1660.* London: Routledge, 1979.

Gabriel
: Gabriel, Alfons. *Die Erforschung Persiens: Die Entwicklung der abendländischen Kenntnis der Geographie Persiens.* Wien: A. Holzhausen, 1952.

GK
: Olearius, Adam. *Gottorffische Kunst-Cammer Worinnnen Allerhand ungemeine Sachen So theils die Natur theils künstliche Hände hervor gebracht und bereitet.* Schleswig: Holwein, 1666.

H/S
: Henkel, Arthur, and Albrecht Schöne. *Emblemata:*

Handbuch zur Sinnbildkunst des XVI. und XVII. Jahrhunderts. Ergänzte Neuausgabe, 2nd ed., [1st ed. 1967]. Stuttgart: J. B. Metzler, 1976.

Judson   Judson, Jay Richard, and Carl van de Velde. *Book Illustrations and Title-Pages.* Vol. 2, *Corpus Rubenianum Ludwig Burchard.* London and Philadelphia: Miller & Heyden, 1978.

Münster   Münster, Sebastian. *Cosmographey: das ist Beschreibung Aller Länder Herrschafften und fürnemesten Stetten des gantzen Erdbodens.* Basel, 1598.

PR   Olearius, Adam. *Persianischer Rosenthal. In welchem viel lustige Historien scharffsinnige Reden und nützliche Regeln. Vor 400. Jahren von einem Sinnreichen Poeten Schich Saadi in Persischer Sprach beschrieben.* Schleswig: Johann Holwein, 1654.

Tanavoli   Tanavoli, Parviz. *Lion Rugs: The Lion in the Art and Culture of Iran.* Basel: Werner Druck AG, 1985.

VNB   Olearius, Adam. *Vermehrte Newe Beschreibung der Muscowitischen und Persischen Reyse.* Edited by Dieter Lohmeier. 1656 ed., *Deutsche Neudrucke 21.* Tübingen: Max Niemeyer, 1971.

VISIONS OF PERSIA

I

Adam Olearius and the Journey to Muscovy and Persia

June 25, 1637 A.D. (or 1047 in the year of the Prophet) was an extremely hot and dry day in the city of Qazvīn, Persia. Qazvīn's mayor waited at the city gates — along with an honor guard and fifteen dancing girls clothed in silk gowns adorned with pearls and jewels — as a delegation of one hundred Germans approached on horseback, followed by a train of camels. After the official greeting, the foreigners were led through the streets of the city to the cheers of the populace, accompanied by musicians playing drums, cymbals, and pipes, and acrobats performing cartwheels and somersaults. When the procession reached the *maidan,* or city square, the crowd surged forward: everyone wanted to see what would come out of the delegation's *ketzawehan* ("Weiber Kisten"), the curtained palanquins carried by camels in which Persian noblewomen normally travelled unseen through the country (Figure 1.1). Since the Germans, or "Frenki" (*farangi*), were on their way to the capital in Isfahan, the crowd expected these boxlike litters to contain the foreign delegation's presents for the Shah: most likely beautiful German virgins or exotic curiosities from the sea ("Meerwunder"). However, when the curtains of the palanquins were pulled back, there were no such marvels to be seen — instead, out stumbled a small group of nauseous, bearded German men, who had been too sick to ride horseback, and who complained

1.1 Detail from Jan Struys's *Reysen door . . . Persien* (1676).

bitterly about motion sickness and camel stench. The stunned Persian onlookers could only laugh at the absurdity of the situation and at their own dashed expectations.

The original reads:

Als wir einen guten Büchsenschuß von der Stadt / kamen 15. Junge Weibes Personen uns entgegen geritten / waren statlich außgeputzet / mit bunten sammet und seiden Röcken bekleidet / mit güldenen und seiden / vom Kopff über die Schultern herunter fliessenden Tüchern / umb den Halß aber mit Perlen / und allerhand Geschmeide behangen. Sahen mit unverhülleten offenen Angesichtern (welches bey ehrlichen Weibes Personen nicht im Gebrauch) die Deutschen frisch in die Augen / und hiessen uns mit lachenden Munde wilkommen. Es waren aber die fürnembsten Sängerinnen und Tänzerinnen in der Stadt [. . .] Als wir abstiegen / kam das Volck heuffig und in grossem gedränge zugelauffen / zu sehen was wir doch in den Ketzawehan oder Weiber Kisten führeten. Dann sie hatten einer dem andern weiß gemachet (wie sie darmit sehr fertig) daß die Deutschen etliche schöne deutsche Jungfern / Item seltzame Meerwunder dem Könige zum Geschenck mit gebracht / als sie aber sahen / daß nur Krancke und bärtige Leute heraus krochen / lieff die ihnen eingebildete Meynung auff ein gelächter und vexiren hinaus.[1]

When we were about a gun-shot's distance away from the city, fifteen young women came riding toward us. They were splendidly decorated; dressed in colorful velvet and silk skirts, with golden and silken cloths that flowed down from their heads over their shoulders; around their necks they had pearls and all kinds of jewelry. With uncovered open faces (which is not the custom with honorable women) they looked the Germans straight in the eye and welcomed us with great smiles. They were the most important singers and dancers of the city. [. . .] When we descended from our horses the people came running in groups and much pushing was done in order to see what we had in our ketzawehan or ladies' palanquins. They had namely told one another — as they are wont to do at any time — that the Germans had brought some beautiful German virgins and strange marvels from the sea as presents for the king; but when they saw that only sick and bearded persons crawled out, their fantastic opinions ended in laughter and embarrassment.

This scene — recounted in Adam Olearius's *Vermehrte Newe Beschreibung der Muscowitischen und Persischen Reyse* of 1656 and reminiscent of a "Monty Python" sketch — is a humorous example of what may occur when members of one society encounter a different one: things are not always what they seem, expectations remain unfulfilled, and serious matters may easily turn into farce. The opposite is also true; especially in the age of incipient European colonialist expansion, seemingly innocent encounters can lead to misunderstandings that may just as easily turn into tragedy.

A truly Baroque work, the *Vermehrte Newe Beschreibung der Muscowitischen und Persischen Reyse* (The Expanded, New Description of the Muscovite and Persian Journey) combines a number of disciplines within its 800-page folio text and 120 engravings: a scholarly proto-ethnography, it also contains information on geography, biology, linguistics, history, and natural history. Olearius's text belongs to a genre of travel writing that seeks to acquire eyewitness information about a relatively unknown part of the world. He sets out to write about Persia for a German–speaking public eager to learn about an area which had been largely outside of their mental scope except for some mention in classical works.

Edward Said's concept of Orientalism is a useful point of departure in assessing how Olearius perceives Persian society. While the German author does not fit Said's definition of a typical nineteenth-century Orientalist with colonialist aims, his work both betrays stereotypical views of Persia, and also seeks to repudiate European prejudices concerning the Orient:

> "Orientalism" is the generic term to describe the Western approach to the Orient; Orientalism is the discipline by which the Orient was (and is) approached systematically, as a topic of learning, discovery, and practice. But in addition . . . the word . . . designate[s] that collection of dreams, images, and vocabularies available to anyone who has tried to talk about what lies east of the dividing line.[2]

Adam Olearius's travel account analyzes Persia in at least two ways. As a humanist scholar, he methodically classifies customs, dress, and language. A German Protestant, educated in the Greco-Roman tradition, he also assesses Persian culture using the standard Western prejudices toward an Islamic people. Olearius portrays the people and their customs using visual tropes, often in dramatic form, for his audience. As Said notes:

> The idea of representation is a theatrical one: the Orient is the stage on which the whole East is confined. On this stage will appear figures whose role it is to represent the larger whole from which they emanate...The Orient then seems to be, not an unlimited extension beyond the familiar European world, but rather a closed field, a theatrical stage affixed to Europe.[3]

The idea of a theater also finds an echo in the work of the cartographer Abraham Ortelius, especially his *Theatrum Orbis Terrarum* (1570), and can serve as an appropriate metaphor for the work of the German author. The theatrical arts combine the spoken word and a visual spectacle, and it is no coincidence that the Baroque era sees the rise of opera, an art form that mixes genres and blurs boundaries between them. The interplay between word and image is a fundamental component in the production of representation in Olearius's account, and it supports his claim that his observations were drawn from life.

IMAGES OF PERSIA: THE CLASSICAL TRADITION

Since the fifth century B.C. Persia existed in the minds of the Western world as a literary construct derived from antiquity, endlessly varied, copied and emended. The works of major writers such as Xenophon (*Cyropaedeia* and *Anabasis*) Herodotus (*Histories*, fourth century B.C.), and the Roman Quintus Curtius Rufus (*Historiae*, which includes the story of Alexander the Great)[4] form the treasure chest from which generations of scholars, scholiasts, commentators, and students obtained their knowledge of Persia.

Others who wrote on Persian matters included Strabo, the geographer, and Pausanias, whose travelogues included Persian sites. Lastly there was Ammianus Marcellinus, a late-Roman, non-Christian professional soldier and officer who served four Roman emperors. His *Res Gestae* included campaigns against the Persians as well as campaigns against the tide of Germanic tribes that had begun to enter the Roman Empire from the East.

In the seventeenth century, three major accounts were written about Persia, but they were all by men who had never been there: Barnabas Brissonius, who issued *De regio Persarum principatu* in 1606; Pietro Bizzarri, who published *Rerum Persicarum Historia*, also in 1606; and Johannes de Laet, author of *Persia, seu Regni Persici Status* in 1633. An English expedition from around 1630, led to an eyewitness account by Thomas Herbert published in 1634, after the Holstein embassy had already left, and to which Olearius refers in his narrative.[5]

In recording their contacts with Persia, these writers had one common point of reference. As Westerners reporting on the East, as Greeks or Romans, as observers of the differences between their civilizations and that of the Persians, their standards of measure were those of the West. Herodotus's remarks about the worldview of the Persians provide a wry commentary regarding their ethnocentricity:

After their own nation they hold their nearest neighbors most in honor, then the nearest but one — and so on, their respect decreasing as the distance grows, and the most remote being the most despised. Themselves they consider in every way superior to everyone else in the world, and allow other nations a share of good qualities decreasing according to distance, the furthest off being in their view the worst.[6]

In his own narrative of the great encounters between Greeks and Persians of the early fifth century, the Greek historian sets up a dichotomy that would influence how Persia would be seen in literature until the time of Adam Olearius. The encounter between "us" and "the other" — the small Greek democracies and the powerful Persian Empire — or as Herodotus says, between "Greece and the East . . . and especially the causes of their conflict," are major themes of his work.[7] The cause of the conflict is the attempt by four Persian kings over two generations to expand their empire, and the defense of the various Greek citystates against them. Books V–IX chronicle the history of the Persian invasion of Greece in 490 and 480 B.C. and the final defeat and disillusionment of the Persians.

But there is more to this conflict. Herodotus presents two ways of viewing the world in his narrative: first, the cult of the simple and good (*modestia*) as practiced by the Greeks is confronted with the pride (*superbia*) of the Persians. Secondly, those who obey only laws — the society of Greeks — are confronted with those who obey an absolute monarch. Those who sacrifice themselves voluntarily for the survival of their country are contrasted with those who fight out of fear and for rewards.[8] The fact that the Greeks won at Marathon and at Salamis proves to generations of readers of Herodotus that there are virtues that belong to the West and negative attitudes that remain associated with the East. Emblematic situations are created from the narrative of Herodotus that are passed down over the centuries, and that shape the representation of "the Persian" for generations of Europeans.

EARLY–MODERN EUROPEAN TRAVELERS TO PERSIA

The *Cambridge History of Iran* summarizes four main reasons for contact between Europe and Persia during the period 1350–1736:

1) The "religious incentive" (at the end of the thirteenth century Dominican and Franciscan friars were allowed to establish themselves in certain parts of Persia);
2) "The desire for concerted military action by both East and West against the Ottoman Turks";
3) "the commercial incentive";
4) "travelers who passed through Persia on their way to or from India or beyond."[9]

In Alfons Gabriel's study on European travelers to Persia over the ages, the author notes that German travelers also followed these four basic categories listed above.[10]

The first German who reported on Persia was the Bavarian soldier Hans Schiltberger (1473), who experienced the country as a captive (cf. Gabriel, 46). His account of the country was very straightforward, and reflected his background and lack of education. An Austrian nobleman who traveled to the area in 1589, Hans Christoph von Teufel, was one of the few travelers to find the country ugly and inhospitable, in contrast to the prevailing view that considered the land to be green, fruitful, and blessed with mineral wealth:

Und teucht mich, dass Persien in unsern Ländern gar zu beschrein sey und schier eines so grossen berueffss nicht wuerdig, dieweill es ein sehr unfruchtbares, sehr (doch von kahlen, fölsigen pergen) gebürgigs landt und nach Arabia deserta und Arabia petrea ich khein so hässliches landt gesechen. (Gabriel, 65)

And thus I think that Persia is too much praised in our lands and is not really worthy of such a great reputation because it is a very infertile, very mountainous country — however of bald and rocky mountains — and I have not seen such an ugly country other than *Arabia deserta* and *Arabia petrea* [=that part of Arabia which is desert, and that which consists of rocks].

The Holy Roman Emperor Rudolf II sent two embassies to Persia.

The first one was to be a return visit to honor the delegation sent by Shah Abbas I in 1600 to courts of Europe. Rudolf II appointed a nobleman, Stefan Kakasch von Zalonkemeny, to be the first ambassador of the Holy Roman Empire to Persia. Unfortunately, after he died en route, almost the entire embassy was killed — only the secretary, Georg Tectander, lived to write a report (in 1608) on the happenings. Perhaps the most celebrated German traveler after Olearius was Engelbert Kaempfer, who on his way to the Far East at the end of the seventeenth century wrote an excellent account of his journey.[11] However, since the work was written in Latin, it has not received the attention it deserves.

A number of other European travelers should also be noted in passing: the Englishmen Anthony Jenkinson (1557), Anthony and Robert Sherley (1598), and Thomas Coryat (1615); the Italian Pietro della Valle (1617); the Spanish diplomat, García de Silva y Figueroa (1614); and from France, the merchants Jean Baptiste Tavernier (mid-seventeenth century) and Jean Chardin (ca. 1670). They all left reports of their adventures that reflect their particular talents and interests in the country. The Catholic monk, Raphaël du Mans, was firmly convinced of the superiority of Western thought and was in general unimpressed by the achievements of Persian civilization.[12] These are but a few of the Europeans who traveled to Persia in the Early-Modern Era, and whose accounts give evidence of the fascination — and possibilities for profit — that the land held for a few intrepid souls.

THE HOLSTEIN MISSION TO PERSIA

The story of the Holstein expedition to Persia begins in 1633 at the midpoint of the Thirty Years' War when Duke Frederick III (1597–1659), ruler of the small Northern German duchy of Holstein-Gottorf, was contacted by the Hamburg lumber merchant, Otto Brüggemann. The latter proposed a commercial venture that would put the tiny territory on the map, as it were, and eliminate all its debts. He proposed to convince Shah Safi I of Persia to export his country's silk via the Volga, through Russia and the Baltic States, to Gottorf, which would then sell it to Northern Europe. Brüggemann's project was strengthened by two factors: his brother-in-law, Rudolf Stadler, the Shah's personal watchmaker, had assured him that the time was right for such an endeavor. Also, Tsar Mikhail I, whose permission was essential — and who needed hard currency — was more likely to permit representatives of a small, relatively non-threatening duchy such as Holstein-Gottorf to travel through his country, as opposed to delegations from larger rivals, such as Sweden or England.

The plan seemed worth exploring further, since the war had blocked off the traditional routes through Southern Germany by which Northern Europe obtained its silk, and the Turkish monopoly of the trade had led to exorbitantly high tariffs. Moreover, an overland route through Muscovy would be much cheaper and shorter than shipping silk via the Cape of Good Hope. Frederick decided to send an embassy to the Shah's capital in Isfahan; Brüggemann was to lead it, accompanied by the doctor and poet Paul Fleming (1609–1640), along with approximately one hundred support personnel. Adam Olearius, was chosen to chronicle the mission as its official secretary.[13]

Olearius, born Adam Öhlschlegel in 1599, the son of a tailor, had distinguished himself as a student of theology, philosophy, and the natural sciences at the University of Leipzig. In addition, his facility for learning languages made him a good choice to chronicle the journey. The entire mission described by Olearius lasted from 1633–1639 and was comprised of two parts. The first section, 1633–1635, describes the embassy's voyage to Moscow, negotiations with the Tsar — who demanded a higher transit fee than expected — and the return of some of the leaders of the delegation to Gottorf in order to secure Duke Frederick's approval for the increased payment to the Russian monarch. The second part, 1635–1639, began inauspiciously, when the ship of the Holsteiners was shipwrecked during a storm near Reval in present-day Estonia. After securing the Tsar's approval, they made their way down the Volga on a specially built ship named the *Friedrich*, under constant threat of attack by Tatars and Cossacks. Upon reaching the Caspian Sea a storm once again destroyed their ship, but most of the entourage survived. The members of the embassy were able to proceed to Shemakha, the Persian point of entry, where a three-month waiting period ensued. Olearius was able to profit from this interval by beginning his study of the Persian language, and becoming familiar with the country's customs. The delegation had to contend with more adversities after their arrival in Isfahan. An altercation with a foreign delegation of "Indians" (actually Uzbeks) developed into an all-out melee, in which scores of both parties were killed. In addition, Rudolf Stadler, Brüggemann's brother-in-law, who was to support the Holsteiners' request, killed a thief who had broken into his house. The Shah, who wished to keep the watch-maker at his court permanently, offered to pardon him for having killed a Muslim, in exchange for his own conversion to Islam. When Stadler refused, the thief's relatives hacked him to death with their sabers in the *maidan* of Isfahan (Figure 1.2).

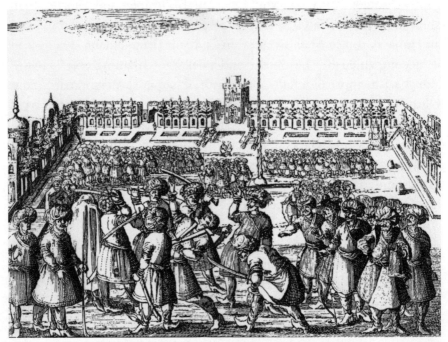

1.2 Execution of Rudolf Stadler from Adam Olearius's
Vermehrte Newe Reysebeschreibung (1656).

Paul Fleming wrote a poem commemorating the event, in which the victim's Christian steadfastness (*constantia*) was praised. At other times, the Holstein entourage was invited to a number of extravagant feasts held in their honor and taken on hunting expeditions. Olearius was able to observe the country's court society and manners first-hand during his five-month stay. Acquaintance with Armenian merchants and Portuguese monks, who had lived in the capital for many years, provided him with more information and complemented his own experiences.

The leader of the delegation, on the other hand, distinguished himself by his insensitivity to Persian culture, and general boorishness.[14] Otto Brüggemann probably realized that the venture would not prove very profitable, even though the deliberations were proceeding well enough. A number of incidents took place in which Brüggemann insulted his hosts. On the return trip he even tried to convince the Tsar's envoy that Russia should conquer Persia's silk-producing region of Gilan. It reached the point where Olearius, in fear of his life, hurried back to Gottorf ahead of the rest of the entourage, in order to begin proceedings against Brüggemann for gross neglect of his diplomatic duties. Found guilty, Brüggemann was executed in 1640.

After the embassy returned to Germany in 1639, a Persian delegation was sent by Shah Safi to Gottorf. The Persian embassy arrived in Holstein in order to discuss details of the proposed agreement, express the Shah's friendship to the Duke, and invite further contact. As it turned out, the few bales of silk that they presented to Duke Frederick as a present from the Shah were the only amounts of the precious material that Gottorf would ever obtain from the mission. There were a number of reasons for the failure of the venture, aside from Brüggemann's diplomatic failings: the long, dangerous route; the high tariffs required by the Tsar, as well as by the Swedes, who controlled shipping along the Baltic; the fact that Dutch and Armenian traders already controlled the silk trade in Isfahan; and most significantly, the reality that Persia did not produce enough silk to make the venture profitable.

OLEARIUS'S TRAVEL ACCOUNT

The title page of the *Vermehrte Newe Beschreibung der Muscowitischen und Persischen Reyse* (1656) gives a summary of the author's intention:

Worinnen die gelegenheit derer Orter und Länder / durch welche die Reyse gangen / als Liffland / Rußland / Tartarien / Meden und Persien / sampt dero Einwohner Natur / Leben / Sitten / Hauß =Welt=und Geistlichen Stand mit fleiß auffgezeichnet. (*VNB*, III)

> Where the location of places and countries through which we trav-
> elled, such as Latvia, Russia, Tartary, the countries of the Medes
> and Persians, as well as the nature, life, customs, domestic, worldly,
> and spiritual conditions are conscientiously described.

The work claims, therefore, to be not only a geographic account of a journey, but an ethnography, in the modern sense of the term, since it depicts the "nature" and customs of the peoples encountered and studied along the way.

Olearius is a typical Baroque writer in that he is still deeply respectful of classical and Renaissance sources. He cites them copiously and compares them to each other, thus paying homage to the scholarly tradition. However, he does so with the critical attitude of a seventeenth-century scientist, whose own experiences and scholarly observations make the correction of faulty source material imperative. His attitude, which might seem rather predictable to a modern-day reader, represented a significant step forward for the scholarly world of his age. In medicine, for instance, Harvey's new theory of the circulation of blood was only gradually freeing itself from the views of the second-century physician Galen. An example of Olearius's critical methodology occurs during the storm in the Baltic, near the beginning of the journey. Olearius notes that seasickness could not be caused by saltwater, as the humanist Pontanus maintained, but rather by the motion of the waves, since the crew felt the same effects later on the freshwater Caspian Sea. Similarly, after a discussion with two Samoyeds of a Siberian tribe, Olearius speculates that sailors who had claimed that there were "monsters" living along the Siberian coast were wrong. They had simply seen natives of the region. During the winter, these indigenous people wore big furskins over their heads, making it appear that they were "headless;" and their "huge feet" were most likely snowshoes.

In the interest of science, Olearius's methodology is that of a comparatist. He juxtaposes the customs and social structures of the people he meets with those of his native land. At times he even expresses admiration for some of their traits though they are so different from his own. Olearius does not claim to possess all the answers, and he consults with scholars and native informants of the lands he visits. The most practical and lasting result of the trip was the production of superior maps of the areas to which he traveled. Olearius corrected previous depictions, many of which were considerably flawed. His trip also led him to dismiss the Ptolemaic system of the world, which still found adherents during his lifetime. The *Vermehrte Newe Beschreibung* includes large, detailed fold-out maps describing Persia and the Caspian Sea, as well as Moscow and the course of the Volga. The latter — which was used until well into the eighteenth century — so impressed Tsar Mikhail by its exactitude that he later attempted to enlist Olearius into his service. Even a cursory comparison of Sebastian Münster's 1544 woodcut map of Muscovy (Figure 1.3) with Olearius's engraved map of the course of the Volga (Figure 1.4) shows the rapid development of cartographic methods over the span of a century.

The very structure of his work is evidence of the multiplicity of its purposes, for it is many texts at once. It not only treats the landscape, flora, and fauna of a region, but it also becomes a travel advisory. It discusses the history of an area, providing stories from classical sources as well as legends and present-day folktales. It is also a lively adventure story. In voice, it alternates between first-person accounts of the journey itself and third-person descriptions. One section might deal with the adventures that befell the expedition (such as a shipwreck, or imminent attacks by Cossacks or Tatars) and the next section would discuss a region's flora and fauna, and the past and present history of the peoples who are encountered. A description of the Persian "natives" and their "nature" is really a codification of his human hosts: it follows the description of Persian fauna. On the one hand, the author is impressed by the curiosity and intelligence of the Persians he meets:

> Die Perser sind von Natur mit statlichen Ingenii und guten Verstande begabet / seynd scharffsinnig und lehrhafft / daher gibt es unter ihnen viel treffliche Poeten / welche nachdenckliche Dinge schreiben / und halten in gemein die freyen Künste in hohen Werth. [. . .] Sie . . . erzeigen sich gegen einander / und sonderlich gegen Frembde gar freundlich / gebrauchen im reden sonderliche Höfflichkeit und Demut. (*VNB*, 589)

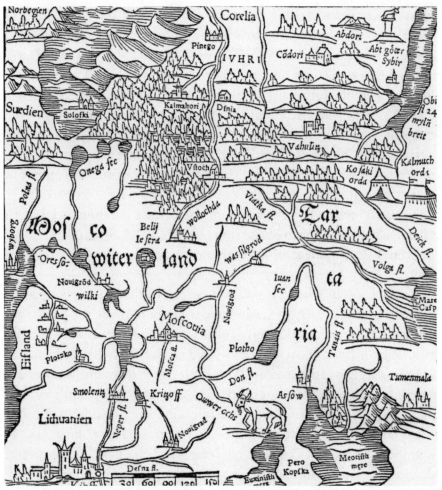

1.3 Map of Russia in Sebastian Münster's *Cosmographia* (1544).

By nature the Persians are gifted with remarkable perspicacity and a good mind; they are sharp-witted and good teachers, therefore there are many excellent poets among them who write reflective poetry; in general they have a high regard for the liberal arts. [. . .] They . . . are very friendly toward each other, especially toward foreigners, their speech is remarkably polite and kind . . .

The Persians are also known to be fierce warriors, they are very clean, and the streets are remarkably safe.

On the other hand, in spite of his admiration for certain traits,

1.4 Map of the Volga from Adam Olearius's
Vermehrte Newe Reysebeschreibung (1656).

Olearius, as a devout German Protestant, cannot help but attack Persian character traits, especially those dealing with religion, morality, and sexual behavior — he goes into great detail when discussing the latter.[15]

> With regard to sexual conduct, Persian males are abnormal. They are too sexually promiscuous (not only do they take many wives, they also frequent brothels); they are perverse as well, since the greatest sin, sodomy, is rampant among them. This corporeal licentiousness is only to be expected, since their leaders — both worldly and spiritual — are depraved. (cf. *VNB*, 593)

Olearius notes that Shah Safi, his host, was not only a typical Oriental despot, but was suspected of engaging in homosexual acts; and he states that "ihr falscher Prophet / Mahumed / weil er selbst ein geiler Hund . . . [versicherte] daß solche Wollust ein groß stück von der Frewde im ewigen Leben seyn werde / wodurch die Religion bey dem einfältigen Volcke desto angenehmer gemacht worden" (their false prophet Muḥammad since he himself was a horny dog . . . [gave assurances] that carnal relations would play a large part in the afterlife, so that the religion would appeal more to the simple folk, *VNB*, 593).

Olearius also tells the amusing story of a woman who filed for divorce, on the grounds of her husband's impotence. Actually, Olearius uses the term *impotentia*. When dealing with risqué subjects, Latin is used for the sake of women and young people who read his work:

Und als der Kasi den Mann gefraget / warumb er / nach dem ihm seine beschaffenheit wissend / ein Weib genommen? hat er geantwortet: Daß sie ihm den Rücken kratzen solte. Darauff sie; Ich habe dir lang gnug den Rücken gekratzet / bin aber von dir niemahls wieder gekratzet worden. (*VNB*, 610)

When the judge asked the man why he had taken a wife if he knew about his condition, the man answered: he wanted her to scratch his back. She replied: "I've scratched your back long enough, but have never been scratched in return."

Sexual deviance is often aroused by dancing, "which they love beyond measure," ("über die massen beliebet") and enhanced by cannabis seeds and leaves, that "strengthen nature in preparation for the games of Venus" ("welche die Natur stärcken / und zum Venus Spiel brünstig machen sol," *VNB*, 594). On the other hand if one drinks too much *kahwae* or coffee-water, carnal desires are completely extinguished.

The German embassy had its own sexual encounters while in Persia, which fully correspond to the traditional Western stereotypes regarding exotic eroticism. Shah Safi's "Eahtemad döwlet," or Grand Vizier, invited the visitors to a banquet held in a setting which corresponded fully to a European's notion of what an Oriental feast should entail (Figure 1.5).

Whoever stood in the middle of the banquet room could see himself reflected from hundreds of large and small mirrors set into the walls; a fountain shot water upward, "higher than a man's height" (cf. *VNB*, 531); women's clothing from many different nations, as well as European paintings hung from the walls; musicians played in the background, while the Shah's female dancers performed acrobatic, sexually arousing feats for the guests.[16] The evening, however, did not end with such visual stimulation. On the left side of the engraving we may observe the three seated German ambassadors, one of whom is watching the entertainment. The dancers were expected to perform sexual favors for the foreign guests in specially prepared rooms. Since he characterizes it as a "Thorheit" (foolishness), Olearius seems not to have been interested in acceding to his host's invitation. Only after

1.5 "Sarü Tagge's" banquet for the Holstein Embassy from Adam Olearius's *Vermehrte Newe Reysebeschreibung* (1656).

presenting this erotic situation does our narrator explain that their host, the Grand Vizier Sarü Tagge, could not participate in the festivities, since he was a eunuch. Tagge had raped a young boy, and when the boy's father complained to the Shah, Tagge castrated himself in order to save his life.[17] This episode marks the poles of Persian culture: as the site, on the one hand, of voluptuous, erotic encounters, and of unnatural cruelty and despotism on the other hand. Having condemned the Persian practice of openly maintaining houses of prostitution, Olearius is conveniently silent regarding the reaction of his fellow envoys to Tagge's invitation — the book, after all, while seeking to entertain, is also meant for the moral edification of its Western readers.

The reader of modern texts, who is used to studying disciplines such as geography, linguistics, biology, and ethnography, in separate, compartmentalized form, is confronted with a Baroque excess of information within this 800-page folio text. The *Vermehrte Newe*

Beschreibung was a success because of its method, organization, and careful presentation. It appealed to a wide audience whose knowledge of the area had often been derived from reports that had changed little since classical antiquity. A number of emblematic mottos and sayings, many taken from Saʿdi's *Gulistān* are interspersed throughout the work, in accordance with the century's proclivity for moral edification: not only were readers taught about different countries, they were also taught how to be a better person. All these factors account for the work's popularity. Besides six different German editions in the seventeenth century, the travel account was also translated into Dutch (1651), French (1656), Italian (1658), and English (1662).[18]

THE ILLUSTRATIONS IN THE
VERMEHRTE NEWE BESCHREIBUNG

Another reason for the success of the *Vermehrte Newe Beschreibung* are the numerous illustrations included in the work, some of which were even drawn by Olearius himself. After his return to Gottorf, he personally supervised the layout and production of the engravings. The title page emphasizes the language of pictorial representation: the customs of the observed peoples "[sind] mit fleiß auffgezeichnet und mit vielen meist nach dem Leben gestelleten Figuren gezieret" (depicted with diligence and are decorated with many figures mostly drawn from life) (*VNB*, III). These illustrations, then, support the scholarly aspirations of the account in a number of ways. For example, a discussion of linguistic differences between Arabic, Persian, and Turkish is complemented by a comparison of the respective alphabets. Frequently, illustrations are used for their entertainment value, to highlight what might be termed the most adventurous moments of the journey. The storm in the Baltic is depicted with the poignant detail of a drowning person's hand still sticking out of the water; the disaster on the Caspian Sea is portrayed at the moment of greatest danger, just as the mast is shattered into many pieces. Olearius notes the perils of the journey from Narva to Reval (in present-day Estonia), by recounting recent wolf and bear attacks in the region. At the center of Figure 1.6 a rabid wolf attacks a peasant lying prostrate on the ground, next to another victim. A dead tree, with a jagged, broken-off trunk (probably

1.6 Effects of a wolf attack near Narva (present-day Estonia) from
Adam Olearius's *Vermehrte Newe Reysebeschreibung* (1656).

a symbol of death) frames the picture on the right-hand side, while
almost the entire left portion depicts the consequences of the attack.
What appears to be a page of a book inserted into the left foreground
of the engraving shows the front and back bust of a victim — an open-
eyed corpse, gazing directly at the viewer — worthy of any modern-
day slasher movie. The upper right-hand corner of the page is slightly
peeled back, to underline the temporal displacement, that is, to show
the aftereffect of the attack.

In another depiction we see that even a relatively innocuous subject such as a cityscape is not what it seems (Figure 1.7). The Persian
city of Kashan is characterized by the prominent front and back view
of a tarantula in the bottom left-hand corner. The five to six scorpions
hiding on top and alongside the cartouche are not so readily identifi-
able. The viewer who does not notice these creatures at first is, in a
way, invited to confront in a pictorial representation the danger that
the author himself experienced in real life. Olearius notes that he
alone, out of the entire entourage, was bitten by one of these scorpions
on the neck, and describes the symptoms he experienced. He then
advises that a victim should try to kill the animal that inflicted the bite

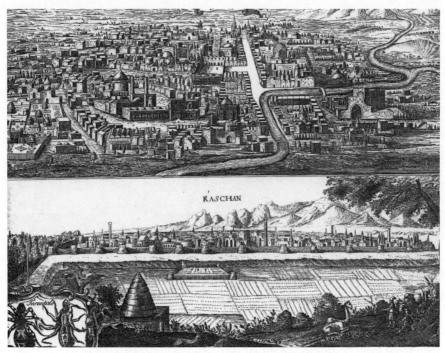

1.7 View of Kashan from Adam Olearius's
Vermehrte Newe Reysebeschreibung (1656)

and place it against the wound. According to the law of "sympathies" the poison in the human would be attracted back to the scorpion, and a cure would follow. Olearius mentions that a specimen scorpion, which he took back to Gottorf, is in the Duke's *Kunstkammer* or cabinet of curiosities: the Oriental danger is thus immobilized and tamed, on display.

OLEARIUS'S ACTIVITIES IN GOTTORF

When the Persian delegation sent by Shah Safi made ready to leave Gottorf, a number of delegates defected, including the secretary, Hakwirdi. This was to prove most fortuitous for Olearius, since he was then able to perfect his knowledge of Persian, as well as check the information he had acquired abroad with a cultured, native informant. Most importantly, Hakwirdi helped Olearius to translate the celebrated Persian poet Sa'di's *Gulistān* (1258), under the title *Persianischer Rosenthal* (Persian Valley of Roses, 1654), which had great resonance among the German literary public. This translation, along with the travel account influenced such German Baroque authors as Grimmelshausen (*Simplicissimus*), Lohenstein (*Ibrahim Bassa* and *Ibrahim Sultan*) and Gryphius (*Catherina von Georgien*) and, in the following centuries, Montesquieu (*Lettres Persanes*), and Goethe (*West-östlicher Divan*).

Besides preparing the different accounts of his own journey, editing other travel accounts, and the poetic works of his prematurely deceased friend Paul Fleming, and working on a (never published) Persian–Turkish–Arabic dictionary, Olearius's other duties in Gottorf kept him extremely busy until his death in 1671. He was appointed court librarian by Duke Frederick, and given the task of cataloging and expanding the ducal collection. He was admitted into the "Fruchtbringende Gesellschaft," an organization committed to the development and purification of the German language. Olearius's interest in the sciences led him to build an astrolabe, a microscope, a telescope, and his crowning achievement, a giant globe. This globe, ten feet in diameter, was hollow and seated twelve people inside, who could then watch the movement of the stars put into motion by an ingenious hydraulic system. The globe was later presented to Peter the Great.[19] All these achievements contributed to Olearius acquiring the sobriquet "the Holstein Pliny."

In addition, Olearius was charged with developing the Duke's *Kunstkammer*, made up, in large part, of mementos from the trip to Russia and Persia. It consisted of bizarre objects (scorpions preserved in oil, minerals, fossils, and stone relics), which were organized and presented in a controlled environment. Unfortunately, this carefully assembled collection was dispersed in the eighteenth century, but items from the Gottorf collection were eventually integrated into the Danish National art museums.[20]

II

Adam Olearius and the Early-Modern Frontispiece

The preface to Olearius's *Gottorffische Kunstkammer* (The Gottorf
Cabinet of Curiosities) of 1661 — with its insistence on the
concepts of writing and drawing, as well as the word and the
"Wunderbuch" — contains a number of themes that can be applied to
Olearius's ideas on the genre of the frontispiece (also known as
engraved title page):

Wenn ein kluger Vater oder fleissiger Praeceptor seinen Kindern
und Schülern etwas in Wissenschaft beybringen und sie lehren wil /
thut ers nicht nur mit dem Munde / sondern auch mit der feder /
schreibet und mahlet ihnen vor allerhand Figuren und
Abbildunge[n] / und wil durch das Kleine was Grosses andeuten
und zu verstehen geben . . . Ein Astronomus zeiget auff einem
kleinen Hand Globo Coelesti die Beschaffenheit des grossen
Himmels mit allen seinen sichtbaren Cörpern / da ein punct einen
grossen Stern bedeutet. Imgleichen auch ein Geographus bildet auff
einer kleinen Erdkugel oder Globo terrestri ab den gantzen Kreiß
der Erden / mit allen Landschafften / Seen und Strömen / da auch
ein Punct eine Stadt / eine Linie einen Strom / und ein Platz eines
Daumens breit eine gantze breite See abbilden muß.

 Eben auff solche Art handelt unser allgemeiner Vater im

Himmel und klugester Lehrmeister GOTT der Herr mit uns seinen Kindern und Schülern. Dann er uns neben seinem geoffenbarten Worte das grosse Wunderbuch die Welt mit den zwey grossen Blättern nemlich Himmel und Erden vorgeschrieben / daß wir darinne studiren / und dadurch etwas grösseres erkennen lernen sollen / nemblich / Ihn den Schöpfer selbst / seine Majestät und Allmacht.[21]

When a clever father or an industrious preceptor wants to introduce his children and students to something in the arts and sciences and wishes to teach them he does it not only by means of his mouth but also with the pen; he writes and paints all kinds of figures and pictures before them and wants to allude to, and make them understand, something grand by showing them something small . . . An astronomer shows on a small hand-globe, a *globo coelesti,* the make-up of the great Heaven with all its visible bodies, where a point means a star. In the same way a geographer represents on a small terrestrial globe, *globo terrestri,* the entire circle of the earth with all its landscapes, seas, and rivers where a point must describe a city, a line a river, and a thumb-size dot an entire broad sea.

In the same fashion our Common Father in Heaven and cleverest of all teachers, the Lord God, acts with us, His children and students. Because beside His revealed Word He wrote for us the great Book of Wonders, the World, with its two great pages Heaven and Earth, so that we may study in it and thus learn to recognize something much greater, namely Himself, the Creator, his majesty and power.

Two ideas from the above quotation deserve closer investigation. First, there is the concept of microcosm and macrocosm: something small (for example a dot on a globe) stands for something else, larger than itself (a city). That is to say, individual objects of study or curiosities of nature — that are collected and presented to a reader or observer — represent a greater whole, and these objects are all interconnected by means of the great chain of being, which has God at its summit. An analogy is established: God teaches humans by means of natural wonders. In turn, adults (read: males) instruct children by means of words and images, thus creating yet another chain or connection. In studying natural wonders and reading the "Wunderbuch" (Book of Wonders), a person desiring knowledge may come closer to understanding the works of God. In like fashion, a frontispiece acts as a visual microcosm of the larger book — the textual macrocosm — that it introduces.[22] The frontispiece is meant to intrigue the reader with its complex set of visual images (taken from classical coins and medals, from devices and emblems, from Egyptian hieroglyphs and Medieval treatises), but these images can only be fully decoded after reading the book that follows.

Second, following the Horatian precept of *aut prodesse aut delectare poetae volunt* Olearius wishes to entertain while instructing; he thus emphasizes the dual role of the word (be it spoken or written) and of the image in his didactic program. A teacher both implies and needs an audience, and here the conceit of *theatrum mundi* overlaps with the notion of microcosm and macrocosm. Nature in all its various manifestations (animal, vegetable, and mineral) must be displayed on a stage — be it the "stage" of the title page; or the compartments of a *Kunstkammer,* into which the exotic objects are placed for people to examine. As we shall see, the idea of the stage plays a crucial role in frontispieces. Classical architecture provided the basic model for the majority of Renaissance and Baroque title pages: an arch or gateway, resting on a platform, or plinth, symbolized the formal entrance to the work within, a design that recalls the structures of allegorical tableaux used for triumphal entries into Italian and Dutch Renaissance cities, in order to honor the hero of the day.

The twentieth-century Spanish critic José Montesinos characterizes the Baroque as "el arte de no renunciar a nada" (the art of not rejecting anything),[23] and this phrase holds true for our subject, in the sense that all the disciplines are brought onto the stage of Olearius's world: ethnography, history, natural science, geography, architecture, and literature.

THE FRONTISPIECE: THE DEVELOPMENT OF A GENRE

The early development of the frontispiece or illustrated title page in Europe takes place during the late-fifteenth and early-sixteenth centuries, and reaches its height by the late-seventeenth century.[24] This genre went hand in hand with the flowering of the book trade and spread with the migration of engravers throughout the continent. Northern Mannerist art had the greatest influence on the artistic vocabulary used by the engravers, who would generally illustrate the artistic program outlined by the author of a book. As we shall see, this is the formula that was employed with our author's works as well: Olearius would decide which elements to include in his frontispieces, and then have an engraver produce the image itself.

In their study on the development of the frontispiece, Margery Corbett and Ronald Lightbown are primarily concerned with the growth of the genre in Early Modern England, but their observations can be applied to the engraved title page on the European Continent as well. They note four different types of designs:

1. Frontispieces that are divided into geometrical compartments, a feature which seems to be German in origin;

2. Frontispieces that have a single design. For example, those depicting a particular scene, an arrangement that also seems to have been a German invention. In the 1520s, "the Lutherans of Germany . . . had seized on these types of title pages as a means of pictorial propaganda for their religious beliefs . . . in Reformation Bibles . . . we find the first title pages whose iconography bears more than an illustrative relation to the text, in that their images are deliberately chosen for doctrinal and controversial significance" (*CF,* 3);

3. Title pages in which a single cartouche dominates. The School of Fontainebleau, where this type of design originated in the 1530s, had a predilection for Mannerist irrationality and illusionism. In these types of designs one finds interlocking, complicated scroll-work and strapwork, a "form of design imitating the three-dimensional scrolling of intertwined lengths of soft leather, with the edges curling forward around the inscription;"[25] garlands and masks surrounding fantastic architectural structures; and grotesque figures and monsters taken from classical mythology;

4. The architectural title page is the most monumental of the four types of designs, and has the most three-dimensional character.

Of the antique architectural forms which were used, "from the first, the most popular of all was the classical recess flanked by wings, standing on a base and surmounted by a pediment" (*CF*, 4). The title was normally inscribed within a cartouche, which was attached to the overall architectural frame. Another important aspect of this arrangement was the introduction of sculpture-like allegorical figures or personifications into the overall design (cf. *CF*, 5).

The shift from the technique of the woodcut to engraving on copper around the middle of the sixteenth century, marked an important moment of transition for the frontispiece. Whereas woodcuts involved the use of movable type for its titles and allowed the borders of a title page to be used for different editions or even for other books, engraved title pages were commissioned for specific books (although details could be altered in subsequent editions). Engraving also allowed for greater pictorial detail and better illusionism than the woodcut. It was only after the use of engraving that frontispieces came to be independent images, filled with complicated allegorical and symbolic programs, which were then often followed by a title page consisting entirely of text. The design of the frontispiece was deliberately chosen to epitomize the text which followed it: "It was the vehicle for the thoughts of the author on his work, but might also seek to give an indication of its scope, and include pictorial representations which could be understood only by perusing the book, thus stimulating the reader's curiosity. All the themes were carefully interwoven into the set patterns for the design of title pages, according to an inner logic, to make up the meaning of the whole" (*CF*, 35).

To understand how the Early Modern frontispiece functions, it is useful to first examine some of the different elements that were instrumental in its development.

The Device

"The device (French, *devise*; Italian, *impresa*; in Latin usually rendered as *symbolum*)" (*CF*, 10) is a combination of a picture and a personal motto. A private adage or clever aphorism was linked to a heraldic image, and the fusion resulted in the device, that is, a personal message by means of which a knight would define himself. The device developed from the chivalric tradition of fourteenth-century France and made its way into Italy during the French invasions of the fifteenth century. The genre became very popular among the Italian nobility, who observed French aristocrats wearing their personal devices on their uniforms or shields. As a result, Paolo Giovio published his *Dialogo dell'Imprese* (Florence, 1555), which soon became a European bestseller. It was the first of a long line of books that provided theoretical advice and examples of devices. Giovio's treatise emphasized the fact that only illustrious men could wear devices that scholars or poets invented for them. The meanings of these inventions should not be immediately evident (especially to the common folk); the reader or observer, when trying to understand a device, should have the sensation of unraveling a mystery or figuring out a puzzle. A craftsman, i.e., painter or goldsmith, would then supply the visual form of the idea that the learned scholar created. Other celebrated works in this genre included *Le imprese illustri* by Ruscelli (1566); the *Insignivm, Armorvm, Emblematum, Hieroglyphicorvm, et Symbolorvm, que ab Italis Imprese nominantur, explicatio* by Abraham Fraunce (1588); the *Devises héroiques* of Claude Paradin (1551); and the *Imprese heroiche et morali* of the Italian Gabriello Simeoni (1559). The moral devices (of these last two authors) — which discuss general qualities and characteristics such as courage, nobility, obligation — lead us to the genre of the emblem.

Emblems and Hieroglyphs

The emblem is an art form that also combines pictorial and verbal elements, but strives for universal applicability. Like the device, it is derived from the accumulated knowledge derived from classical Greece and Rome, ancient Egypt and the European Middle Ages.[26] The first work of this genre, the *Emblematum Liber* which gave the name to the concept "Emblem," was printed in 1531. Written by the Milanese legal scholar Andreas Alciatus in Latin, and published in Augsburg by Heinrich Steyner (who apparently added pictures to the text — drawn by Jörg Breu — in order to make the work more intelligible for the non-scholarly audience), the book's success caused it to be translated soon thereafter into French (1536), German (1542), and Spanish (1549).[27]

> Griechisch ἔμβλημα und emblema im klassischen Latein meinten freilich das Angesetzte oder Eingesetzte, Mosaik- und Intarsienwerk. So, als Bezeichnung für verzierende Einlegearbeit, für abnehmbaren Metallschmuck an Gefäßen hatte noch Alciatus es aufgefaßt; auch die metallenen Schilde und Plaketten der Impresen, mit denen man Hüte und Gewänder schmückte, hat er wahrscheinlich darunter verstanden, vielleicht die in Bücher eingeklebten Bibliothekszeichen, die Verlegersignets, möglicherweise sogar den Schmuck der Rede durch 'loci communes', die schon Quintilian mit den Emblemata verglichen hatte. (*H/S*, XVIII)

> Greek ἔμβλημα and emblema in classical Latin meant that which has been added or inserted, mosaic work or intarsia. Alciatus had still defined it in such a manner, namely as designation for decorative intarsia work, for detachable metal ornaments on containers; he probably included also the metal shields and plaques of impresas with which people decorated hats and clothes, perhaps also library identifications, the signets of publishers, maybe even the ornament of speech by *loci communes* [commonplaces] which already Quintilian had compared to emblemata.

The emblem was truly a product of its age, and reflected the concerns of the Renaissance scholars who created the collections of various types of *emblemata*. Of chief concern to the first humanists in Italy was the desire to understand the mysteries of antiquity, especially ancient Egyptian hieroglyphs, which were thought to represent a secret language. These scholars wished to interpret the bizarre letters and signs that could still be seen on Egyptian obelisks, sphinxes and lions, and which Herodotus, Plato, Diodorus Siculus, Plutarch, and other classical writers had written about. The *Hieroglyphica* — a work written in Greek by the author Horapollo (or Horus Apollo Niliacus) around the fourth century A.D. in Alexandria — gave great impetus to this movement (it arrived in Italy in a Greek version in 1419, and was subsequently translated into Latin in 1517). The key to deciphering the hieroglyphs had apparently been found. It was supposed to provide access to the original wisdom of early man, and to the secrets of the world ordered by God. Although Horapollo claims to have been born at Nilopolis, he did not have an accurate understanding of Egyptian hieroglyphics: he interpreted them according to the allegorical system, by means of which an image represented a certain idea e.g., a crocodile stood for evil.

Nonetheless, works seeking to unravel the mysteries of the Egyptians soon appeared — by such noted scholars as Marsilio Ficino (*De Mysteriis Aegyptorum*, 1483) and Francesco Colonna (*Hypneroto-machia Poliphili*, 1499) — and started a vogue. Soon the humanists, who had wanted to research and understand antiquity, also wished to make it come alive, by using "hieroglyphics" — that only the initiated understood — to ornament medals, coins, columns, triumphal arches, as well as objects of daily use. Pythagorean symbols were added to the hieroglyphs, since metaphors and allegories of the ancients supposedly derived from the wisdom of Egyptian priests; representations on ancient coins were interpreted as hieroglyphics; Biblical imagery, medieval animal and plant books, cabalistic number mysticism, and Old Testament motifs, ancient mythology and medieval allegory were all used as potential sources for the applied hieroglyphics of the Renaissance.

The hermetic character of Horapollo's book and the hieroglyphic secret writings helped in the formation, acceptance, and dissemination of the emblem (which in turn adopted the pictorial aspect of Egyptian writing, and added a textual explanation below the image). Inventors of emblems tried not to reveal the obvious, but wanted to reveal the significance hidden in the picture. In short, emblematics became a kind of language, that scholars and then readers of the vulgar tongue deciphered in books and then applied to a number of fields in daily life. Arthur Henkel and Albrecht Schöne, whose work *Emblemata* reproduces the emblems from approximately fifty of the most popular Early Modern emblem books, provide a good definition of the emblem in the introduction to their work. Three parts are needed to compose an emblem:

1. The *pictura* (also known as *icon, imago, symbolon*) is a small wood-cut or copper engraving that could show a plant or animal; a

figure taken from mythology, the Bible, or history; or a popular saying or moral derived from a fable. A seventeenth-century scholar, Bohuslaus Balbinus, noted in 1678 that "Nulla res est sub Sole quae materiam Emblemati dare non possit."[28]

2. Above the *pictura* one finds a short *inscriptio* (*motto, lemma*), which usually quoted classical authors, Bible verses, or popular sayings.

3. Located beneath the image is the *subscriptio*, which explains the *pictura*, and often draws a lesson from it. Usually it is in the form of a prose text or an epigram. (cf. *H/S*, XII)

Many of the epigrams were derived from the *Anthologia Graeca*, a collection of over six thousand epigrams, written from the seventh century B.C. to the tenth century A.D.[29] The *subscriptio* provides the solution to the "mystery" posed by the inscription and the image, and tries to draw a general or universal moral. The *res picta* of the emblem is *res significans*, that is, the image directs the reader toward an interpretation which has ethical, theological, or practical implications. Together, the three parts of the emblem fulfill the double function of showing and explaining, representing and interpreting.

Emblematics is based upon the belief that the initiated reader can discover the secret relationships existing in the world — like the viewer, who can understand the different elements that are contained in the microcosmic world of the frontispiece. As Henkel and Schöne note:

> wenn für den Idealtypus gilt, daß das emblematische Bild eine potentielle Faktizität besitzt und eine ideelle Priorität gegenüber dem auslegenden Text, der einen höheren Sinn in ihm entdeckt, eine in der Res picta gleichsam angelegte Bedeutung aufschließt, so wird man das zurückbeziehen müssen auf die typologische Exegese und das allegorische Verfahren der mittelalterlichen Theologie, die alles Geschaffene als Hinweis auf den Schöpfer verstand und die von Gott in die Dinge gelegte Bedeutung, ihren auf die göttliche Sinnmitte hingeordneten heilsgeschichtlichen Bezug aufzudecken suchte. (*H/S*, XVI)

if it is true for the ideal type that the emblematic picture possesses a potential facticity and has an ideal priority vis-a-vis the exegetic text (which discovers in it a higher meaning, and unlocks a significance that is rooted in the res picta) then this fact must be referred back to the typological exegesis, and the allegorical proceedings of medieval theology; the latter understood all creation to be an allusion to the creator; and it strove to uncover the meaning put by God into the objects [created by Him]; it sought to uncover their relationship to the history of salvation, its reference to the divine center of meaning.

Both Catholic and Protestant circles subscribed to this concept and attempted "to connect the Bible and Nature, history, art as a cosmos of signatures, and to understand the world as mundus symbolicus."[30] Readers believed that God's message could be gleaned from correctly interpreting the visible phenomena, whose hidden messages could be deciphered in "das grosse Wunderbuch die Welt," as Olearius notes in the introduction to the *Gottorffische Kunstkammer* (*GK*, 3b).

The genre of the emblem book had a European-wide success from the sixteenth to the eighteenth centuries, during which time over two thousand emblem books were published in the fields of education, morality, politics, religion, and even erotic arts. Some of the most influential emblem books were *Emblemata* by Joannis Sambucus (Antwerp, 1564); in France, Guillaume de la Perrière's *Theatre des bons engins, auquel sont contenuz cent Emblemes* (Paris, 1539) and Barthélemy Anneau's *Picta Poesis* (Lyons, 1564); the *Emblemata* of Nicolaus Reusner (Frankfurt, 1581) and the *Symbola* of Joachim Camerarius (1593, 1595, 1596, 1604); in England, Geoffrey Whitney's *Choice of Emblemes* (1586) and Henry Peacham's *Minerva Britanna or a Garden of heroical Deuices, furnished, and adorned with Emblemes and Impresa's of sundry natures* (1612).

The Stage and the Actors

Early-Modern title pages often incorporate the feature of the triumphal arch in order to signify the symbolic entry into the written work. Derived from the portal that served as the entrance to ancient walled Roman cities, this architectural feature (in conjunction with ornamentation, such as cartouches, swags of garlands, and obelisks) marked the formal, monumental opening that led the reader to the interior of the book.

> However it is a mistake to assume that such forms are always or only triumphal arches, since a constant feature on the title page is the continuous high plinth which runs across the opening. In fact, these designs often closely resemble a type of Renaissance architectural structure made for triumphal entries in the Netherlands and in Italy in the sixteenth century. This was the stage on which an allegorical tableau was presented in honour of the hero of the day. It was set in a free-standing architectural framework with the central area usually flanked by columns which supported the cornice and the pediment; the whole was raised on a substantial base so that the spectacle could be seen and was placed in a prominent position beside the route of the procession. The term used to describe it by Corneille de Schryver in his account of the entry of Philip of Spain into Antwerp in 1549 is *pegma*; in the French and Dutch editions of his work it is also called a scaffolding. (*CF,* 7)

In the German-speaking world, the most famous woodcut series in this genre — although not a frontispiece per se — was made to commemorate the deeds of Emperor Maximilian I, who had himself represented in the style of ancient Roman triumphal processions. The royal historiographer, Johann Stabius, created the iconographic program (using symbols from Horapollo's *Hieroglyphica*), and the woodcuts were then prepared by Albrecht Dürer (See *CF,* 8).

In a frontispiece, the plinth created the stage for allegorical tableaux on which the actors "performed." That is, it provided the architectural space on which the historical figures or personifications — chosen to symbolize the material of the book's subject matter — were displayed for the viewer:

> The juxtaposition of spiritual symbols, of allegory and myth with the factual world was a commonplace of visual art; it was characteristic of the tableau mounted on its *pegma* and of the contemporary masque. Similarly on our title pages there is an interplay of symbol

and reality; indeed they derive much of their impact from the interaction of the different spheres of imagery. Reality may be represented by historical characters, living people, the stuff of geography and
astronomy, architectural views. (*CF*, 42)

The figures who appeared on the *pegma*, or plinth, were derived
from a number of sources. In the fourteenth century, antiquarians and
scholars began to collect classical coins and medals. These objects celebrated great events, depicted mythological figures, and were thought
to provide accurate portraits of historic individuals, such as Roman
emperors.[31] The reverse of these ancient coins often depicted allegorical subjects, such as gods or the fates. Along with figures taken from
classical mythology, allegorical personifications inherited from the
Middle Ages (such as the Arts, or the Vices) also found their way onto
the title pages.

In 1593 an unillustrated edition of Cesare Ripa's *Iconologia* was
published in Rome, and this book became the standard work on allegorical personifications for the following two centuries. It was originally meant to serve as a handbook for writers and for organizers of
ceremonies and pageants, but it soon became a manual used primarily
by artists.[32] The work included more than 1,250 personifications,
arranged alphabetically, from *Abbondanza* (abundance) to *Zelo* (zeal).
Since Ripa was a member of two literary academies in Italy, the personifications in his work were derived from classical literature and
statues, hieroglyphs, emblems, and a large number were even invented
by Ripa himself. Ripa "not only relates in extreme detail how personifications should look, but he also explains why they should be depicted precisely as he describes them. The moralizing nature of his 'spec-
ifications' often becomes evident in these explanations."[33] By 1603 the
first illustrated edition appeared, and again it showed the primacy of
the author, who enjoined the artist, Cesare d'Arpino, to follow the dic-
tates of the text. The *Iconologia* thus was an important reference work,
not only for princely ceremonies (triumphal entries, weddings, pageants) and works of art (statues, paintings, and frescoes), but it also
served as a source for the frontispiece, which often used personifications as simulated sculptures in niches flanking the archway, or on the
plinth itself.

The Portrait

Finally, a portrait of the book's author could appear on the frontispieces as well.

> An old tradition led to . . . [its] inclusion. During the Middle Ages living authors often had themselves portrayed on presentation copies of their manuscripts. In the case of the printed book such portraits were long placed on the verso of the title page and in the seventeenth century we frequently find an engraved portrait following the engraved title page. But from the first decade of the sixteenth century we also find the portrait of the living author transferred to the title page itself. (*CF,* 43)

After the advent of copperplate engraving, an author's portrait would often be updated several times during his lifetime, in order to have as accurate a likeness as possible.

In Olearius's case, his likeness appears in all the editions of his travel account. In the first edition of 1647, his portrait appears on both the frontispiece (above the ceremonial arch in a separate cartouche) and as a separate engraved portrait, three pages later. On the engraved portrait by August John, Olearius is depicted at age forty-five in an oval frame (Figure 2.1). His bust is turned toward the left, while his right hand rests on his hip and his elbow sticks out rather jauntily. He wears an elaborate lace collar and a doublet. Below the portrait one finds his personal motto still within the oval frame. Below the frame, in a separate cartouche (engraved with the date, and with a swag of fruits and flowers on either side) we read a separate dedicatory poem, written in Latin by his friend Polycarpus Wirth. A cartouche above the portrait depicts the hand of God holding an olive twig above the author's head: a word play on "Olearius" most likely.[34] On either side of the oval the geographical areas through which the author travelled are represented: on the left, a wooden structure, perhaps a Russian farmhouse, is surrounded by trees; to the right we find a Persian hostel ("Gasthaus") and a *chinar* tree (plane-tree).

The 1656 edition of the travel account includes a separate engraved portrait of the author, five pages after the frontispiece

2.1 Engraved portrait of Adam Olearius from the *Offt Begehrte Rejsebeschreibung* (1647).

(Figure 2.2). The depiction of the by now fifty-five-year-old man is more sober and staid than in the earlier image, which showed a more active Olearius. Here the *Hofbibliothecarius* and *Hofmathematicus* — whose titles of office have been added to the inscription encircling the oval — fingers his chain of office. The collar is simpler, and the luxurious robe, with its deep folds, belongs to an established member of the court, who exudes an aura of respectability and accomplishment. The face is also more careworn (with larger bags under the eyes) and the author's white hair is yet another sign of his age and distinction. One may also note the plainness and austerity of the entire image: no flora or landscapes detract from the portrait itself (as in the previous version), having been replaced by thin horizontal lines. The personal motto is still contained within the oval, while the dedicatory verse below also remains the same, albeit appearing on an illusionistic drapery, which appears to have been nailed below the frame. The engraver's name, "C. Rothgießer," appears in the bottom right corner,

2.2 Engraved portrait of Adam Olearius from the *Vermehrte Newe Reysebeschreibung* (1656).

but no date is included. The portrait in the frontispiece was thus a visual method of representing or even creating an image of the self, and prefigures the author's self-representation in the written text that follows.

A frontispiece was designed with a specific book in mind. It was not meant to stand alone as a general statement, since its complicated iconographic program was directed at (or even implied a dialogue with) the text that followed — the written words would make clear what the images symbolized on the frontispiece. In the case of especially recondite imagery, this process of interpreting the imagery on the frontispiece could either occur explicitly in a short poem or prose text called a *frontispicii explicatio,* that immediately followed the title page; or the meaning would become evident in an implicit manner as the reader made his way through the text and became familiar with the subject matter. Finally, after having read the entire work, the symbolism on the title page could be reexamined and fully understood in retrospect (so to speak), in light of the knowledge acquired from the reading of the text.

OLEARIUS AND THE FRONTISPIECE

Olearius's Frontispieces for the Gottorf Court

Upon returning from his journeys, Olearius was appointed court librarian and mathematician, in charge of maintaining the library as well as developing the Duke's cabinet of curiosities. Olearius's travel account was a European bestseller, and was translated into Dutch, English, French, and Italian soon after its publication in 1647. The enlarged second edition of the journey, which appeared in 1656 included more than 120 engravings in an 800-page book, most of which were "drawn from life," as he emphasizes in the introduction to his account. In order to coordinate the publication of this massive work, Olearius had three printing presses installed in his house, and required that the engravers live and work there, under his direct supervision. Typically, he would design a title page and then have a professional engrave it. The two men who are most associated with his frontispieces are: August John, his former drawing teacher from Leipzig, and Christian Rothgießer from Husum.[35] As an official and respected member of the Gottorf court — as *Secretarius*, then *Hofmathematicus* and *Hofbibliothecarius* — one of Olearius's duties was to create and commission works that would glorify his patron: first Olearius's main benefactor, Duke Frederick III of Holstein-Gottorf (1616–1659), and then his successor, Duke Christian Albrecht (1659–1694). Frontispieces served this purpose admirably, since by definition, they sought to be monumental, awe-inspiring works that aimed to spark the viewer's interest. There are two main categories of frontispieces that Olearius designed: those made to commemorate official functions at the court, and those that resulted from his literary activities.[36] Among those of the first category — relating to his official duties — we can begin with the frontispiece for the ballet *Von*

Unbeständigkeit der Weltlichen Dinge / und von Herrligkeit und Lobe der Tugend (Concerning the Changeability of Worldly Things, and the Wonder and Praise of Virtue, Schleswig, 1650), engraved by Christian Lorenzen Rothgießer, following a design by Adam Olearius (Figure 2.3).[37]

The ballet was written to commemorate the wedding between the Landgraf Ludwig von Hessen and the third daughter of the Duke and

2.3 Frontispiece to the ballet
Von Unbeständigkeit der Weltlichen Dinge (1650).

Duchess of Schleswig-Holstein, Maria Elisabeth. The work is a good example of courtly self-representation during the German Baroque. The image on the frontispiece is contained within a cartouche, beneath the text of the title. The bride and groom — who both wear classical clothing — stand on a stage beneath an archway, and strike theatrical poses. Flaming hearts, symbolizing their union, are at the apex of the arch, below which Cupid pulls back a curtain to reveal their coats-of-arms and an anagram formed from a union of their names, which creates a play on words: the bride's initials form "MEL," or "honey" in Latin.[38] On the following page, the allusion is made clear in the text: "In unser beyder Liebeswunden / Wird lautter süsses Honig funden." (In the love wounds of the two of us / Nothing but sweet honey will be found.)[39] The text following the title page consists of approximately fifty pages. The ballet was comprised of three acts that contain an intricate mythological and allegorical program that explained the subject matter of the performance and included the texts of the songs. The wedding guests participated in the ballet as well, playing personifications of "Virtues" or "Vices," "The Four Seasons," etc. The piece culminated in the final act, entitled "Vergänglichkeit . . . [wird] überwunden durch Nachruhm" (Transience. . . [is] conquered by fame). My description can only provide a brief overview of the entire ballet, but what it demonstrates is, once again, the manner in which the symbolism of the frontispiece tries to contain the subject matter of the text that follows.

When Duke Frederick III died in 1659, Olearius designed the title page for the "Leichbegängnis" (Funeral procession) of 1662 to commemorate the event (Figure 2.4). The theatricality of the memorial is emphasized, as rather misshapen putti pull back the curtain to reveal the title text within an imposing architectural framework. The busy iconographic program contains such typical Baroque symbols and architectural motifs as serpentine columns and ivy-enlaced obelisks resting on unstable spheres (above which float — in midair — a crown of royalty and a winged sphere, symbolizing transitory Fame). Along with the banderolles ("Schriftfahnen") on the obelisks and the mottos inscribed on the cloths attached to the bases of the structure, the allegorical personifications in the side niches serve to underline the message of the image as well: the triumph of death (but with a happy end

2.4 Frontispiece to the *Hochfürstliche Leichenbegengniß* (1662).

for the deceased). We find, on the left, a standing skeletal figure of Death holding the imperial orb, and, on the right, another figure of Death, holding a scythe, and attempting to knock down a crypt door with its foot. Each of the swags above the niches contains a skull at its center, a motif that is repeated at the very top of the structure, where two putti seated on the "S-volutes" hold shields emblazoned with a skull and crossbones. Between the cherubs at the very top of the image we find the religious summation to the Duke's life: the Hebrew letters for "Jahweh" enclosed within a cloud, cast their divine light onto the kneeling figure of the Duke, who kneels above his personal motto: "Non est mortale quod opto" ("That which I wish for is not mortal"). As Wolfgang Müller has demonstrated, this motto was derived from the collection of religious emblems assembled by the Jesuit priest Hermann Hugo (1588–1629), the *Pia Desideria, emblematis, elegiis et affectibus . . . illustrata* of 1624.[40] Although originally compiled in

CHRISTIANO-ALBERTINÆ.
INAVGVRATIO.

Catholic Antwerp, "das Andachtsbuch . . . war auch im lutherischen Holstein verbreitet, es entsprach in seinem gesamten Inhalt auch der lutherischen Überzeugung, daß der Menschenseele die individuelle Selbstläuterung anbefohlen und möglich sei" ("the devotional book . . . was also popular in Lutheran Holstein; in its contents it corresponded to the Lutheran conviction that the human soul was ordered to engage in individual self-purification, and was capable of it.")[41]

Below the motto we find the elaborate coat-of-arms of Schleswig-Holstein, affixed above the title and name of the deceased, which in turn is placed above a southern view of the Gottorf castle in the cartouche below. A link is established between earth at the very bottom of the image and heaven at the top, with the Duke serving as intermediary figure, connecting the two realms. In other words, the central placement of the Duke's attributes — his home, name, heraldry, and figure — allows the viewer to grasp the entire span of the deceased's life (and death) at a single glance.

When Duke Frederick's successor, Christian Albrecht, inaugurated the University of Kiel in 1665 Olearius did not write the pamphlet in honor of the event — this task was carried out by a certain Alexander Julius Torquatus à Frangipani, a baron who had been employed at the Swedish court.[42] However, Olearius did design the iconographic program of the frontispiece (Figure 2.5), which depicts the Duke in Parnassus, seated on a dais. He is surrounded by the nine Muses and receives homage from Apollo, who kneels before him. The ruler wears a laurel wreath on his head, and holds an olive branch of peace in one hand, and a neck-iron in the other, which he has removed from the god. The Duke crushes a Gorgon/Medusa head underfoot — symbolizing war. He is showered by flowers, perhaps roses, that fall from the horn of plenty which is held by a cupid. The cupid is astride an eagle flying above the assembly, and trumpets the Duke's accomplishments against the background of a resplendent sun that shines forth despite the clouds in the sky. The sun and flowers symbolize the good will of the emperor, who, along with God, blesses the enterprise (as the banderolle "Cum Jova et Caesare" implies).

2.5 (*Opposite*) Frontispiece for the founding of Kiel University (1666).

Olearius's Frontispieces: Literary Works

Olearius was involved in the publication of many literary works, including an edition of his friend Paul Fleming's collected poetry, after the latter's early death in 1640.[43] Olearius was also associated with the translation of Virgil's *Eclogues* into German: Oswald Beling, *Verdeutschete Waldlieder / Oder 10. Hirtengespräche Des aller fürtrefflichsten Lateinisch: Poeten Virg. Marons / In Deutsche Verse übersetzet . . . und mit schönen Kupfferstücken gezieret . . . Heraus gegeben Durch M. Adam Olearium* (Schleswig, 1649) (Forest Songs translated into German, Or ten conversations among shepherds by the most excellent Latin Poet Virgilius Maro translated into German verse . . . and ornamented with beautiful copper engravings . . . published by Adam Olearius). Since Virgil's ten eclogues — the *Bucolica* — were considered to be classics of the pastoral poetry genre, German Baroque authors considered it necessary to have a good translation of the work in German. "Martin Opitz forderte Olearius dazu auf, als dieser ihm 1630 in Leipzig seine Aufwartung machte, Olearius gab den Auftrag später an seinen vielversprechenden, aber jung gestorbenen Schüler Oswald Beling (1625–1646) weiter, half aber wohl auch selbst nach. Trotz ihrer stilistischen Qualitäten blieb die Übersetzung ohne Wirkung" (Martin Opitz encouraged Olearius to do this when the latter paid him a courtesy call in Leipzig in 1630; Olearius later gave the task to his promising student Oswald Beling [1625–46] who, however, died young; he probably helped in the translation. In spite of its stylistic qualities the translation had no resonance.)[44]

The title page (Figure 2.6) — engraved by Christian Rothgießer and most likely designed by Adam Olearius — shows a single outdoor scene with a shepherdess and a flute-playing shepherd facing each other in the foreground (representing the work's subject matter) and an outdoor scene with dancing shepherds in the middle and background. Between the foreground figures, the title is written on a cloth, suspended from two tree branches. As we have seen, this motif of the cloth or scroll of paper was a very popular feature on Early Modern frontispieces. It was derived from the practice of depicting titles which seemed to be carved onto tablets, "a conceit that appealed to the Renaissance cult of antiquity" (*CF,* 20).

2.6. Frontispiece to Oswald Beling, *Verdeutschete Waldlieder* (1649).

Olearius also published the travel account of his friend, Johann Albrecht von Mandelsloh, who, like Fleming, accompanied the embassy to Persia. Although Mandelsloh claims to have travelled to India and the Spice Islands, he actually sailed home along the African coast and died soon after returning to Europe.[45] On the title page, engraved once again by Christian Rothgießer, (Figure 2.7), an ivy-enlaced obelisk raised in Mandelsloh's memory dominates the scene, and leads the viewer's eye upward, toward the heavens (where the author, it is assumed, now resides). The obelisk is vine-covered and rests on four spheres, which in turn are located on a base with the inscription: "Vivit post funera virtus" (Virtue lives on after the funeral rites). At the top of the obelisk, winged Fame trumpets the deceased's accomplishments. The very tip of the monument is crowned by a winged sphere, again, signifying the author's renown.[46] A large, elaborate cartouche — with palm fronds sticking out from the sides — contains the title of the work: *Johan Albrecht von Mandeslos*

Johan Albrecht
Von Mandelsloss.
Morgenlendische
Reise.
Beschreibung

Viuit post
funera
virtus

C. Rothgießer fecit

Morgenlendische Reise Beschreibung. The cartouche is capped by a medieval jousting helmet on top of which we find the head of a Moor, who has two daggers stuck into his eyes. This is a particularly violent image of Christian mastery over the infidel — who is blinded to the true faith — and is perhaps a trophy-like remnant from the Crusades. While the dark clouds in the sky contribute to the mood of sorrow that the image strives to depict, the notion of wonder for the young author's achievements is expressed in the scene by the group of international admirers gathered around the base of the monument, all of whom gaze up at the cartouche.

At the extreme left, we see the frontal view of a dark-skinned "Hassanist oder Indostaner" holding a shield and bow in his right arm and with a double-handled dagger stuck in his belt.[47] Next to him stand two Europeans (Germans), both of whom turn their backs to the viewer. Their clothing, swords, walking stick, and spurs betoken their status as nobles — and remind the viewer that Mandelsloh is an aristocrat as well. In the right foreground four more men look up at the cartouche. At the extreme right, a Russian boyar (or nobleman) wearing a bearskin hat, with his hand on his hip, is shown in three-quarter profile. Next to him we see the profile view of a turbaned Persian with his left arm outstretched, and pointing up at the column. A Persian saber hangs from his left side. Partially obscured, a Dagestani Tatar, holding a bow and furry shield, stands next to him; while at his side the viewer can see the head, shoulders, and left arm of yet another Persian wearing a turban. In short, the "iconic" individuals on the frontispiece are meant to represent both the various parts of the world Mandelsloh actually (or supposedly) traveled to, and the international fame accrued to the author because of his many voyages. Intrigued by the image, the reader is then supposed to be spurred on to read the text, in order to find out more about the author's adventures across the globe.

2.7. (*Opposite*) Frontispiece to J. A. von Mandelsloh,
   Morgenländische Reyse-Beschreibung (1668).

Flugblätter

Another method used in Europe to disseminate information about foreign peoples during the Early-Modern Era was the *Flugblatt* (broadsheet or broadside). A broadside usually consisted of a single sheet of paper that combined a woodcut illustration and a text, imprinted on one side of the paper. It was a medium directed at the illiterate classes that needed a visual cue to understand some kind of dramatic event. The subject matter of these *Flugblätter* was very broad, and could include news about battles, both at home and abroad; an astrological prediction or the sighting of a comet; the birth of a monstrous creature (be it animal or human); the execution of a famous criminal; tales of witches, devils, or other supernatural beings; and religious or political propaganda. The introduction of new technology in the fifteenth and sixteenth centuries in Europe — movable type and the printing press — made the large scale production of *Flugblätter* possible. No longer the sole realm of the privileged classes, printed matter became popular across Europe: broadsides continued to be used for over two centuries to spread news to a large audience. As Dorothy Alexander notes, the counterpart of the *Flugblatt*:

> was the *Flugschrift*, which can be translated as "flying writ" or "flying pamphlet." These pamphlets were popularized by Martin Luther. They were intended for a more limited audience with the ability and leisure to read longer tracts. Sometimes these pamphlets consisted of a mere four pages, with a woodcut gracing the first page, but occasionally they numbered as many as thirty-two pages, folded from one large printed sheet. But the prevalence of illiteracy or limited reading knowledge made the broadsheet the preferred medium for the general public, much as the tabloid newspaper is today.[48]

Emperor Maximilian I (1459–1519) made use of both genres, *Flugblatt* and *Flugschrift*, as a form of self-representation and political propaganda. During the early sixteenth century, the most talented minds were involved in the production of broadsides.[49]

The mid-sixteenth century also saw the development of the periodical newssheet, which was an adaptation of the broadside. While the customary single-leaf broadside, issued intermittently, thrived during times of social political, or religious turmoil, the need of merchants and politicians for accurate and consistent reports of current events resulted in the issuance of periodical sheets. During the Thirty Years War the intermittent broadside saw a revival, but it reached its final phase and demise in the subsequent decades. It was not until after the Thirty Years War that the daily newssheet made its appearance . . . *Neue Zeitungen* ("new happenings") . . . reported new discoveries, inundations, disasters, trade restrictions, trade opportunities, peace settlements, openings of hospitals, and so on.[50]

In Europe, broadsheets were often employed to report on the Ottoman threat during the sixteenth and seventeenth centuries and to provide a European or German-speaking public information concerning the advance of the Ottoman armies, which were considered to be nearly invincible. That is one of the reasons that their defeat at the hands of a Christian navy at the battle of Lepanto (1571), for example, was considered an event of such magnitude. News of this victory resulted in hundreds of "extra" editions being published across the entire continent.

An account of a Persian victory over an Ottoman army in 1578 is portrayed in a *Flugblatt* by the artist Hans Mack (Figure 2.8). The battle consists of a number of rather confusing scenes, with each scene showing a different moment in the battle. The action takes place between the cities "Caranit" and "Servan." If we read the image from the right foreground to the left middleground, we see the combined Persian and Georgian army driving the "Tvrcken" along with five hundred of their camels, into the Tigris or Tegil river — 50,000 Turks supposedly perished either on land or in the river. On the left-hand side, the Ottoman general, Mustapha Pasha ("Mustapha Bassa"), is portrayed three times. The first depiction shows him seated in the foreground, flanked by two Janissaries, and receiving an embassy of Georgian noblemen, who kneel before him as they offer him treasure. A German viewer would have been particularly interested in the representation of these exotic foreigners, who are depicted as if on display (especially the Janissary holding the rifle, facing the viewer). Above the

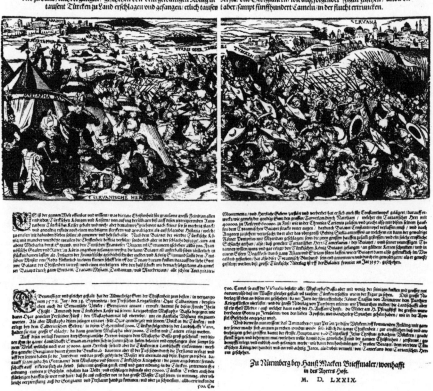

Contrafactur vnd anzeigung der jetzigen grosse n Türckischen Niderlag/dergleichen in 181. Jaren/zu Land/nicht ergangen/geschehen von dem gewaltigen König in Persia/vnd Georgianern/wie auß folgender Figur zusehen/allda vil tausent Türcken zu Land erschlagen vnd gefangen/etlich tausen t aber/sampt fünffhundert Cameln/in der flucht ertruncken.

Zu Nürmberg bey Hanß Macken Brieffmaler/wonhafft in der Apertz Hofe.

M. D. LXXIX.

2.8. Broadsheet of Persian victory over the Ottoman army by Hans Mack (1578).

Ottoman tents, in the left middle ground, the mounted generals — Mustapha Pasha on the left and the Persian, "Ozar Calarinum" on the right — face each other, at least symbolically. In the background, yet another inscription shows "MVSTAPHA" a third time, fleeing the battle with a few of his followers, and leaving the rest of his army to drown in the river. Although the *Flugblatt* depicts a single event, not a universal situation, it does have a quasi-emblematic tripartite structure. An inscription running above the woodcut tells the reader that this is the greatest Ottoman defeat on land within the past 181 years. The image portrays different segments of the battle, which, however, are unintelligible without the benefit of the accompanying text below the picture. The text is divided into two parts: the upper portion reminds the audience of the Ottoman defeat in 1397, whereas the lower portion details how the Persian/Georgian army was able to defeat the mighty Ottoman host. The interrelated portions of the broadside — consisting of image and text — work together in order to provide meaning for the design. A viewer needed to combine all the different segments of the work, in order to fully understand what was being depicted, and the significance of this foreign battle for a European audience.

The Early-Modern Costume Book

Another medium used to depict foreign peoples for a European audience was the illustrated costume book. This type of publication typically displayed the local costumes of European citizens, e.g., nobles, clergy, merchants, warriors, and women at the beginning of the work and then showed examples of exotic folk from around the world wearing their native dress. These latter depictions could be based on eyewitness observations, but the further away the peoples were located, usually the more fanciful the representation. Hans Weigel's *Trachtenbuch* (Costume Book) of 1577, which included a number of illustrations by the artist Jost Amman, is a good example of the genre, and was very popular in the German-speaking lands. The frontispiece (Figure 2.9) to the work is divided into three levels, and contains the subject matter of the work depicted in a condensed visual form, complete with Mannerist strapwork, grotesques, garlands, and allegorical personifications. In the cartouche at the top, the expulsion from the Garden of Eden is depicted: on the right half, Adam and Eve are shown in Paradise, with a unicorn in the middleground between them. The left-hand portion of the cartouche depicts them in furs, being cast out of the garden by the angel. The scene also represents the original reason why humans need to wear clothing, and is an appropriate frontispiece for a book on costumes. The title of the work is placed on an illusionistic cloth, which appears to be nailed onto the lower edge of the cartouche. The inscription promises that the depictions are up-to-date, entertaining, and include clothing of both sexes from the most important regions in the world. Allegorical putti (symbolizing industry on the upper right), and personifications (Mars on the left, not engaged in warlike activity) flank the upper two registers. In the bottom level, within an ornately decorated cartouche, the four corners of

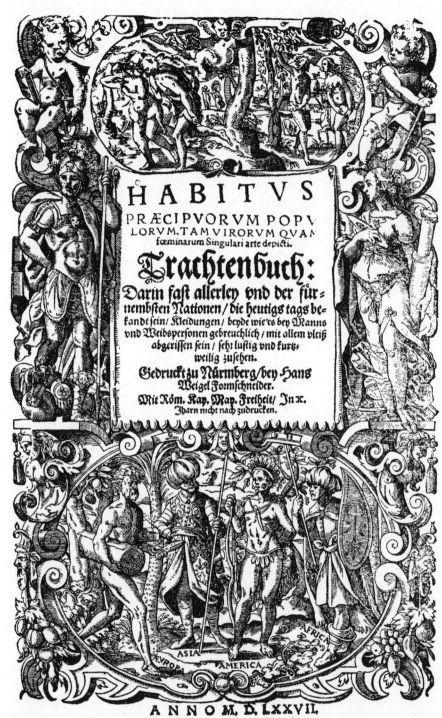

HABITVS
PRÆCIPVORVM POPV
LORVM, TAM VIRORVM QVAM
fœminarum Singulari arte depicti.

Trachtenbuch:
Darin faſt allerley vnd der fur-
nembſten Nationen/ die heutigs tags bekandt ſein/ Kleidungen/ beyde wie's bey Manns
vnd Weibsperſonen gebreuchlich/ mit allem vleiß
abgeriſſen ſein/ ſehr luſtig vnd kurtz-
weilig zuſehen.

Gedruckt zu Nürmberg/bey Hans
Weigel Formſchneider.

Mit Röm. Kap. May. Freiheit/ Jn x.
Jharn nicht nach zudrucken.

ANNO M. D. LXXVII.

2.9. Frontispiece to Hans Weigel's *Trachtenbuch* (1577).

the Earth are represented by male figures, who are identified by inscriptions at their feet and by the flora beside each of them. Entering the scene from the left, in three-quarter profile, a nude European tailor, holding a roll of cloth and scissors, represents Europe. He is the only individual who is active, nude, and not dressed for battle — although his scissors do point rather dangerously at the midsection of his foreign neighbor representing "Asia." Perhaps the nude figure is meant to stand for the author, who will actively clothe the other figures for the benefit of his readers.

At his side, a Persian satrap (governor) standing next to a palm tree represents Asia. Completing the group are a Native American and an Ottoman Turk (standing for Africa, since the Sultan's empire stretched across Northern Africa). The fact that the personifications of the non-Europeans are all prepared for battle — with spears, swords, knives, bow, and shield — underscores the notion that the rest of the world is full of danger. The reader is meant to be intrigued by this element of peril, and should wish to see more such figures delineated in greater detail inside the book. Inside the *Trachtenbuch*, the Persian satrap is portrayed in a full-page format (Figure 2.10) above a

2.10. Persian satrap from Hans Weigel's *Trachtenbuch* (1577).

2.11. Tatar warrior from Hans Weigel's *Trachtenbuch* (1577).

four-line rhymed inscription that stresses the fact that Persia was destroyed by the European conqueror Alexander. The exotic noble lord is accurately portrayed in sixteenth-century dress, implying that the artist had access to recent depictions of Persian costumes. The portrayal of the satrap stands in contrast to that of a Tatar warrior (Figure 2.11), who looks as though he could have stepped directly out of "Asterix and Obelix" instead of from the Central Asian Steppe.

Later costume books — such as Abraham de Bruyn's *Omnium pene Evropae, Asiae, Aphricae atque Americae Gentium Habitus* (Antwerp, 1610) — which had illustrations based on direct contact with the foreign peoples in question, provided more accurate depictions of faraway natives: the "Tartarus gentili more armatus" shown in de Bruyn's work (Figure 2.12) is still as bellicose as the Tatar soldier in the Weigel costume book, but his dress and appearance are based more on reality than on imagination.

2.12. Muscovite and Tatar warriors from Abraham de Bruyn's *Omnium pene Evropae, Asiae, Aphricae atque Americae Gentium Habitus* (Antwerp, 1610).

The four continents were usually represented by female figures, as on the frontispiece to de Bruyn's work (Figure 2.13). A large oval cartouche contains the title, which is written in three languages, thus aiming at an international audience. From upper left, continuing counterclockwise to the upper right side, we find the female personifications

2.13. Frontispiece to Abraham de Bruyn's *Omnium pene Evropae, Asiae, Aphricase atque Americae Gentium Habitus* (Antwerp, 1610).

of Asia (holding a parrot and with a miniature camel beside her); a recumbent Africa (with an elephant and wheat-like hair — derived from the classical association of Egypt as Rome's breadbasket); Europe is astride a bull and has a horse as her attribute; America wears a feather headdress and cloak, as well as a jewel necklace, which represents the riches of the New World. She also holds a bow and arrow and has a tapir as her token. The symbols associated with the personifications of the continents were derived, in part, from Biblical and classical sources, such as Roman coins.[51]

In the frontispiece to Petrus Opmeer's contemporaneous historical work *Opus Chronographicum* of 1611 (Figure 2.14), the personifications of the continents are placed on rounded plinths and act as simulated sculptures. To the left of the title we find Europe holding a sceptre and imperial orb, and Asia with an incense holder; on the right, a nude Africa holds a parasol, and a warlike America grasps a bow and arrow, and wears a feather headdress and skirt. The iconography of the feather skirt has an intriguing history. Scholars have researched this particular attribute of "America," and found that there are no native

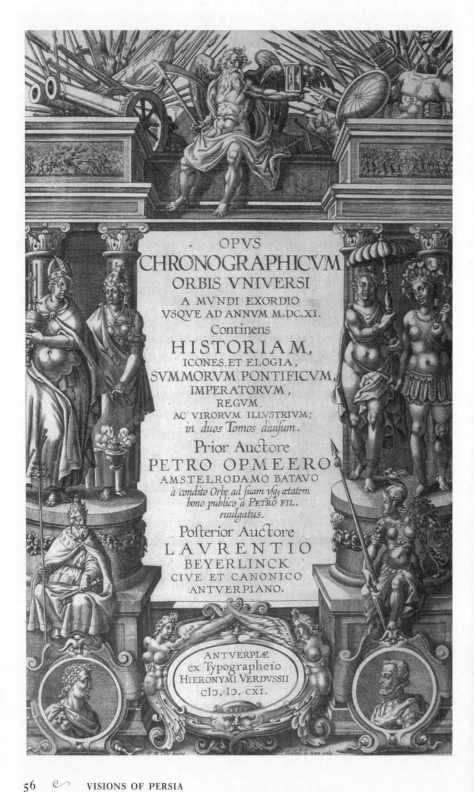

OPVS
CHRONOGRAPHICVM
ORBIS VNIVERSI
A MVNDI EXORDIO
VSQVE AD ANNVM M.DC.XI.
Continens
HISTORIAM,
ICONES, ET ELOGIA,
SVMMORVM PONTIFICVM,
IMPERATORVM,
REGVM,
AC VIRORVM ILLVSTRIVM;
in duos Tomos diuisum.

Prior Auctore
PETRO OPMEERO
AMSTELRODAMO BATAVO
à condito Orbe ad suam vsq; ætatem
bono publico à PETRO FIL.
euulgatus.

Posterior Auctore
LAVRENTIO
BEYERLINCK
CIVE ET CANONICO
ANTVERPIANO.

ANTVERPIÆ
ex Typographeio
HIERONYMI VERDVSSII
cIɔ. Iɔ. cXI.

Amerindian tribes who wore such feather skirts. In fact, the art historian Hugh Honour observes that "the quills of the feathers would have made it a most uncomfortable, if not slightly perilous garment for anyone not standing upright."[52] He points out that this type of object, when opened out flat, resembles a Central American featherwork headdress. When the object was sent back to Europe as an artifact — that is, once the object was removed from its original ethnographic context, "decontextualized," and then "recontextualized" in a different setting[53]— a European, quite understandably, might have thought that it was a skirt. The first representation of Amerindians wearing such attire dates from 1505, and feathered skirts also appear in Hans Burgkmair's woodcuts for Emperor Maximilian I's triumphal procession (1516–1519; print, 1526). It then became a convention to portray America wearing this garment, a custom that has continued even to the present age.

Olearius's Frontispiece for the *Offt Begehrte Beschreibung der Newen Orientalischen Rejse* (1647)

Olearius's travel account was his defining work, and the frontispiece to the first edition, *Die Offt Begehrte Beschreibung der Newen Orientalischen Rejse* (Schleswig, 1647) — engraved by August John — provides the viewer with a mixture of realistic and fantastic images concerning the journey to Muscovy and Persia (Figure 2.15).

The architectural frame — festooned with swags of exotic fruits — is crowned with a profile portrait of Olearius within an oval cartouche, which has been uncovered by a cloth of honor. A Persian silk rug, with a floral pattern (representing the economic incentive for the journey) partially conceals the title of the work. The author's name below the title is unobscured. The rug and the cloth of honor serve a similar function, in that they uncover both the author's image on the entablature, as well as his inscribed name and the title of his magnum opus. The illusionistic cloths denote a process not only of uncovering, but of discovery as well. As in a theater, the curtains are pulled back (on the top and middle registers) to reveal the true subject of the work,

2.14 (Opposite) Frontispiece to Petrus Opmeer's *Opus Chronographicum* (1611).

2.15 Frontispiece to Adam Olearius's *Offt Begehrte Rejsebeschreibung* (1647).

which, appropriately, is located at the very center of the image: the Paradisical scene in the center, which is flanked by exotic natives standing on plinths. These "natives" can be identified as follows: to the right we find a Russian boyar (with a servant half hidden behind him), who stands above a scalloped-shaped cartouche depicting St. George killing the dragon. On the left, a Persian nobleman holds a hooded falcon in his right hand; below him is the symbol of Persia, a lion and a rising sun. In order to understand why our author chose this particular scene — the Garden of Eden — to illustrate the title page of his

2.16 Frontispiece to Basilius Besler's *Hortus Eystettensis* (1613).

travel account, indeed, to epitomize the topic of his work, we need to consult the title page of a different text, one which may have even served as a model for Olearius's frontispiece.

The composition of the frontispiece to the *Hortus Eystettensis* (The Garden of Eichstätt) of 1613 (Figure 2.16) is remarkably similar to the Olearius title page. The work was written by the Nürnberg apothecary Basilius Besler for Johann Konrad von Gemmingen, the "Fürst-bischof" of Eichstätt. Besler's work describes and depicts all the plants found in the prince-bishop's garden, and provides illustrations and names of the vegetation, all catalogued according to the seasonal period of each plant. Besler's frontispiece contains most of the same basic elements as are on the title page to Olearius's travel account: an architectural frame with double columns and Corinthian capitals, that support a pediment. On the upper register, reclining personifications of bounty (on the left) and industry (on the right) flank the center cartouche with the prince-bishop's coat-of-arms. The title of the work is placed on an illusionistic cloth attached to the architectural framework. On the plinths we find wise Solomon on the left (identified by the name inscribed on the cartouche below him); on the right is Cyrus, ancient King of Persia, which, according to the Bible, may have been the land where the Garden of Eden was located. In the central scene, God takes Adam by the hand and shows him the flora and fauna of Paradise.[54] In his introduction to the *Hortus Eystettensis*, Dieter Vogellehner explains why Besler chose this scene for his title page:

> Es ist die Aufgabe des Menschen, das Buch der Schöpfung neu zu lesen und den Versuch zu machen, das Paradies, durch den Sündenfall zerschlagen und an vielen Plätzen der Erde in Einzelstücken zerstreut, wie die Steinchen eines Mosaiks zusammenzusetzen zu einer Enzyklopädie der Schöpfung — wie sie auch der Garten Eden ursprünglich war . . . Die Aufgabe Adams ist es, auch dieses Paradies zu hüten und zu bewahren. Dem Botaniker ist der Auftrag zugewiesen, in der Art eines neuen Adam die Pflanzen zu benennen, zu beschreiben und abzubilden. In einem Garten . . . sollen Pflanzen aus allen vier Erdteilen zusammengetragen und somit ein Abbild und ein Ausschnitt aus dem Paradies geschaffen werden.[55]

> It is the task of man to read the book of creation anew and to try to reassemble Paradise (which has been smashed by Original Sin and has been scattered across the earth like the small stones of a mosaic) into an Encyclopedia of Creation — as was the Garden of Eden originally . . . It is moreover, the task of Adam to care for this Paradise, and to preserve it. The botanist — like a new Adam — has been given the task to name plants, to describe and depict them. In

a garden . . . plants from the four continents are to be collected and thus a reflection and a part of Paradise shall be created.

If we return to Olearius's frontispiece of 1647 (Figure 2.15, page 58), we may now better understand the Paradisical scene at the center of the image: in the foreground, a leopard sniffs at a hare; a lion is with a lamb (as in the Biblical citation); and in the background, an elephant leans against a palm tree. What is implied in this frontispiece (and made visible in the Besler title page) is the presence of Adam — that is, of Adam Olearius, whose image and name are found just above, not within the Garden scene. Adam's function is to name (and illustrate) the exotic wonders and foreign objects for his Western audience. He writes in the "Book of Wonders" for the reading public, and adds to the information contained within the universe, thus fulfilling a quasi-religious function: his role as scholar and explorer is to add to the body of knowledge in the world, and as a new Adam, he too is helping to recreate the lost Paradise on Earth (in word and image) through his encyclopedic travel account.

Olearius's Frontispiece for the *Vermehrte Newe Beschreibung der Muscowitischen und Persischen Reyse* (1656)

The illustrated title page to the second edition of the travel account, the *Vermehrte Newe Beschreibung der Muscowitischen und Persischen Reyse* (Figure 2.17) is even more imposing than that of the first edition; it makes use of an architectural framework that is more complex than the traditional arch and plinth model that we have encountered in most frontispieces thus far. In this depiction, the viewer is placed within what seems to be an atrium-like building, which is oval, colonnaded, and open to the sky. Tops of trees peek above the entablature.[56] Enclosed within this space is another tomb-like structure. Schlee describes it as "eine Art Altar- oder Epitaphaufbau" (a type of altar or epitaph structure),[57] which contains the title of the work clearly displayed as a monumental inscription. Below the title, the date, "*Im Jahr 1656*" is inscribed on a type of plinth that juts into the foreground and has two strapwork grotesques above and below. Flanking this structure, two pairs of iconic figures look out directly at the viewer. At

2.17 Frontispiece to Adam Olearius's *Vermehrte Newe Reysebeschreibung* (1656).

the very left, a Persian servant holds a bowl and flask and stands slightly behind his master, who wears a nobleman's *mandil* (turban) and has a fur draped around his shoulders and knife stuck into his belt. The bearded Russian boyar wears a tall bearksin hat and an embroidered coat with overlong sleeves (designating his lofty status). His servant holds a bow, which rests against the ground, and an arrow that is held at a diagonal angle and that leads the viewer's eye to his master's face. The objects held by the servants emphasize the warlike, uncouth nature of the Muscovites, while emphasizing the more civilized, hospitable character of the Persians. Heraldic shields — hanging above the nobles and attached to fluted columns with Corinthian capitals — show a lion (designating Persia) and, as in the frontispiece of the first edition, St. George killing the dragon (denoting Muscovy). Above the inscription a grotesque mask spews forth garlands of exotic fruits, which represent the flora from the visited lands. Flanking the mask, and resting on the entablature, two containers emit flames and smoke, perhaps signifying a valuable product encountered during the voyage, namely *naphta* (oil or petroleum) from the region near Baku. The shape of the oil containers is also reminiscent of the incense holder, which, as we have noted, is an attribute of Asia personified (See Figure 2.13 page 55).

Crowning the entire image — above the grotesque mask — is a cartouche whose image portrays Olearius's religious convictions (in contrast to the 1647 travel account, which depicted Olearius's profile in the cartouche). Inscribed within the oval frame of the cartouche is the author's personal motto, taken from the Bible: "*In consilio tuo ducis me*" (You lead me through your counsel), an inscription that we have already encountered in Olearius's engraved portrait above (Figures 2.1 and 2.2, pages 36 and 37). The scene shows a robed man standing on a globe, who grasps a cord that is held by a hand emanating from the clouds. The man can be construed as Olearius, but it could also represent any individual who believes in the true faith, and allows himself to be guided by God. It thus becomes a general statement that portrays and does not portray our author. The image indicates the author's faith in God, who has accompanied him throughout his travels, and reinforces the notion of the Great Chain of Being. The explorer writes his observations into his magnum opus, the travel account — just as God writes in "das grosse Wunderbuch die Welt" (*GK*, 3b).

It is also important to note that in this title page, the connection established between author and heavenly being is clearly depicted and supplements the textual proclamation of the author's faith. The frontispiece to the 1647 edition only implied the religious dimension of the work: it depicted the author's profile in the cartouche, and did not show God in the Paradisical scene — in contrast to the title page of Besler's *Hortus Eystettensis,* in which God leads Adam through the Garden of Eden. In other words, as Olearius became older, and more devout, he shifts the emphasis from depicting himself (as in the 1647 edition) to a more general portrayal of himself (in the present frontispiece) in which he is not immediately recognizable as Olearius. Here the religious message predominates.

The Foreign Editions of the Travel Account

The frontispieces to the foreign editions of Olearius's travel account, do not, as a rule, attain the artistic level of the German works. Compositionally they are much simpler, and the artists who executed the engravings were less skilled than August John and Christian Rothgießer. In short, they have a cruder feel to them than the last two engraved title pages we have examined.

The engraved title page to the English translation, *The Voyages and Travels of the Ambassadors* (London, 1662),[58] depicts the engraved portraits of the main individuals associated with the journey. The bust of Duke Frederick III occupies the place of honor at the center of the page, since he is the patron of the expedition. Around his portrait, clockwise from the upper right-hand corner are the portraits of Frederick III, Crusius, Brüggemann, Olearius, and Mandelsloh.

The title page to the Dutch edition of 1651 also depicts five individuals and is more interesting than the English version (Figure 2.18).[59] In this depiction, above the inscribed title, we find a rather dour representation (actually a portrait) of the expedition's leader,

2.18 Frontispiece to Adam Olearius's *Beschrijvingh Van de Nieuwe Parciaensche oste Orientaelsche Reyse* (1651).

Otto Brüggemann, contained within an oval cartouche, placed on an entablature at the top of the page. On his right is the three-dimensional bust of Frederick III, who is not placed in the center, perhaps because the Dutch Republic did not place as high an emphasis on aristocracy — the Dutch readers might have identified with the bourgeois merchant rather than the noble. The other depictions are not portraits of actual individuals, but iconic figures representing the main regions through which the embassy traveled. A bust of a turbaned Persian rests on the entablature as well. On the plinth below stand the full-figure representations of a Muscovite — on the left — holding a mace in his right hand; and on the right, a Tatar with a knife at his belt and a quiver of arrows slung over his shoulder. These warlike figures hold a crude, square map showing the regions through which the Holstein embassy traveled in the account, including "Lituania, Moscovia, Tartaria, Astracan, Mare Caspium, Persia" along with the neighboring "Armenia, Natolia, Pontus Euxinus, [and the] Mare Mediterraneum." This emphasis on the map reflects the interest that a Dutch audience would have had in the improved cartography that Olearius produced of the region. Above the map, the inscribed title provides Olearius's

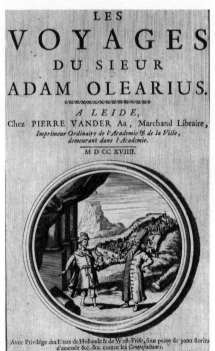

2.19 Frontispiece to Adam Olearius's *Les Voyages du Sieur Adam Olearius* (1727).

name, along with that of the translator, and emphasizes the "Copere fyguren" included within the work.[60]

A French frontispiece of 1727 emphasizes the neo-classical tradition and deemphasizes the pictorial aspect of the representation (Figure 2.19). The title and publication information occupy the upper half of the page, whereas the image is contained within a circular frame. The theatrical aspect of the depiction is accentuated: a curtain has been pulled back and gathered up on the upper left, in order that the viewer may observe the spectacle. On the left side of the image, columns resting on bases, and lying on the ground in fragments, suggest classical antiquity. The iconic representatives — a very misshapen Persian and a bearded Muscovite — are located in the center of the scene, while in the background Mt. Barmach and the city of Derbent are portrayed, most likely chosen since they lie at the border between the two regions.

III

Adam Olearius and the Persianischer Rosenthal

The *Persianischer Rosenthal* (Persian Valley of Roses) of 1654[61] is Adam Olearius's German translation of the celebrated Persian poet Sa'di's *Gulistān* (The Rose Garden) of 1258 A.D. (A.H. 656). This particular work can be said to epitomize the genre of the frontispiece in that it combines the written and pictorial elements in an especially clever manner and reproduces the subject matter of the text in a condensed, visual form. Olearius's translation, the importance of which was later acknowledged by Goethe in his *West-östlicher Divan*,[62] was accomplished with the assistance of a Persian intellectual named Hakwirdi. Hakwirdi had defected from the Persian embassy sent by Shah Safi I to Gottorf in 1639, and ended up living at Olearius's house and teaching him Persian. The *Gulistān* — a collection of short moralistic tales, aphorisms, proverbs, and Sufic lore collected by Sa'di — has been popular in Iran ever since it was written. Appearing a few years after the end of the Thirty Years War in the German-speaking lands, the *Persianischer Rosenthal* parallels the publication of the *Gulistān* in the sense that each work speaks to an audience that has recently suffered from the ravages of war. As Naime Bishr observes in his study on the *Persianischer Rosenthal*: "1258 überrannte Dschingizchans Enkel Bagdad, brannte Stadt und Land zu Schutt und Asche und mordete die Bevölkerung, den Kalifen und seine Familie. Mit dem Tode des letzten der seit 750 herrschenden Abbasiden kam das islamische Grossreich sowohl wie das symbolisch die Einheit des Islams verkörpernde Kalifat zu Ende" (In 1258 Genghis Khan's grandson overran Baghdad, reduced the city and the countryside to rubble and ash and killed the populace, the Khalif, and his family. With the death of the last of the Abbasids — who had been ruling since 750 A.D. — the Islamic Empire as well as the Caliphate, which symbolized the unity of Islam, came to an end).[63] Bishr also notes: "Das bald nach dem Blutbad niedergeschriebene 'Rosenthal' ist daher ein Zeitdokument, das von einem stets das Praktische betonenden Verstandesmenschen verfasst worden war" (The "Valley of Roses" written soon after the bloodbath is therefore a document of its time composed by a man of reason who always stresses the practical, Bishr, 66).

The *Gulistān* provides its readers with pragmatic guidelines for living, that are presented in an entertaining manner. Ever the didact, Olearius praises Sa'di as a "lustiger Kopff" (funloving spirit; *PR*, A3r) and then by way of appealing to a classical authority, who also supports the combination of teaching and entertainment, Olearius goes on to cite Horace's celebrated dictum: "Aut prodesse volunt, aut delectare poêtae, Aut simul & jucunda & idonea dicere vitae" (Poets either want to be useful or provide enjoyment, Or at the same time want to say pleasant things and things which are useful for life; *PR*, A3v). In order to fully appreciate Olearius's role in the translation of Sa'di's text, and to better understand how the images function in the engraved title page to the *Persianischer Rosenthal,* our analysis of Olearius's frontispiece will be preceded by a discussion of the work's background and the history of its translation.

THE POET SA'DI

Shaykh Muslih al-Din Sa'di Shirazi (c. 1213–1292) — known as Sa'di — grew up in the Persian city of Shiraz, the main city in the province of Fars.[64] He spent part of his life in Baghdad, studying traditional Islamic religion at the Nizamiyya Madrasa, before travelling throughout the Islamic world (from North Africa, through the Middle East, and perhaps as far as India and Central Asia). Sa'di is a celebrated Sufi mystic and author of lyrical poetry (*ghazals*) and odes (*qasidas*), best known for both his *Būstān* (The Orchard, 1256–1257), written entirely in verse, and for the *Gulistān*, primarily a work of prose that also includes short poems and aphorisms in verse. These last two works — which blend personal experience, humorous insights, and aphorisms of an ethical/didactic nature — have contributed to Sa'di's reputation as one of the most popular poets of classical Persian literature.

In his preface to the reader Olearius specifically mentions how beloved Sa'di's works are in Persia, and praises the poet's ability to write eloquently about God and spirituality, despite the fact that he is a Shi'i Muslim:

Er ist gleich seinen Landesleuten in dem Mahumedischen ver-führischen Glauben und Aaly Secte aufferzogen. Daher er in diesem Buche / welches sonst lustige Historien und auß demselben gute Lehren in sich hält / bißweilen etliche mahumedische Stücklein mit einwirfft / die man an seinen Ort muß gestellet seyn lassen / und sich darbey verhalten / als Virgilius bey des Ennij[65] Schrifften / da er auß dem Koht schöne Perlen laß. Sonst gibt er seinen Eifer und Andacht in seiner Religion an vielen Orten zuerkennen / und redet bißweilen von Gott / und seinen Wercken / und wie der Mensch sich verhalten soll / nach seiner Art so wol / als ein Christe thun mag / ja beschämet mit seinen geistlichen Gedancken offt manchen Christen / wie zu ersehen auß dem anfang seiner Vorrede . . . Die Warheit der Historien / die Saadi beschreibet / anlangend / kan es wol seyn / daß sie nicht alle also / wie er sie erzehlet / sich begeben haben. (*PR*, B1v)

He was raised like his compatriots in the seductive belief of Mohammed and the sect of Ali. That is why in this book, which otherwise contains entertaining stories and within them good teachings, he sometimes introduces Mohammedan concepts which one has to leave be, and one has to behave in this manner like Virgil with the writings of Ennius when he picked beautiful pearls from out of the dirt. Otherwise he shows his zeal and devotion within his religion in many places and he sometimes talks of God and His works and how man should behave so well — in his own way — as a Christian might do; he even shames many a Christian with his spiritual thought as we can see from the first words of his preface . . . Concerning the truth of the stories described by Sa'di, it is indeed possible that not all of them occurred in the same manner in which he tells them.

This quotation underscores the religious relativism in Olearius's orientalism. On the one hand — in deference to his Christian audience and as a dependent of the Gottorf court — he disparages Islam. We see this in his use of such terms as *verführischer Glauben* (seductive belief) and the inference to *Koht* (dirt). In his preface to the *Persianischer Rosenthal*, Olearius even observes: "Man sihet wie weit es der Teuffel mit den Kinderen des Unglaubens bringen können" (One can see how far the devil can get with the Children of Unbelief, *PR*, B1r). On the other hand, when Olearius writes that Sa'di speaks of "Gott und seinen Wercken," he implies that the poet's spirituality transcends the bounds of Islam. It is interesting to note Olearius's use of the word "Gott" rather than the name "Allah." Perhaps this choice of terminology was made in order to establish a common ground between the Christian God and the God of Muslims. The simple fact that Olearius shows admiration for a distinctly Muslim expression of spirituality, casts his work as the forerunner to the comparative religious studies like those carried out by such Enlightenment philosophers as Herder and Voltaire.[66]

EARLY–MODERN EUROPEAN TRANSLATIONS OF THE *GULISTĀN*

Olearius writes that he acquired his copy of the *Gulistān* "von einem ihrer Molla oder Pfaffe-Namens *Mahebali*" (from one of their mullahs or priests by the name of *Mahebali*) in Shemakha (*PR*, B1r). Upon his return to Gottorf, he then translated the work with the assistance of the Persian Hakwirdi, his friend and counterpart (as the former secretary of the Persian embassy). Hakwirdi lived in Olearius's house for five years and, along with his son, eventually converted to Christianity in an elaborate, public ceremony, no doubt intended to confirm the superiority of Christianity over Islam.[67] Olearius, whose knowledge of Persian was rudimentary upon his return from the journey to Isfahan (having had only three months' instruction while in Shemakha) benefitted greatly from having an educated native informant assist him not only with the translation but also with the interpretation of Sa'di's work.

> Worbey ich gerne bekenne / daß in übersetzung dieses Buches ich
> für mich zu wenig gewesen / wenn ich nicht der Perser Gebräuche
> theils selbst gesehen / theils von obgedachten alten gelarten und der
> Sachen wolkündigen Perser Hakvvirdi ferneren Bericht / so wol auß
> dessen Munde als auß den bey sich habenden Schrifften empfangen
> hätte. Er hat zwar anfänglich und vor seiner bekehrung mit allen
> ihren traditionen und Satzungen / weil er wol merckte / daß sie den
> Stich nicht halten / und von uns verlachet werden möchten / nicht
> recht herauß gewolt / als er aber in unsern Glaubens Artickelen
> recht unterichtet / und getaufft worden / hat er sich besser herauß
> gelassen / und von ein und anderen jedoch behütsam / daß er nicht
> gerne zum Schimpff seines Vaterlandes sondern vielmehr auß
> mitleiden der armen verführten Leute blindheit beklagende / deut-
> lichern nachricht gegeben / welches mir dann in erklärung der
> dunckelen Orter wol zu statten gekommen. (*PR*, B3v)

In which I gladly confess that in translating this book I alone would not have been good enough had I not partly observed the customs of the Persians firsthand, and partly received further information from the previously mentioned old scholarly and knowledgable Persian Hakwirdi — both orally and from the writings he carried with him. In the beginning and before his conversion he did not want to reveal all their traditions and prescripts because he noticed that they do not stand up to scrutiny and might have been ridiculed by us. But when he had been properly instructed in our articles of faith and had been baptized, he gave out more information of this and that, however, carefully, so that he did not give out information to the detriment of his fatherland but rather as he lamented with compassion the blind-ness of the poor seduced populace; that in turn helped me to explain obscure points.

While Olearius acknowledges Hakwirdi's assistance, he also manipulates his Persian friend's voice in the propagandistic con-frontation between the great religions. That is, he speaks for Hakwirdi, who — according to Olearius — feels that the customs of his home-land do not measure up to those of his adopted country. It is only after Hakwirdi has been baptized that he supposedly agrees to aid Olearius "out of pity for the poor seduced [Muslim] people, lamenting their blindness." This notion of the other's blindness is reminiscent of the cartouche in the frontispiece to the Mandelsloh travel account above (Figure 2.7 page 46), in which the bust of a Moor is depicted with daggers stuck in its eyes. Here — instead of a pictorial representation of the other, who exists in spiritual and religious darkness — we have a textual disclaimer, considered all the more valid, since it is being stated by a convert to Christianity.

Our author writes after Martin Opitz's *Buch der deutschen Poeterey* (1624) — a poetics that stressed the importance of the German language — and during the era of the "Sprachgesellschaften."[68] These were language academies charged with fostering the development of the German language that had been modelled on the language academies in Renaissance Italy, such as the "Accademia della Crusca" (founded in Florence in 1582). In the *Persianischer Rosenthal,* the entire enterprise of translation is cloaked in highly metaphoric language. Olearius notes that it was the head of the "Fruchtbringende Gesell-schaft" himself ("der Schmackhaffte") who asked him to translate the *Gulistān* into German, and not into Latin. Nationalist sentiment is underlined in the idea that "our German language that used to lie beneath the dust of contempt now shines forth once again":

Das ich aber diesen Persianer in einem Teutschen Mantel herein führe / und in unser Hochteutschen Muttersprache hören lasse / hat mich theils veranlasset / das hohe Haupt der Fruchtbringenden Gesellschafft / der Schmackhaffte / welcher bey auffnehmung meiner unwürdigen Person / als sie vernommen / daß ich diß Werck unter Händen hätte / gnädig an mir geschrieben; daß ich wol thun würde / wenn ich dasselbe nicht in Lateinischer / sondern in unser Teutschen Muttersprache / welche gleichsam unter dem Staube der Verachtung jtzt wieder herfür gläntzet (wie selbige Wort lauten) beschreiben / und den Persianer Teutsch reden lehren würde. (*PR*, B2v)

That I lead this Persian inside in a German mantle and make him speak in our High German mother tongue is partly due to the illustrious Head of the Fruitbearing Society, the *Schmackhaffte* [the one who has good taste], who when accepting my unworthy person [into the society] heard that I was working on this opus, and deigned to write to me that I would do well not to complete it in Latin but in our German mother tongue which has recently reassumed splendor from under the dust of disdain (as he said), and that I should teach the Persian to speak German.

"Der Persianer" in the quote above is an ambiguous term, since it could stand for either Sa'di or the text of the *Gulistān* — or even Hakwirdi. This Persian is to be "led inside, wearing a German coat," and Olearius is charged with teaching "the Persian to speak German."

If we read "the Persian" to mean the "text," then it already "spoke" different European languages: three translations of Sa'di's *Gulistān* already existed in Europe before Olearius's German version. The first translation into a European language was carried out by André du Ryer, a French nobleman, who learned Turkish, Persian, and Arabic while on several diplomatic missions to the Near East. Du Ryer completed the first translation of the *Gulistān* into French: *Gvlistan ov l'Empire des Roses Composé par Sa'di, Prince des Poëtes Turcs & Persans* (Paris, 1634).[69] Du Ryer's translation then served as the basis for the first translation into German, Johan Ochsenbach's *Gvlistan. Das ist, Königlicher Rosengart: Des persischen Poeten Sa'di. Durch Johan Friderich Ochssenbach, aus Dem Frantzösischen in Das Teutsche gebracht* (Tübingen, 1636).

Olearius is aware of these previous versions. In his preface, he even mentions "Andreas *du Ryer* and Friederich Ochsenbach zu Tübingen," (*PR*, B3r) and their translations of the *Gulistān*. Yet he rightly points out that their translations are incomplete, that they misunderstood sections of the original, and that like copyists of manuscripts in general, they perpetuated mistakes in their translations.[70] In his study of the European translations of the *Gulistān*, Behzad also observes that in "*l'Empire des Roses* vermissen wir über die Hälfte der 'Golestan'-Geschichten. Du Ryer macht aber den Leser seines 'Gvlistan' nicht darauf aufmerksam, daß es sich um eine unvollständige Wiedergabe des persischen Textes handelt" (In *L'Empire des Roses* we are missing more than half the stories of the 'Golestan.' Du Ryer, however, does not inform his reader that he is dealing with an incomplete rendering of the Persian text. Behzad, 28). Behzad goes on to discuss more problems with the du Ryer translation, before remarking: "Auf die Ochsenbachsche Übersetzung, den *Rosengart,* braucht hier nicht eingegangen zu werden. Sie lehnt sich eng an die französische Wiedergabe an und weist so die gleichen Mängel auf." (We don't need to deal with the translation by Ochsenbach, the *Rosengart [Garden of Roses]*. It follows the French translation closely and thus shows the same defects. Behzad, 30).

Three years before the publication of Olearius's translation, a Latin version of the *Gulistān* by the German Orientalist and scholar, Georg Gentius, appeared in Amsterdam.[71] Gentius's *Gulistān* — *Mvsladini Sa'di Rosarium Politicvm, Sive amoenvm sortis hvmanae theatrvm, De Persico in Latinum versum, necessariisque Notis illustratum A Georgio Gentio* (Amsterdam, 1651) — was a faithful adaptation of Sa'di's work, and included the original Persian text along with its Latin translation. As Behzad notes in his study of the different translations, "Das *'Rosarium Politicum'* des Gentius stellt das extreme Gegenstück zu 'l'Empire des Roses' dar: eine fast wörtliche Übersetzung des beigegebenen persischen Textes, die, abgesehen von wenigen hinzugefügten Wörtern, welche der Übersetzer der Deutlichkeit halber in den Text einführt, nur dort von der Vorlage abweicht, wo es sich um sprachliche Mißverständnisse handelt oder wo Gentius die fremden Anspielungen und Doppeldeutigkeiten nicht recht begriffen hat . . ." (The *Rosarium Politicum* of Gentius is the extreme opposite of *L'Empire des Roses*: an almost verbatim translation of the attached Persian text which — aside from a few added words that the translator adds for the sake of clarity — only deviates from the original when it is a question of linguistic misunderstandings or when Gentius has not quite grasped the foreign allusions or double entendres . . . Behzad, 30). Although Olearius's *Persianischer Rosenthal* is a fairly accurate translation of the Persian original, he added certain chapters and used specific terms that were "adapted" for his German-speaking audience.

As was mentioned earlier, the *Gulistān* contains a number of pithy, witty epigrams and aphorisms that contributed to the work's popularity in Germany. Naime Bishr remarks that:

> Seine knapp und treffend übersetzten Epigramme und Schlussreime wurden bald zu deutschen Sinngedichten, die in den verschiedenen Sammlungen — z. B. in der 1780 von Christian Wernicke unter dem Titel *Überschrifften* in Leipzig herausgegebenen — begeisterte Aufnahme fanden. Herders Neigung zum Epigramm veranlasste ihn, in den ersten drei Büchern seiner *Morgenländischen Dichtungen* hauptsächlich zu Sa'dis Schlussreimen zu greifen . . . Unter den weniger berühmten Dichtern des 18. Jahrhunderts sind Gleim, Hagedorn und Gotthilf Heinrich Schubert zu nennen, die ebenfalls von Sa'dis Gedichten inspiriert wurden und dem *Persianischen Rosenthal* seinen Ruf in der Nachwelt sicherten. (Bishr, 77–78)

His taut and well-translated epigrams and end-rhyme poems soon became German epigrams that found an enthusiastic reception in different collections, for instance in the 1780 Leipzig edition by Christian Wernicke entitled *Headings*. In the first three books of his *Oriental Poetry* Herder's preference for the epigram caused him to use mainly Sa'di's end rhymes . . . Among the less famous poets of the eighteenth century Gleim, Hagedorn, and Gotthilf Heinrich Schubert ought to be mentioned; they, too, were inspired by Sa'di's poetry and helped secure the future reputation of the *Persianischer Rosenthal*.

The genre of the aphorism — or "apophthegma," to give the Greek term — was considered an especially useful tool for instruction and advice. Like emblems, it was deemed necessary that apophthegmata be clever and "sharp," if they were to be memorable and successful.[72]

Some of the types of aphorisms which were current in the literature of the day were concerned with practical advice for individuals (members of the bourgeoisie, merchants), who wanted to climb the social ladder and learn how to behave at court. The *Gulistān* was considered a rich source of "Oriental wisdom" and its maxims were then gathered into collections of such sayings. The genre of these types of "self-help" books was not confined to the German-speaking lands; it was part of a European-wide tradition that included such works as Baldassare Castiglione's *Cortegiano* (written 1513–18, pub. 1528); Baltasar Gracián's *Agudeza y arte de ingenio* (1642), and *El oráculo manual y arte de prudencia* (1647); and various French works that were meant to help the bourgeoisie learn how to behave at Louis XIV's court.

Behzad provides the literary background in which the *Persianischer Rosenthal* appeared:

> Der Hauptbegriff, unter den diese Absicht und Tendenz des Olearius zu stellen ist, heißt Apophthegmata, 'oder auff Teutsch genandt / Klug- und Hoffreden',[73] wie ihn Zincgref übersetzt. Dem Übersetzer stellt sich so der 'Golestan' als eine reichhaltige und brauchbare Quelle, eine 'Schatzkammer' rhetorischer und poetischer Motive dar. Zweckentsprechend numeriert Olearius denn auch die Geschichten und alleinstehenden Sentenzen und versieht die Übersetzung mit einem ausführlichen Satzregister, das unter verschiedenen Stichwörtern auf den stofflichen Inhalt des 'Rosenthal' hinweist. Damit rückt der 'Rosenthal' in die Nähe von Sammlungen wie Zincgrefs 'Apophthegmata', Lehmans 'Florilegium Politicum' (1643) und Harsdörffers 'Ars Apophthegmatica', um nur die bedeutendsten jener Sammlungen zu nennen, die den Hofrednern und Hofpoeten als Hilfsbücher dienten und den höfisch orientierten Leser, der sich 'nach Höfflichkeit gesprächsamb zu erzeigen' wünschte, mit Unterhaltungs- und Gesprächstoff versahen. (Behzad, 52–53)

> The main rubric under which the intention and tendency of Olearius is to be classified, is called Apophthegmata 'or, clever and courtly sayings in German' as Zincgref translates them. Thus the *Golestan* offers itself as a rich and useful source, a 'treasury' of rhetorical and poetical motifs. Appropriately Olearius enumerates the stories and individual aphorisms and includes in the translation

a voluminous index of sayings, which, in its various entries refers to the contents of the *Valley of Roses.* Thus the *Valley of Roses* comes close to such works as Zincgref's *Apophthegmata,* Lehman's *Florilegium Politicum* (1643) and Harsdörffer's *Ars Apophthegmatica,* to name only the most important of those collections which served the court lecturers and court poets as secondary sources, and which provided material for conversation and entertainment to the courtly reader, who wished to show that he had 'refined conversational ambitions.'

Behzad also mentions the influence of the *Gulistān* on the genre of the "Mirror of Princes," another type of self-help book, but which sought to teach monarchs how to rule effectively: "Man findet beinahe alle Motive des Saadischen 'Golestan' beispielsweise auch im 'Klugen Hofmann' — um einen kurz nach dem 'Rosenthal' erschienenen, von Harsdörffer übersetzten Fürstenspiegel zu nennen" (Nearly all the motifs of Sa'di's *Gulistān* can also be found in the *Prudent Courtier,* to name just one of the Mirrors of Princes that appeared shortly after the *Valley of Roses* and was translated by Harsdörffer.)[74]

The essence of the *apophthegma* leads us to the frontispiece of Olearius's *Persianischer Rosenthal.* Olearius defines *apophthegmata* as "kurtz und scharffsinnige Reden . . . da man mit wenig Worten viel zu verstehen gibt" (short and astute speeches . . . in which one gives much to understand in a few words, *PR,* B2v). This definition bears restating. An *apophthegma,* using few words, tries to convey a great deal of meaning ("viel zu verstehen gibt"). One can argue that the words of the aphorisms try to convey mental images or pictures, i.e., situations with which a reader can identify and from which s/he can learn. In a sense, then, the *apophthegmata* are the verbal equivalent of the images on the frontispiece — both genres try to convey a great deal of information in a condensed form, be it verbal or pictorial.

Turning now to the engraved title page, we can say that Olearius wishes to convey "a great deal" through images rather than words. In this context, we may also recall the Horatian dictum of *ut pictura poesis* (as is the picture, so is the poem). The frontispiece represents a variation of that concept: as is the poem, so is the picture. That is to say, in this depiction in particular the written words determine the choice of images on the title page . . . the frontispiece is, namely, a microcosm of the written text which follows it.

THE FRONTISPIECE OF THE *PERSIANISCHER ROSENTHAL*

Sa'di's *Gulistān* is divided into different books, or chapters, each of which is devoted to a specific topic. Within each book are stories (along with poems and aphorisms) which relate to that book's topic. The eight books of Olearius's *Gulistān* are the following:

Das erste Buch. Von der Könige Gemüther und Sitten.
Das ander Buch. Von der Derwischen oder Persischen München Art und Sitten.
Das dritte Buch. Von der Geruhsambkeit und Herrligkeit eines befriedigten Gemüthes.
Das vierdte Buch. Von der Nutzbarkeit der Verschwiegenheit.
Das fünffte Buch. Von der Liebe und der Jugend.
Das sechste Buch. Von der Schwachheit und dem Alter.
Das siebende Buch. Von der Kinder Zucht und guten Sitten.
Das achte Buch. Von Art und Weise wol wissen mit Leuten umbzugehen: Hält in sich etliche Sprichwörter und feine Regeln / so der mensch im allgemeinen Leben zubeobachten hat.

Book One: On the Character and Conduct of Kings
Book Two: On the Ethics of Dervishes
Book Three: On the Virtues of Contentment
Book Four: On the Advantages of Silence
Book Five: On Love and Youth
Book Six: On Feebleness and Old Age
Book Seven: On the Effect of Education
Book Eight: On the Conduct of Society.[75]

What makes this particular frontispiece such a good example of the entire frontispiece genre, is the manner in which Olearius and the engraver Christian Rothgießer are able to represent the different book headings in visual form. Each element of the engraved title page stands for one of the books in the *Gulistān*, that is, each of the Persian figures represents a particular topic and thus stands for the entire set of stories and morals within the particular book devoted to that topic. Together the separate figures embody the entire text, providing a visual table of contents.

The first impression that one receives from the engraved title page (Figure 3.1) is one of confusion, due to the number of "actors" who appear in the depiction: there are twenty figures in the upper level and at least eighteen in the lower one. In place of the simple formula that we have encountered in previous title pages — in which two (or four)

3.1 Frontispiece to Adam Olearius's
Persianischer Rosenthal (1654).

figures stand on a plinth, and the title of the work is enclosed within a central arch — in this frontispiece, instead, a number of persons are positioned around the title of the work, which is itself inscribed on a majestic lionskin at the center. Setting aside the analysis of the lionskin for the moment, let us first consider the different components of the frontispiece.

An architectural framework serves as the organizing structure for the composition. In the foreground, two squared columns topped by large round spheres create a kind of formal entrance to the scene. Between them a lionskin is suspended. Steps which descend to a lower courtyard in the center of the image lead to a row of squared columns with Corinthian capitals. Above these columns, and enclosed by a balustrade we find yet another section. This area, which is contained in the upper level of the composition, represents a quarter of the entire space in the composition.

These numerous sections serve to depict the various Persians, who, like actors, perform their scenes for the viewer in different areas of the stage. The theatrical motif is reinforced by the curtain-like lionskin, as well as the literal, bunched curtains at the top of the page, which are attached to the tasseled ropes in the corners. Additional curtains enclose the scene on the upper right-hand side of the image. The concept of the curtain (which here is drawn back in the frontispiece) also appears in the preface to the *Persianischer Rosenthal*. Olearius has Sa'di specifically use the term curtain when referring to the quality of God's mercy:

> Vorrede SCHICH SA'DI über den Gülustan oder Rosenthal. Im Nahmen des barmhertzigen Erbarmers! LOb sey dem großmächtigsten und allerhöchsten GOtt. . . . Dann sihe / der Regen seiner unendlichen Barmhertzigkeit ergeust sich überall. Und es stehet der Speisenreiche Tisch seiner Gnaden über den gantzen Erdboden auffgedeckt und zubereitet. Er zerreist nicht die Ehrendecke (a) unter welcher unsere Mißhandlungen verborgen liegen. Er entzeucht uns nicht umb unser Sünde halben unser täglich Brodt und Lebens Mittel.

Olearius's footnote "a" reads:

(a) Im Texte stehet das Wort . . . perde eine Gardin oder Vorhang /
und wil so viel sagen / Gott machet unsere Sünde so wir in geheim
begehen / nicht stracks offenbahr und uns für der ehrbaren Welt zu
Schande. (*PR*, E4r-v)

Preface of Sheik Sa'di for the *Gulestan* or *Valley of Roses*. In the
name of the Merciful. Praise be to the mightiest and highest God.
Behold, the rain of His unending mercy flows everywhere. And the
full table of His grace is set all over the entire globe and is ready. He
does not tear away the covering of glory (a) under which our mis-
deeds are hidden. He does not take away from us our daily bread and
sustenance because of our sins.

(a) In the text there is the word . . . *perde,* a covering or a curtain, and
it means that God does not immediately make known the sins we
commit in secret and [does not] put us to shame before the honorable world.

God does not pull back the *perde* (translated as "Ehrendecke,"
"Gardin" or "Vorhang," *parda* in Persian) to reveal the sinner's sins for
the whole world to see. God sees everything, and has no need to pull
back the curtain or cloth. However, as the author of this translation
and inventor of the frontispiece, Olearius does indeed pull back the
curtain on this text, in order to display not only the entertaining
stories of Sa'di, but also to reveal the Persians with all their sins and
frailties.

A viewer would most likely read the title in the frontispiece first,
since it is inscribed on a white background, which stands out against
the surrounding shades of grey. From there one could proceed to the
top portion of the image — the area above the lionskin and below the
bunched curtain — in which the first book of the *Gulistān*, "Von der
Könige Gemüther und Sitten" (On the Character and Conduct of
Kings), is represented. It is interesting to note that just as this book
occupies approximately one quarter of the entire *Gulistān*, the upper
portion occupies about a quarter of the entire composition. This sug-
gests yet another correspondence between the textual and the pictorial realms. The section concerning kings is situated in the place of

honor, at the top of the composition. Accordingly, the ruler is positioned at the center of this space: the Shah, seated in his *divan-khana* (council room), holds court and listens to a supplicant kneeling before him to his right. The consequence of his judgment is visible on the left-hand side of the image; there, a man is being chased by a member of the court, who wields a stick to punish him. This demonstrates the double character of kings, who either punish or reward. The stories in the corresponding book are concerned with the foibles and the temperament of sovereigns, with their adventures, as well as with the various encounters their subjects have with them. Two representative stories capture the moralistic tone of these types of tales. The nineteenth chapter, "Von einem / der zu Hoff gerne seyn wolte / und hernach elend davon kam" (Concerning someone, who wished to live at court, and who later escaped from it, a wretch) recounts the sad tale of a poor man who rose to become a confidant of the Sultan, and then, due to the jealous slander of enemies, lost all his possessions. At the end of the tale, a colorful aphorism serves as a moral to the story:

> Kanstu nicht leiden / daß ein Scorpion dich sticht /
> So steck auch / wo er sitzt / ins Loch den Finger nicht. (*PR*, 19)

> If you cannot tolerate the bite of a scorpion
> do not put your finger into the hole where it sits.

The relative significance of this account for Olearius is underlined by the fact that an illustration in the text refers to this particular story and shows a man sticking his finger out at a scorpion with a raised tail.

Another tale — entitled "Einer grebet einem andern eine Grube und fält selbst drein" (Someone digs a hole for another and falls in it himself) — tells the story of Zain al-Khan, the advisor of Shah Safi, who accuses other nobles of plotting against the Shah, and who is himself killed by the Shah. This tale is one of two that Olearius identifies in the preface as his own work, thus an addition to the *Gulistān*, which was not in the original. Here the German author gives free rein to his storytelling abilities, and incorporates recent events into the framework of the thirteenth-century text. He does this perhaps to show not only that he is up-to-date, but that little has changed since the stories were first written: Oriental despotism is still the norm in this part of the world.

After considering the upper portion of the frontispiece, the viewer's eye can follow the descending curved lines to the bottom of the image: from the ropes attached to the lion's forelegs down to its tail, which is playfully curved in a reverse S-shape . . ."S" for Sa'di? The bottom register also occupies a quarter of the entire composition. In this foregrounded space we find three Persian men, who stand for Books Two through Four of the *Gulistān*.

Book Two, "Von der Derwischen oder Persischen München Art und Sitten" (On the Ethics of Dervishes), is represented by the dervish kneeling in prayer at the bottom left. Book Three, "Von der Geruhsambkeit und Herrligkeit eines befriedigten Gemüthes" (On the Virtues of Contentment), is shown by the man at the center middleground, who holds a bowl above different types of fruit. The man seated on the steps to his right, holds his hand in front of his mouth, and represents Book Four, "Von der Nutzbarkeit der Verschwiegenheit" (On the Advantages of Silence). By the left-hand pillar a man and a woman, who is being caressed under the chin, stand for Book Five, "Von der Liebe und der Jugend" (On Love and Youth). Here we may observe an interesting strategy on the part of Olearius. In Sa'di's *Gulistān*, the tales speak of the love or affection between a man and a young male. However, in the introduction to his translation, Olearius notes that he has substituted the term "girl, lover, person, or human being" for "youth," so that it will not offend young people who read the book (cf. *PR*, B3v). He goes on to observe: "In addition, it sounds less agreeable to Germans, who are strangers to such matters, than to Persians." Finally, he seems to say that the cause for this form of affection may lie in the fact that honorable Persian women are hidden from the sight of men. The entire passage reads:

> Ich wil auch dem günstigen Leser unangedeutet nicht seyn lassen / daß ich an etlichen Orten sonderlich im fünfften buche / da von der Liebe geredet wird das Wort . . . Peser / welches einen Knaben bedeutet / bißweilen ein Mägdigen / Bule / Person oder Mensch verdolmetschet / damit es nicht etwa der Jugend / wenn sie es lesen werden / Ergerniß gebe. Zu dem klinget es auch in den Ohren der Teutschen / denen solche Sachen frembd / unangenemer als bey

den Persern. Dann es ist dieselbe Art Völcker von langen Zeiten her im schändlichen Beruff gewesen / daß sie Knaben / *qui muliebria pati erant assueti, wie Q. Curtius* von des *Darij* Königes in Persien Hoffstadt redet / gebrauchen. Es können die Perser auch bißweilen sich in schöne Knaben also verlieben / daß sie auff selbige mehr / als auff Jungfern Bulen Lieder machen / wie im gedachten fünfften Buche klärlich zu sehen : Sie sollen auch offt / welches mancher nicht gläuben würde / solche Knaben ohne Geilheit und böse that so hertzlich lieben können / daß sie selbige als Jungferen hertzen und küssen. Vielleicht fält die Liebe (ohne welche wenig junge Leute gefunden werden) auff die Knaben daher / weil dieses ihnen stets die Jungferen und Ehrliche Weibes personen aber gar nicht unter Augen kommen / denn es heist doch: *Oculi sunt in amore duces. Item, ardescitque tuendo.* (*PR*, B3v–B4r)

I do not want to hide from my dear reader that in some places, especially in the fifth book where I speak of love, I sometimes translated the word . . . peser which means a youth with the word girl, lover, person or human being so that young people when they read it do not take offence. Besides, it sounds more disagreeable to the German ear to whom such things are not known than it does to the Persians. Because these people have had a nefarious reputation of long standing that they use boys '*qui muliebria pati erant assueti,*' as Q. Curtius tells of the court of King Darius. It happens that Persians fall in love with beautiful boys in such a manner that they write more love songs to them than to virgins, as one can see clearly in the fifth book. Sometimes, it is said — which some people might not believe — they love such boys without lust and evil deeds so heartily that they embrace and kiss them as though they were young women. Maybe Love (which few young people can do without) falls upon boys because they are constantly in their sight whereas they never see virgins and honest women; isn't there the saying: *Oculi sunt in amore duces. Item ardescitque tuendo.*

In Safavid Persia, the tradition of love or affection between a man and a youth was expressed in both poetry and in visual representations — but at times it was also used in an allegorical sense, namely to express the Sufi mystic's love for God.[76]

However, Olearius may not have been aware of this layer of meaning. Indeed, Faramarz Behzad, in his study of Olearius's translation, initially argues this point of view:

> Die adäquate Erfassung der Geschichten, in denen die sufische Liebe zum schönen Jüngling thematisch wird, setzt wegen dieser unterschiedlichen — symbolischen, scherzhaften und moralisch-didaktischen — Verwendung des homoerotischen Motivs im Grunde ein viel tieferes Eindringen in die sufische Terminologie und Motivik voraus, als es von einem Übersetzer des 17. Jahrhunderts zu erwarten ist. Sie als Erzählung über die profane Liebe aufzufassen und mithin der Thematik gegenüber eine distanzierte Haltung einzunehmen, liegt nahe. (Behzad, 95)

> An adequate comprehension of the stories, in which the Sufi's love for the beautiful boy becomes the theme, presupposes because of that differentiated — symbolic, jocular, and moralistic-didactic — use of the homoerotic motif a much deeper understanding of Sufi terminology and motivation than one can expect from a seventeenth-century translator. One might easily interpret it as a story of profane love and therefore distance oneself from it.

Further on, however, Behzad comes to the conclusion that Olearius's friend and colleague, Georg Gentius, must have been aware of this Sufi practice — and since Gentius knew about the tradition, Behzad contends that Olearius must have been familiar with it as well. The critic summarizes the argument by concluding that Olearius knew the *Būstān* — and Gentius's Latin translation of the *Būstān* — in the third book of which love is expressed for a youth. Behzad contends that Olearius must have discussed this topic with Gentius, who in turn must have known about the intricacies of Sufic mysticism and allegory, especially since he spent seven years in the Ottoman empire and travelled through the area.

> Im übrigen kann kein Zweifel daran bestehen, daß . . . [Gentius] während seines siebenjährigen Aufenthalts in der Türkei, wo er die

Werke Saadis kennenlernte, von Sachkennern auch über die Eigentümlichkeit der sufischen Liebe zum schönen Jüngling unterrichtet worden ist. Der Bezug dieser Liebe zur Gottesliebe konnte ihm, wenn nicht in allen Details, so doch etwa in Analogie zur platonischen Schönheitsschau, nicht entgangen sein.

Olearius hat nun, wie gesagt, den 'Bustan' gekannt. Er hat mit seinem gelehrten Freund Gentius, dessen Übersetzung er zu Rate zog, in Verbindung gestanden. Er hat den 'alten gelarten und der Sachen wolkündigen Perser Hakvvirdi' 'fünff gantzer Jahr' in seinem Hause gehabt. Auch Olearius wird also um den Bezug der homoerotischen Motive des V. Buchs zur Gottesliebe gewußt haben. Verhält sich schon Gentius dem Sachverhalt gegenüber schweigsam, so nimmt es nicht wunder, wenn Olearius eine angemessene Übertragung und entsprechende Erklärung des Originaltextes unterläßt. Hatte er mit Rücksicht auf das religiöse Gefühl seines breiteren Lesepublikums schon seine Wiedergabe der Glaubensvorstellungen des heidnischen Dichters rechtfertigen müssen, so durfte er freilich damit rechnen, daß man den religiösen Gleichnischarakter einer derart anstößigen Gewohnheit als massives Ärgernis empfinden würde. Anders als du Ryer verzichtet der Reisebeschreiber vermutlich nur ungern auf die Mitteilung einer so 'curiosen' Sitte der Perser, weil er stets darauf absieht, dem auf das Exotische gerichteten Wissensdrang seines Publikums entgegenzukommen. (Behzad, 104–105)

Besides, there is no doubt that [Gentius] during his seven years' stay in Turkey, where he got to know the works of Sa'di, was also informed by those who knew about the peculiarities of Sufi love for the beautiful youth. The relation of this love to the love for God cannot have escaped him, if not in all its details then at least in analogy to the Platonic conception of beauty.

Olearius, as we said, knew the *Būstān*. He was in contact with his learned friend Gentius whose translation he consulted. He hosted the "elderly, wise, and knowledgable Persian Hakwirdi" in his house "for five entire years." Thus Olearius, too must have known about the relationship of the homoerotic motifs of Book V to the love of God. If already Gentius does not speak about the matter it does not surprise us that Olearius does not undertake an adequate translation and explanation of the original text. He already had to justify his retelling of the beliefs of the heathen poet, because of the religious feelings of his larger reading public; he could count on the fact that the character of religious parable in such an objectionable habit would give great offence. In opposition to du Ryer, the travel writer probably did not like to refrain from communicating such a "curious" custom of the Persians because he is always intent on meeting the drive for knowledge of his public, which appreciates the exotic.

In short, we can also determine that the specific Sufi message has been ignored by the German author, who normalizes the discourse for fear of offending the sensibilities of his reading public.

Book Six, "Von der Schwachheit und dem Alter" (On Feebleness and Old Age), is represented by the old man to the very right-hand side of the image, who is separated from the young woman by the pillar. The physical separation of these persons reflects the literary topos of older men being unable to obtain a youthful companion, or to keep a young wife happy and satisfied. To give an example of the kind of tale found in this book, I will mention the second, entitled "Lieber wird ein junges Weib / einen scharffen Pfeil ertragen / Als sich mit dem Alten plagen. Ob er schon liebt ihren Leib" (A young woman will rather tolerate a sharp arrow than bother with an old man even if he loves her body.) This tale tells of a rich old man, who marries a young woman, who leaves him for a poor, young man and ends up happier. The aphorisms which accompany the tale underline this message:

Ob dein Gemüt böß und frech von Lastern ist /
Erdulde ich es doch / dieweil du schöne bist.
Viel lieber in der Hell' ich mit dir leide Pein /
Als mit dem Alten ich im Paradieß wil seyn. (*PR*, 118)

Zippollen stincken zwar / doch einem gleichwol deucht /
Wenn man sie etwan auß des Schönen Munde reucht /
Den man wol leiden mag / es angenehmer fält /
Als Rosen / so die Hand des Heßlichen für hält. (*PR*, 119)

Even if your mind is is nasty and full of vices
I tolerate it because you are beautiful
I should rather suffer pain in hell
Than be in Paradise with an old man.

Onions do stink, however, if one has to smell them
Out of the mouth of the beautiful young man
Whom one likes very well one thinks that it is more agreeable
Than roses offered by an ugly man.

The scene in the center background depicts the topic of Book Seven: "Von der Kinder Zucht und guten Sitten" (On the Effect of Education). Standing between the two main pillars, and partially obscured by one of the lion's paws, a mullah (teacher) leans on a staff and reads from the Koran. His pupils are seated in the courtyard. Some are behaving: they hold copies of the Koran in their hands and rock back and forth as they chant the holy script. Others are misbehaving: partially hidden by the lion's tail, a boy is bent forward on his hands and knees . . . his feet are tied to a rod, which is held by two other figures, and the miscreant is about to be beaten on the soles of his feet. This topic of boys being disciplined at school was also commonly found in Persian manuscript paintings, suggesting that Olearius may have been familiar with such representations.

Book Seven of the *Persianischer Rosenthal* — concerned with education — includes the story of a teacher who is fired because of his excessive severity toward the pupils in his charge. He is later rehired after his successor cannot control the class, because of his "Englische Frömmigkeit" (angelic piety; *PR*, 125). An illustration that accompanies the story is divided into two sections (cf. *PR*, 126). These portray the positive and negative effects of the two teaching styles. The entire scene takes place in the interior of a *masjīd* (mosque). On the left-hand side (as on the frontispiece), there is a scene of children learning and swaying side to side, while the teacher hits a boy on the soles of his feet with a stick. In contrast, on the right side the boys are shown fighting, and choking each other. One child even throws a book into the air, and, to compound the outrage, a ripped book lies on the ground. The tale, not surprisingly, reinforces, as morally just, the use of force for the sake of a positive learning environment. The scene in which the learning proceeds smoothly is the one depicted on the frontispiece, since, all in all, Olearius is very impressed with the Persian educational system.

Book Eight is entitled "Von Art und Weise wol wissen mit Leuten umbzugehen: Hält in sich etliche Sprichwörter und feine Regeln / so der mensch im allgemeinen Leben zubeobachten hat" (On the Conduct of Society). As far as I am able to determine, this book is not represented by any specific images on the frontispiece. However, since the topic of this last book is proper conduct itself — which is to be learned from aphorisms — perhaps the cumulative effect of the other seven chapters produces the subject matter of the eighth book. That is to say, the preceding sections, which all include specific rules for living in society, create a general set of guidelines. Since the overall message of Sa'di's work concerns how to conduct oneself in society, the visual message of the frontispiece taken as a whole can stand for the content of Book Eight.

Before leaving the *Persianischer Rosenthal*, I would like to briefly mention a tale in the section that includes fables by the storyteller Luḵmān that concerns a lionskin.[77] We read:

Die 29. Fabel. // Hunde zerzaussen ein Löwen=Fell.

Es funden etliche Hunde im Walde ein Löwen=Fell / nnd [sic] fiengen an dasselbe zubegnagen und herumb zuzerren. Als dieses ein Fuchs / so ohngefehr fürüber gieng / ersahe / sprach er: Wenn dieser noch im Leben wäre / so würdet ihr sehen das seine Klawen so lang / ja noch länger als ewer Zähne wären. Hiermit wird angedeutet / wie es bißweilen unter den Menschen pfleget herzugehen / daß mancher nach seinem Tode den Lästerern herhalten und seinen Nahmen schenden lassen muß / weil er sich nicht mehr verantworten kan. (*PR*, 190)

The 29th Fable: Dogs tear a lionskin apart

Some dogs discovered a lionskin in the forest and began to gnaw at it and drag it around. When a fox that was passing by observed this, he remarked: If he were still alive then you would see that his claws

are long, yes, even longer than your teeth. This is supposed to suggest what sometimes occurs among humans, namely that certain
individuals have to suffer slander and have their name dragged
through the mud after their death, because they can no longer
defend themselves.

This story is the only one in the entire *Gulistān* in which a lionskin is
mentioned, and if we read the tale in light of the frontispiece, we may
ask whether it has any bearing on the lionskin portrayed so promi-
nently on the title page. Perhaps Olearius is commenting on the fact
that Sa'di's name and reputation — like a lionskin — are held up to
the public's scrutiny . . . the Persian author's name and the title of his
work are, after all, inscribed on the hide. This may be an ironic comment on the part of the German author: if Sa'di were alive, he would
be able to defend himself and his name, but since he is dead, he must
submit to the judgment of his readers. Nonetheless, the image of the
lionskin offers other possible interpretations.

The figure of the lion, whether alone or in conjunction with the
sun, was considered to be a symbol of Persia, as we have seen in the
frontispieces to Olearius's travel account to Muscovy and Persia — in
both the 1647 and the 1656 editions (Figures 2.15 and 2.17, pages 58
and 62). In Persia there is a long tradition of utilizing lion imagery,
primarily as a sign of royal authority.[78] This practice will now be examined briefly.

The Lion: Mithraism, Islam, and the Safavids

"In a cuneiform tablet of the fifteenth century B.C. that contains a
treaty between the Hittites and the Mitanni, Mithra is invoked as the
god of oath . . . Mithraism was the worship of Mithra, the Iranian god
of the sun, justice, contract, and war in pre-Zoroastrian Iran . . .
Before Zoroaster (sixth century B.C. or earlier), the Iranians had a poly-
theistic religion and Mithra was the most important of their gods."[79]
During the earliest period of Mithraism, the god Mithra was associated with contracts and oaths. Later, he was identified with the powers
of heavenly light, as the enemy of evil and darkness. "With the expansion of the Achaemenian Empire [559–330 B.C.] Mithraism first

spread to surrounding areas such as Babylon and Asia Minor, and in the latter was associated with veneration of the Greek sun god, Helios. In the first century A.D., Mithraism took root in Rome and gradually entered all of Western Europe, North Africa, and the entire Black Sea region" (Tanavoli, 12). Roman soldiers, in particular, worshipped Mithra (whom they called Mithras) in his aspect as a god of light and victory, and erected shrines to him throughout the empire. Dedications to Mithra ceased almost entirely, however, after Emperor Constantine's victory at the battle of the Milvian Bridge in 312 A.D., and the subsequent adoption of Christianity as the imperial religion.

The Mithraic creation myth involves Mithra sacrificing a bull. A lion — symbolizing the element of fire as well as purification — is often represented in reliefs which depict this event. An astrological relationship between the lion and the sun also exists, inasmuch as the lion is considered to be the symbol of Leo, which in turn is the house of the sun (cf. Tanavoli, 38). "Lion and sun come together in Persia in the image of Mithras with a lion's head. He is entwined six times by a snake, symbolizing the path of the sun through the encliptic, and he holds the globe of the sun. The lion is sometimes represented resting a forepaw on the globe of the sun."[80]

These Mithraic influences survived into the Islamic era as well, and became even more prevalent with the Safavid dynasty (1501–1736 A.D.). The founder of the Safavid state, Shah Isma'il, imposed Twelver Shi'ism as the national religion in order to foster national identity and set the new state apart from its Sunni neighbors (i.e., the Uzbeks to the East, and the Ottomans in the West). Despite the injunction against figural representation in Islam, after the advent of the Safavid empire lion imagery became strongly associated with 'Ali, the First imam (in Twelver Shi'ism): "The Shi'ites call 'Ali b. Talib the 'Lion of God.'"[81] This association is represented in a number of artistic objects that are used to this day, especially in religious ceremonies. For example, during the Shi'ite mourning festival of Ashura, which commemorates the martyrdom of Husayn, it is customary to see metal standards, outfitted with small lion figures, and embroidered banners (*alam*), which depict lions, being paraded through the streets.[82] During this festival, at noon, the moment of Imam Husayn's death, "a man dressed as a lion may appear to flagellate himself and pour dirt or straw on his head.

The costumed figure impersonates the lion that Imam ʿAli rescued and that arrived too late at [the battle of] Karbala. Lavish productions have at times featured tame lions in this role" (Tanavoli, 28).

Stone Lions

Another object with the same religious association was the stone lion. Stone lions were placed in graveyards or *imamzadahs* (tombs of descendants of the imams), above the graves of the deceased. However, the deceased who was accorded such an honor was no ordinary person. He had to be someone considered either a martyr for the "true" religion; or be a great champion or hero (*pahlavan*). The deceased's relationship with ʿAli continued into death, through the medium of the stone marker, which served as a token of prestige or a sign of his devotion. The stone lion thus had both a secular function (reminding the viewer of the deceased's prowess and leonine strength) as well as a religious one (associating him with the Imam ʿAli). "Virtually all lions are placed on the grave parallel to the deceased. Since Iranian Moslems are buried with the head to the east and the feet to the west with the face turned toward the south or Mecca, the lions are also oriented east-west" (Tanavoli, 29).

The lion also possessed an ancient apotropaic function, and was meant to protect the object with which it was associated.[83] Figure 3.2 depicts one of these seventeenth-century stone lions, located in the

3.2 Stone lion in the *Imamzadah Ahmad*, Isfahan (17th century).

Imamzadah Ahmad in Isfahan. The deceased warrior's attributes (dagger, pistol, sword, and shield) are carved onto the side of the memorial and are the visual tokens of his prowess in battle (See Tanavoli, 29–30).

The combination of the lion and sun motif — besides appearing together in the Mithraic cult — became widespread in Persia after the advent of Islam. Examples of this combined motif are on Seljuk and Mongol works of the thirteenth century, on objects such as ceramic tiles, coins, inlaid ewers, and vases (Figure 3.3). "The oldest extant

3.3 Bronze Ewer (13th century).

3.4 Silver coin from the reign of Keykhosrow (13th century).

coin bearing the lion and sun motif (Figure 3.4) was struck in the time of Ghiyas ad-Din Keykhosrow, one of the Seljuk shahs who ruled in the seventh century A.H. (thirteenth century A.D.)" (Tanavoli, 36).[84] After the advent of the Safavids, the lion and sun became the customary symbol to represent royal authority and the state. Most copper coins in the seventeenth century depict this symbol (Figure 3.5). Olearius also talks about the political function of this symbol: "Die Sonne haben jetzo die Perser für ihr Insigne, und zwar auff einem Löwen Rücken gemahlet / wie ich solches in unterschiedlichen örtern in Persien an den Wänden angemahlet antraff" (The Persians now have the sun for their symbol, depicted upon the back of a lion as I

3.5 Copper coin (17th century).

have seen painted upon the walls in different places in Persia, *VNB*, 633). Other Early-Modern European travelers to the area — such as the German Engelbert Kaempfer and the Frenchman Jean Chardin — report seeing this symbol of royal power carved on ancient Persian buildings, painted above palaces, and depicted on royal standards.[85] This tradition continues into the modern age as well: the sun and lion (holding Imam 'Ali's sword, the Zu'l-Faqar) was the official symbol of Iran, from 1836 to the end of the Pahlavi dynasty in 1979.

This Persian practice of associating the religious symbolism of the lion with 'Ali, and representing it on objects — whether secular or religious — parallels the contemporaneous European custom of applying emblems to select items, that is, using the language of symbols to decorate objects such as coins, standards, and banners. In the secular realm, as we saw earlier in our discussion of the influences on the frontispiece genre, "hieroglyphic" inscriptions were used to create personal devices for the European nobility. Religious symbols — such as the cross, the Lamb of God, the pelican as a sign of Jesus's self-sacrifice — were commonly used to decorate flags, articles of clothing, etc. Even Jesus's epithet as the "Lion of Judah," for having triumphed over death[86] finds its counterpart in 'Ali's epithet as the "Lion of God."

Shah Safi I, as leader of both Twelver Shi'ism and Persia, made ample use of the lion/sun symbols, in order to stress his religious connection with Imam 'Ali and to reinforce his secular powers as ruler. According to Olearius, Shah Safi — named in honor of Shaykh Safi al-

Din (1252–1334) of Ardabīl, founder of the Safavid order — was a representative and head of a religion, "Gleich wie der König in Franckreich sich nennet *Regem Christianissimum,* und der König in Spannien *Regem Catholicum*" (Just as the King of France calls himself Most Christian King and the King of Spain calls himself The Catholic King, *VNB,* 632). Although Shah Safi did not claim that he was the sun (as Louis XIV would most famously proclaim), in his official correspondence he supposedly made use of cosmic imagery and forms of address that had a long tradition in Persian royal missives. Olearius mentions that Shah Shapur of Persia[87] — in a letter written to Emperor Constantine in the fourth century A.D. — referred to himself as "*particeps siderum, frater Solis & Lunae*" (member of the constellations, brother of the sun and the moon) and "jetzo ihre Gewonheit auch an Europeische Potentaten / so ferne sie in Freundschafft an sie schreiben / fast dergleichen Wort gebrauchen" (that now they use almost the same words when writing to European princes–if they write in friendship, *VNB,* 632).

In other words, Olearius saw Persian symbols as the counterpart of European heraldic symbols, and informed his reader of the parallels between the iconographic traditions in Persia and Europe. The Persian sun/lion symbol becomes intelligible for a European audience, when it is represented as a symbol of royalty. The lion — in the form of a hide — fulfills this role as well, since it was chosen to serve as the physical representation of Persia. The title, *Persianischer Rosenthal,* appears on the lionskin; more precisely, the animal's (interior) surface contains the writing, which provides the information about Persian society and customs. Perhaps, the absence of the sun on the frontispiece could be accounted for by the presence of the Shah, who embodies the cosmic imagery.

The Lionskin

Upon first seeing the depiction of the lionskin on Olearius's frontispiece, the viewer wonders what the significance of a skinned lion may be. Is this an Orientalist image, intended to show the power of the European over the exotic other? The most famous classical image that relates to this topic is that of the Nemean Lion, the animal killed by

Hercules, who then wore the skin of the beast as a trophy. In an emblem by the Spaniard Diego de Saavedra Fajardo (1584–1648) that uses this topic as its theme (Figure 3.6), the *inscriptio* reads: *Fortior Spoliis* ("Mächtiger durch die Beute," or "More Powerful through Spoils"). The message provided here could also be applied to the Spanish colonialist enterprise, which advocates territorial conquest. Inasmuch as the Holstein mission to Persia was unsuccessful from an economic standpoint, the lion's hide could represent a kind of wish fulfillment. That is, since the Northern Germans were not able to conquer or exploit the Persians, the lion (read: Persia) is defeated symbolically. Slain and flayed, exposed to the European audience, the lion/skin serves as a background on which the German author inscribes the story.

3.6 "Fortior Spoliis,"
Emblem from Diego de
Saavedra Fajardo, *Idea de un
Príncipe Político Christiano*
(1640).

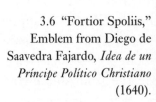

Vencido el Leon supo Hercules gozar de la vitoria, ve-
stiendose de su piel, para sugetar mejor otros monstruos.
Assi los despojos de vn vencimiento arman, y dejan mas
poderoso al Vencedor, y assi deben los Principes vsar de
las vitorias, aumentando sus fuerzas con las rendidas, y
adelantando lo grandeza de sus Estados con las puestos
ocupados. ...

Mächtiger durch die Beute

ALS Hercules den Löwen vberwunden / wuste er sich des
siegs Meisterlich zu gebrauchen / dan mit desselbigen haut
bedeckete er sich / auf das er desto leichter andere wunderthier
vberwiltigen möchte. Also machet nach erlangten sieg der
raub / den obsiger desto mächtiger / vnd versihet jhn mit mehr
wehr vnd waffen: vnd müssen die Fürsten sich jhres Siegs also
zu gebrauchen wissen / damit jhre macht durch die ergebung
der Soldaten grösser werde / vnd durch eroberung der Stätte
vnnd Schlösser mit seinen waffen sein Landt vermehret vnd
erweitert werde. ...

Nonetheless, the depiction of an animal hide on the Early-Modern European frontispiece did have certain precedents, ones that did not necessarily imply domination or subjugation. The skin of an animal could be chosen for its symbolic attributes and the title of the work inscribed upon the stretched-out hide. We have already seen how cloths and drapery were used in this way. As regards the choice of a lionskin on the *Persianischer Rosenthal*'s frontispiece: a possible model could have been provided by the work of Peter Paul Rubens, who was celebrated for his innovative frontispieces, and whose work was well-known to the artists and engravers who worked at the Gottorf court.[88]

RUBENS AND THE FRONTISPIECE

Rubens's contributions to the frontispiece genre were many. On the one hand, he applied principles from his painting style to the engraved title page. As we have seen, in sixteenth-century frontispieces — such as Weigel and Amman's *Trachtenbuch* (Figure 2.9, p. 52) — Mannerist concepts tend to dominate. Figures are crowded into separate, compartmentalized niches, with a superfluity of detail. As Jay Judson observes:

> The figures were too tall for their surroundings and their proportions distorted as was the space. The tomb-like structures or building façades in or upon which the figures and titles were placed were mannered and cluttered with unreal decorative motifs. This vocabulary was set in an unreadable space close to the foreground plane. The maniera style prevailed in the designs made for books published by the leading Antwerp houses until as late as 1613, when the Plantin Press published Rubens's first title page.[89]

In contrast, the figures in Rubens's title pages are more three-dimensional, they have normal proportions, and are portrayed in an intelligible space. Often, Rubens imbued his depictions with dramatic light effects, which gave a sense of movement to his work. These innovations were adopted by other artists in the late 1620s and early 1630s.[90]

Furthermore, Antwerp's importance as one of Western Europe's

3.7 Peter Paul Rubens, oil sketch for frontispiece to Balthasar Cordier's *Catena Sexaginta Quinque Graecorum Patrum in S. Lucam* (Antwerp, 1628).

leading publishing centers during the late-sixteenth and early-seventeenth centuries — due primarily to the Plantin Press — ensured that Rubens's ideas were disseminated throughout Europe. Although Rubens continued to use artistic motifs from the sixteenth century, he modified them and created a new idiom. As Judson remarks, Rubens "transformed the overly decorative architecture, the exaggerated postures and poses of the figures and the unclear space of the sixteenth- and early-seventeenth-century frontispieces into monumental architecture with three-dimensional figures moving in a readable illusionistic space. In short, he applied his innovative painting ideas to book illustration." Judson further notes that Rubens's "new painterly notions were never allowed to dominate the printing. This was due to his close collaboration with Balthasar Moretus, a genius in maintaining the balance between the artistic concept of the title page and typography. The concerted effort of these men brought book illustration into line with seventeenth-century concepts of art" (Judson, 74).

Rubens's influence on the frontispieces produced at the Gottorf

3.8 Cornelis Galle, engraved frontispiece to Balthasar Cordier's *Catena Sexaginta Quinque Graecorum Patrum in S. Lucam* (Antwerp, 1628).

court can be deduced when one compares the Flemish master's work to that of August John, for example. In the latter artist's engraved title page of Olearius's 1656 travel account (Figure 2.17, p. 62), the figures of the Persians and Muscovites are very Rubenesque in their three-dimensionality and monumentality, although Rubens would have defined the space behind the figures more clearly.

The idea for placing the title of the *Persianischer Rosenthal* on a lionskin may have been derived from Rubens's frontispiece for Balthasar Cordier's *Catena Sexaginta Quinque Graecorum Patrum in S. Lucam* (Antwerp, 1628). Rubens completed the oil sketch for the frontispiece (Figure 3.7),[91] from which Cornelis Galle later engraved the title page (Figure 3.8). Judson notes that:

This in-folio book contains commentaries by the Greek Church Fathers on the Gospel according to St. Luke. [. . .] The title of the Catena in S. Lucam is inscribed upon an ox's skin which is held up on the left by an eagle, the attribute of St. John, and on the right by a lion, the emblem of St. Mark. The ox's head is in the middle and directly beneath St. Luke who holds a scroll presumably containing his Gospel. (Judson, 249–250)[92]

The oxhide was chosen as the attribute of St. Luke, and the skin provided a convenient locus for the inscription of the title. Here, I would argue, the animal hide does not suggest relationships of power or dominance (as may be the case with the lionskin).

Judson's study points out that Rubens was not the first artist to depict an animal hide in an engraved title page. The frontispiece for *Vestigi delle Antichità di Roma* (Prague, 1606), by the artist Aegidius Sadeler portrays a flayed she-wolf, chosen because of its association with ancient Rome (Figure 3.9). Perhaps the animal skin reinforces the choice of the work's subject matter: the vestiges of Rome, with the wolfhide itself a vestige that symbolizes the city. The antiquity of the monuments described in the book are also echoed in the choice of the hide. The ancient buildings — like the hide — are still recognizable for what they once were in the past; although the outlines and essences of the objects may be represented in the image, they have all succumbed to the ravages of Time (who is seated to the right, across from winged Fame).

Another frontispiece that includes a lionskin is Abraham van

3.9 Aegidius Sadeler, frontispiece to the
Vestigi delle Antichità di Roma (Prague, 1606).

Diepenbeeck's engraved title page for Gregorius de St. Vincent's *Opus Geometricum Quadraturae Circuli* (1647), a work that makes ample use of Rubens's artistic vocabulary (Figure 3.10). In this frontispiece, van Diepenbeeck "does not copy a specific design but uses Rubens's idea of combining large and realistically rendered figures who conduct a scholarly experiment with cupids as assistants. Rubens did this in the vignettes for his 1613 *Opticorum Libri sex*. Van Diepenbeeck probably also follows Rubens in placing the title on a stretched-out animal skin with the head in the top center" (Judson, 71).

Rubens's use of the animal skin is thus an expedient: he transforms

3.10 Abraham van Diepenbeeck, engraved title page to Gregorius de St. Vincent's *Opus Geometricum Quadraturae Circuli* (Antwerp, 1647).

a saint's attribute into a medium for writing. It may, in fact, be precisely the medium that he wishes to emphasize. Since animal skins were used for parchment — albeit before Rubens's day — by depicting such a skin on his frontispiece, he reinforces the idea of the written word. Saint Luke and the Gospels are, after all, the nominal subject of the text. While Olearius may also have chosen the lionskin for the sake of convenience and to emphasize the idea of writing, he may also have been underscoring the significance of a trophy — of subjugating a wild, dangerous animal and then displaying it proudly for all to admire. This relationship with reading ties in with the notion of collecting and the development of the *Kunstkammer*. Olearius was, namely, enjoined to collect exotic objects on the mission to Persia, which he later arranged for Duke Frederick III's cabinet of curiosities. There are thus a number of possible interpretations for Olearius's choice of the lion/lionskin. First, it serves its purpose as a dramatic visual introduction to the *Persianischer Rosenthal* and piques the reader's interest in the work. It also stands for the dangerous, exotic land that has been symbolically tamed and displayed for the Western viewer. Finally, the hide is the material on which the author writes his title and his work, while at the same time symbolically representing the material that is being written about.

JAN JANSZOON STRUYS'S TRAVEL ACCOUNT

The motif of flaying was employed in other Early-Modern European frontispieces that were associated with the Orient. A particularly horrifying example of this motif can be seen on the frontispiece to Jan Janszoon Struys's travel account, *Drie aanmerkelijke en seer rampspoedige Reysen, Door Italien, Griekenlandt, Lijflandt, Moscovien, Tartarijen, Meden, Persien, Oost-indien, Japan, en verscheyden andere Gewesten* (Three remarkable and very calamitous journeys through Italy, Greece, Livland, Muscovy, Tartary, Medea, Persia, the East Indies, Japan, and various other areas; Amsterdam, 1676).[93] Figure 3.11 depicts the title page of the German translation of 1678 (*Johann J. Straußens REISEN durch Griechenland, Moscau, Tarterey, Ostindien, und andere Theile der Welt*).[94] The title of the work is inscribed on what seems to be a curtain attached by means of hooks to the top of the image. It is only by looking carefully that the reader notices the upside-down eye-, nose- and mouthholes that separate the first from the last name, that is, the "Johann. J." from the "Straußens." It is not a curtain, but rather the flayed skin of a woman, which hangs suspended from the top of the engraving. The skin from the arms and hands hang down on the sides, and the skin from the feet and arms have been gathered up at the spot where the genitalia would have been.

3.11 Frontispiece to Jan Janszoon Struys's *Reisen durch Griechenland, Moscau, Tarterey, Ostindien, und andere Theile der Welt* (Amsterdam, 1678).

The frontispiece cannot be properly understood unless one consults the text which follows. We have already seen how titles could be inscribed on tablets, cloths of honor, sheets hanging from trees, and on lion- and wolfskins. In the case of Struys's travel account, there is, in the third part of the work, a story about a Polish woman who was part of a Persian nobleman's harem. The woman tried to escape with the assistance of the Polish ambassador in Isfahan, who was subsequently forced to return her to the harem. As a warning to his other wives, the Persian nobleman flayed the woman alive. An engraving in the text (Figure 3.12),[95] which is meant to be read from right to left, depicts the act itself.

In the foreground, on the right-hand side of the engraving, the husband is shown flaying the naked Polish woman. He holds a knife in his right hand, and has begun to gather up her skin in his left hand. Her slippers and clothing are strewn on the floor in disorderly fashion. She is bound to two crossed planks of wood held down by two male servants, and her open mouth cries out in pain. The theatricality of the scene is reinforced by the fact that the entire scene is observed through

3.12 Persian nobleman flaying his Polish wife,
from Jan Janszoon Struys's *Reisen* (1678).

the screen door/window by people standing outside the house.[96]

On the left side of the engraving, separated from the first scene by a column, the after-effect of the punishment is displayed. Again, the theatricality of the spectacle is underlined by the gathered-up curtain — at the side of the archway — that has been pulled to the side. In a deictic gesture, the husband points to the flayed skin which he has nailed onto the wall like a trophy. He still holds the hammer he has used to nail the skin onto the wall: the tools of his barbarity (knife, hammer, nails) are thus emphasized in this depiction inside the book. The ghostlike skin hangs on the wall like a trophy — attached at the wrists and hair — as a warning to the other wives not to disobey their husband. The notion of the scream serves to link the still-living woman on the right side of the depiction, with, on the left, the suspended remnant of her corporeal body that still seems to haunt the living with a final wail. His other wives stand next to him and lament the death of the Polish woman. In order to underline the sorrow in the scene, a dog slinks away in the left foreground, and a child mourns as well — perhaps these were her pet and child?[97]

If we return now and examine the rest of Struys's frontispiece, we see that different narrative elements from the text have been visually conflated in the composition. Following the chronology of the book, one should begin by examining the background, in which we see a European — Struys himself — wearing a loincloth, being led away by warlike Tatars, who are both mounted and on foot, carrying spears. The account notes first what kind of Tatars captured the author and then gives the reason for his nakedness, before recounting the torments he suffered at their hands. The exotics in the depiction are:

> The Dagestan Tartars . . . The men are very robust and able of Body, of a deep swarthy complexion, and terrible to look at. . . . They are great Men-stealers, not sticking if they find opportunity to sell their own Relations, or Children of their nearest Friends, which they bring to the *Turks* and *Persians*. . . . [a] Troop of Horse...fell suddenly upon us, stripped us to the shirts, and ravished the wife of my Contreyman *Brak*, before our Eies, and left her naked. My shirt and Drawers which were left me I gave to the Woman, on whom I had more compassion than on my self. . . . 2 or 3 hours further we were set upon by another Company of Horse, belonging to the *Osmin*. These took us, tied our hands behind our back, made us fast to their Horses Tails, and so to trot after them through Thistles and thorns backwards, so that the Horse men driving on apace sometimes dragged us forward, for it was not possible that we should keep pace with them. After they had brought us a good way, they untied me and binding me fast to a Tree, shot me with their Arrows, which they had broken off and made stumped on purpose to urge me to discover the rest of our Company. But when they could not move me to detect them they continued shooting, that I often wished that they would have dispatched me, and rid me of that misery. The marks and pits remain still in my Body, as I have shown them to many hundreds since my arrival at home. These Torments I endured with incredible patience . . . [98]

In the right foreground, the figure of a bearded European man standing in a St. Sebastian-like pose, depicts the author once again. He is bound to a tree, and is being used as target practice by a group of swarthy Tatar archers, two of whom hold bows and arrows. In the left foreground stand two Persian noblemen, one of whom points at a lifeless, naked body displayed on a bench in the center foreground — only the upper half of this body is visible. This, then, is the corpse of the flayed Polish woman, whose skin serves as a curtain on which the title is written. The corpse is hardly recognizable as that of a woman: there is only the slightest hint of a bare breast. The left arm hangs from the bench at an awkward angle, and reflects the rigor mortis of the body. The upside-down head which hangs over the edge of the bench echoes the upside-down flayed skin-head of the title, which also lolls unsupported. The most significant female marker, the long hair, is absent from both the corpse and the flayed skin, making the body appear sexless, its gender indistinguishable.

The dramatic pose of the Persian husband; the curtain-like skin; the "emblematic corpse" on a "stage" — in a quasi-Benjaminian sense — that is meant to serve as *exemplum;*[99] and the martyr-like European hero, who suffers the slings and arrows of outrageous Tatars; they all serve notice that this is the theater of cruelty. The three European figures, a trinity, as it were, are respectively: naked and dead; unarmed and captured; or badly wounded. The agents of their suffering are clearly recognizable according to their clothing and skin color. The Persian nobles are aligned on the most lefthand — sinister — side of the image. The Tatars stand next to them, in an unbroken line: archers in the middleground and horsemen in the background. The two groups are connected by the bow, a symbol of their bellicosity. The reader/viewer is horrified — and fascinated — by the scenes exhibited on the title page. Like a good movie poster, the image promises to provide the consumer of the text with a tale of Oriental atrocities. The stage is then set for the adventure stories that follow.

Olearius's *Persianischer Rosenthal* makes use of the dramatic image of a lionskin on its frontispiece in order to attract its audience. The viewer is supposed to become intrigued by the portrayed subject matter so that s/he will proceed to the written account. The author's aim is to instruct the reader, and thus depicts scenes that represent Persian customs. Struys's composition is at the opposite end of the spectrum, portraying Oriental cruelty (at its most extreme) on the image that introduces his work. The observer realizes eventually that this author's account will highlight the perils and adventures that the Western traveler experienced in the dangerous Eastern lands. While both these frontispieces share the representation of a flayed skin, each author makes use of his object for a different purpose.

IV

Adam Olearius as Cartographer

The aim of the following chapter will be to analyze the "*Nova Delineatio PERSIAE*," Adam Olearius's new and improved map of Persia and the Caspian Sea that first accompanied the *Offt begehrte Beschreibung Der Newen Orientalischen Rejse* (1647) and was reprinted in the *Vermehrte Newe Beschreibung der Muscowitischen und Persischen Reyse* (1656) as well as in subsequent editions of the travel account.[100] As we shall see, this map represents a significant achievement in the history of cartography, and the story of its realization has not yet been adequately told.

What accounts for the importance of this particular map and why is it necessary to study this depiction of Persia in detail? One of the most significant reasons has to do with Olearius's representation of the Caspian Sea, which he asserted was longer from north to south than from east to west. Practically all previous European maps of the area had depicted the sea as an oval, extending from east to west, an incorrect depiction that had been perpetuated over the ages, following Ptolemy's *Geographia*. Olearius's portrayal thus begins to depict the Caspian correctly, a rather bold move that subjected the author to a great deal of criticism from his contemporaries. However, since this map is "based on his own eyewitness observations," as well as on Persian and Arabic sources, Olearius is able to provide an important chapter in the story of the depiction of this body of water, which, after all, is the largest lake in the world.

As a product of the Early-Modern Age, Olearius's map truly stands at the juncture between two time periods. On the one hand, the document contains echoes of the received learning of its predecessors, especially from classical Greece and Rome, but also, less obviously, from standard geographical texts of the Islamic world. Yet with its emphasis on direct observation and critical objectivity, the map also points the way toward the more exacting "scientific" standards of the Enlightenment.

In discussing the qualities of any given map, Reimer Witt observes:

Modernen und älteren Karten ist aber gemeinsam, daß sie gleichermaßen in der Aufsicht die Erde oder Teile der Erdoberfläche — zumeist in einem bestimmten Maßstab — verkleinert und möglichst wahrheitsgetreu darstellen wollen und sollen. Sie spiegeln in allen Perioden gleichsam das Weltbild und auch die Bildwelt ihrer Epoche wider. Erst das Wissen um Zeit, Voraussetzungen und Zweck ihrer Entstehung erlaubt es, sie im Einzelfall und in den vorgegebenen Grenzen ihrer Ausdrucksform zutreffend zu interpretieren und zu werten.[101]

What modern and old maps have in common is that they want to, and are expected to portray in a reduced scale but as truthfully as possible the earth or portions of the earth's surface from above — usually following a predetermined scale. During all periods they reflect both the world view and the imagery of their particular epoch. Only when one knows about the time, the preconditions and the purpose of their creation can one interpret and evaluate them individually according to the given limits of their means of expression.

Maps are cultural artifacts and represent the knowledge as well as the values of a particular age. This specific map reflects the concerns and attitudes of both its author and of the society in which he lived. The public of mid-seventeenth-century Europe was interested in learning about the exotic, faraway land of Persia, an area of the world which had been in the consciousness of Europeans since antiquity, but about which there was relatively little new information (in contrast to the Ottoman Empire, which had posed a threat for Europe ever since the time of Suleiman the Magnificent). Olearius's map and travel account promised the most recent, up-to-date representation of the country based on his eyewitness observation and on his use of Islamic sources. Whereas recent — mainly Dutch — maps of Persia had simply copied and recopied the same shapes and ideas proposed by learned armchair geographers, Olearius's cartographic representation promised an accurate, informed portrayal of the area by a cultured observer, one who had actually travelled to the area in question. The success of Olearius's travel account was due to the combination of erudition and adventure in the narrative, but the novelty of the work's illustrations and maps were doubtlessly important factors that contributed to its status as a Baroque bestseller.

A map — like a frontispiece — is comprised of both visual and textual elements, combining word and image; it represents a type of text, or discourse, that needs to be analyzed in detail in order to be "read" correctly. As J. B. Harley points out:

> Even after exhaustive scrutiny maps may retain many ambiguities, and it would be a mistake to think they constitute an easily readable language. Maps are never completely translatable. [. . .] In some respects — even after the development of a more sophisticated vocabulary of cartographic signs — maps are no less imprecise than written language.[102]

In a different article, Harley notes:

> From the first I view maps as a kind of language. The idea of a cartographic language is also preferred to an approach derived directly from semiotics which, while having attracted some cartographers, is too blunt a tool for specific historical enquiry. The notion of language more easily translates into historical practice. It not only helps us to see maps as reciprocal images used to mediate different views of the world but it also prompts a search for evidence about aspects such as the codes and context of cartography as well as its content in a traditional sense. A language — or perhaps more aptly a

"literature" of maps — similarly urges us to pursue questions about changing readerships for maps, about levels of carto-literacy, conditions of authorship, aspects of secrecy and censorship, and also about the nature of the political statements which are made by maps.[103]

I too wish to provide a "reading" of Olearius's map of Persia, and of its component parts. These different elements, namely the graphic signs and pictorial icons — consisting of words, numbers, icons, images, and cartouches — need to be interpreted individually, in relationship with each other as well as to the text of the travel account itself. In short, this map must be studied in conjunction with the narrative of the account, and vice versa, in order to arrive at a fuller understanding of both "texts." This type of analysis, the interplay between the visual elements of the map and the textual component within the written work, will allow each type of discourse to shed light upon the other. I shall make selected references between these worlds, primarily using elements from the map to draw parallels with the text and juxtapose them with sections of the text. The map, like a frontispiece, represents another kind of microcosm of the author's journey; it too depicts the entire travel account in a condensed form.

In this context, Olearius's notion of "Reysebeschreibung" can be linked to the pictorial and written aspects contained within the term *ekphrasis*. Svetlana Alpers, who examines the manner in which Dutch Renaissance geographers interpreted Ptolemy's use of this term, observes that:

> To call a picture descriptive at the time was unusual, since description was a term commonly applied to texts. From antiquity on, the Greek term for description, *ekphrasis*, was the rhetorical term used to refer to a verbal evocation of people, places, buildings, or works of art. As a rhetorical device, *ekphrasis* depended specifically on the power of words. It was this verbal power that Italian artists in the Renaissance strove to equal in paint when they rivaled the poets. But when the word "description" is used by Renaissance geographers, it calls attention not to the power of words, but to the sense in which images are drawn or inscribed like something written. It calls atten-

tion, in short, not to the persuasive power of words but to a mode of pictorial representation. The graphic implication of the text is distinguished from the rhetorical one. When we look back at Ptolemy now we have to say that his term *graph-o* was opened up to suggest both picture and writing.[104]

THE DEVELOPMENT OF CARTOGRAPHY IN
EARLY-MODERN NORTHERN EUROPE

One of the distinguishing characteristics of the Early-Modern Era in Europe is the development of cartography. Within a relatively short timespan — approximately the two centuries from 1450 to 1650 — maps develop from the schematic world maps of the Middle Ages to the Early-Modern depictions of a globe that is divided into segments by coordinate grids. The latter results from numerous voyages of exploration.

During the Early-Modern Age, the scientific and artistic achievements of the northern German court of Gottorf resounded across Northern Europe in a manner disproportionate to the small size of the duchy. This was especially true for the cartographic enterprises under Duke Frederick III of Schleswig-Holstein-Gottorf, who, along with his relative, King Frederick III of Denmark, was especially interested in an accurate record of his lands.

While it is not my objective to give a detailed account of the history and development of cartography during the Renaissance and Baroque ages, it may be useful to provide a brief sketch of its evolution as it relates to the map-making activities at the Gottorf court and give some of the reasons for the rise of cartography during this period. This will help to situate Olearius's map of Persia in a European — as well as Islamic — context and will help to explain why the German author's work represents such a significant achievement in the field of cartography and for the mapping of the region. For theoretical issues relating to cartography in general, and in Early-Modern Europe in particular, I shall refer to a number of articles by J. B. Harley, especially those that examine maps as texts or discourses; and those that discuss the hidden power relations within a cartographic text and what he terms the hidden elements or "silences" within a map.

Considered to be the first map published in Europe, Figure 4.1 is taken from the *Rudimentum novitiorum* of Lucas Brandis, published in Lübeck in 1475.[105] It is a typical example of a medieval Christian representation of the world, and depicts the world as a disk. A so-called T-O map, it shows the world divided into three continents, Europe and Africa in the lower half of the map, divided by the Mediterranean, and Asia at the top of the depiction, in the "East." This type of division forms a "T," and the "O" is created by the surrounding oceans. A number of different lands are represented as islands surrounded by water. At the very top of the image a Christian and a Jew debate each other on a hill — Jerusalem — surrounded by the river of Paradise. Adjoining this river we find the mons auri (mountain of gold) and the "tree of the sun and the moon," which are derived from legends associated with Alexander the Great. Persia is also located in the upper right-hand quadrant, far away from the Caspian and the Amazon Sea

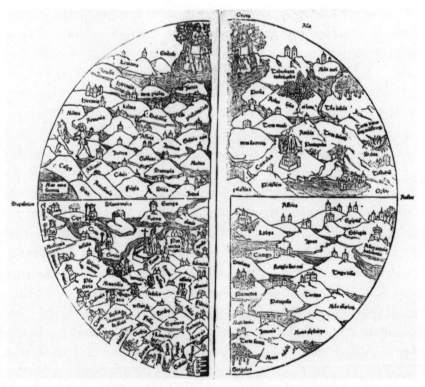

4.1 Lucas Brandis, *Rudimentum novitiorum* (Lübeck, 1475).

(*Mare Amasonearum*) at the very left-hand ("north") side of the map. Above the Caspian we find a devil, which has torn off a man's arm. *Holsatia*, in the lower left area, is located next to *Vinland* (North America?) and is not connected to Denmark (*Dacia*). While the map's date of publication places it at the threshold of the Renaissance, it represents a Biblical conception of the world: thus its aim is an ideological representation, it does not seek to have practical applications for travel.

Soon after this map was published, maps began appearing in Northern Europe that were made according to mathematical principles and projection methods derived from the works of Ptolemy. Ptolemy's tenets for cartography and his system of coordinates — while inexact according to later standards — still marked a significant step forward compared to the medieval conception of the world. Claudius Ptolemy, as librarian in Alexandria during the second century A.D., had compiled a great deal of geographical information about the ancient world, including coordinates for some eight thousand locations. In his *Geography*, "Ptolemy explained three different ways of projecting the three-dimensional surface of the spherical earth onto the two dimensions of a map."[106] Byzantine scholars fleeing the Ottomans at the end of the fourteenth century took the *Geography* along with them to Western Europe, and in 1406, Jacobus Angelus, a Tuscan monk, translated the work into Latin. It soon became a European bestseller, equipped with maps drawn according to Ptolemy's instructions. The Nürnberg humanist Willibald Pirckheimer published an early edition of the work (Strassburg, 1525). The most celebrated editions were published by Sebastian Münster, the first one in 1542, and subsequent versions appeared well into the seventeenth century. Although Ptolemy's descriptions were responsible for perpetuating certain errors — such as the length of the Mediterranean — he encouraged geographers to correct errors and to update their information about the world. Renaissance geographers would then print Ptolemy's maps and add newer maps that incorporated more recent findings next to those of the classical authority. Münster's editions of the *Geography* as well as the *Cosmography* (first edition, 1544) grew ever larger through such additions, the latter work reaching encyclopedic dimensions. Such works, as well as the earlier

4.2 Detail from Olaus Magnus, *Carta marina et descriptio septentrionalium terrarum* (Venice, 1539).

Nürnberg *Weltchronik* by Hartmann Schedel (1493, with woodcuts by a young Albrecht Dürer), sought to include "ancient and modern discoveries in one verbal and visual description."[107] This makes them the forerunners of Olearius's travel account, which attempted to do the same for Muscovy and Persia in the mid-seventeenth century.

We see some of the attempts to correct the Ptolemaic canon in a detail from the *Carta marina et descriptio septentrionalium terrarum* of the Swede Olaus Magnus, published in Venice, in 1539 (Figure 4.2). While the map still contains a number of mistakes, the coasts of Schleswig-Holstein and Denmark are beginning to be represented more exactly. Gottorf is mentioned for the first time on this map; the Swedish and Danish kings are depicted on their thrones, with their royal coats of arms, conferring a stamp of royal authority upon the lands they rule. The map contains a number of colorful images, including lighthouses and a number of different types of ships. In the upper left corner the depiction of a drowned man — being eaten by fish, which in turn are eaten by an even larger fish — underscores the dangers of the sea.

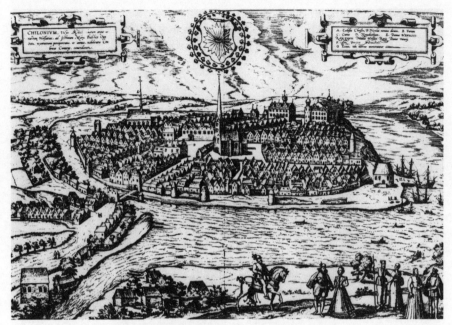

4.3 View of Kiel from the *Theatrum urbium*
by Georg Braun and Franz Hogenberg (ca. 1588).

By 1588, cityscapes had become extremely popular, as in this example of the city Kiel from the *Theatrum urbium* by Georg Braun and Franz Hogenberg (Figure 4.3).[108] Besides providing a view of the city, from an oblique, raised three-quarter perspective, an accompanying text usually gave background information about a city. Inhabitants wearing native costumes — typically couples — are often displayed in the foreground in order to provide an example of local color. In this image, a number of social classes are depicted: nobles, merchants, and a fisherman and his wife.

In the next example, Holstein is represented with "the greatest diligence and accuracy" (Figure 4.4). In this elaborate work by the Dutch cartographer Nicolas Piscator (Amsterdam, 1659),[109] the map of Holstein occupies the center of the image, and is surrounded by four views of castles, six representations of women in native costumes, eleven cityscapes, and two closeups of the area in the upper left- and right-hand corners. With a scale bar that frames the depiction, this map seems to conform to more modern, scientific standards, and is a particularly good example for the mixing of "art and science" in a

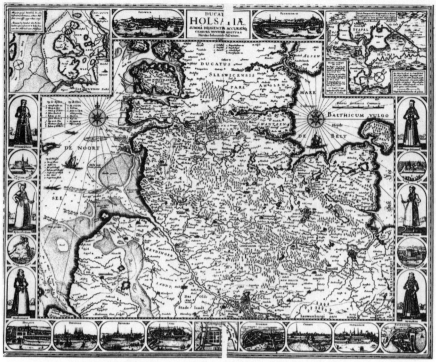

4.4 Map of Holstein by Nicolas Piscator (Amsterdam, 1659).

map. The windrose, and the indications of depths of the coastal waters are meant to have practical applications for seafarers, but the ornamental elements, such as the costumed women, are meant to both inform and be decorative.

CARTOGRAPHY AT THE GOTTORF COURT: ĐUKE FREDERICK III AND THE *NEWE LANDESBESCHREIBUNG* (1652)

During the Early-Modern Age, European potentates strove to consolidate their power and gain a clearer picture of the territories they controlled. This was done in order to gain an awareness of the military and strategic situation of their lands, and the geographical features involved in the defense of an area; to establish fortifications; to mark boundaries, and so forth. In order to take advantage of trade opportunities, rulers founded new cities, established guilds and trading companies, and distributed privileges to associations and individuals. In all these enterprises, geography played a role in facilitating the development of commercial, military, and nationalist activities. J. B. Harley, using a Foucauldian approach to the study of maps, notes that:

> Power is exerted on cartography. Behind most cartographers there is a patron; in innumerable instances the makers of cartographic texts were responding to external needs. Power is also exercised with cartography. Monarchs, ministers, state institutions, the Church, have all initiated programs of mapping for their own ends. In modern Western society maps quickly became crucial to the maintenance of state power. Mapping soon became the business of the state and cartography is early nationalized.[110]

In another article, Harley notes that:

> In Early-Modern Europe, from Italy to the Netherlands and from Scandinavia to Portugal, absolute monarchs and statesmen were everywhere aware of the value of maps in defence and warfare, in internal administration linked to the growth of centralised government, and as territorial propaganda in the legitimation of national identities. Writers such as Castiglione, Elyot, and Machiavelli advocated the use of maps by generals and statesmen. With national topographic surveys in Europe from the eighteenth century onwards, cartography's role in the transaction of power relations usually favoured social elites. The specific functions of maps in the exercise of power also confirm the ubiquity of these political contexts on a continuum of geographical scales. These range from global empire building, to the preservation of the nation state, to the local assertion of individual property rights. In each of these contexts the dimensions of polity and territory were fused in images which — just as surely as legal charters and patents — were part of the intellectual apparatus of power.[111]

Duke Frederick III of Holstein–Gottorf shared many of the same concerns with the rulers of his age. He too was interested in improving the administration and defense of his territory, fostering the economic ambitions of his duchy, and expanding its scope beyond the confines of the North Sea region. His most famous attempt in this regard is the economic embassy he sent to Persia in 1635, whereby he hoped to import Persian silk to Northern Germany via Muscovy.

Frederick's interest in geography most likely developed in Dresden at the court of Saxony, where he was raised. Ever since the sixteenth century Saxony had been a center of geographical activity in the German-speaking lands and Kurfürst August of Saxony (with whom Frederick was related) had been personally involved in the measuring and mapping of his own lands, to the point where he even participated in the surveying process.[112] Frederick III followed suit when he became ruler of Schleswig-Holstein, a position that he shared with his relative, Frederick III, king of Denmark and Norway (r. 1648-1670). While Duke Frederick did not go out into the countryside himself to survey his lands, he made a conscious effort to have Schleswig-Holstein mapped systematically, as soon as possible.

For this task, he commissioned the mathematician and cartographer Johannes Mejer. Mejer, born in 1606 in Husum, studied at the University of Copenhagen under the astronomer Longomontanus, who in turn had received instruction from the celebrated Tycho Brahe. Brahe's astronomical tables and work on triangulation had provided a point of reference for a number of students, including the prominent Dutch cartographer Willem Blaeu. Mejer also received a one-year scholarship from Duke Frederick III to study in the Netherlands, which was the center of cartographic activity in Europe at the time.

Some of Mejer's earliest works, produced around 1640, included maps related to the Duke's economic concerns (such as the herring nets located in the Schlei River); as well as the "Danewerk," a fortification; and a map of the city of Schleswig. In 1642 the Danish monarch charged Mejer with mapping the West coast of Schleswig--Holstein, a commission that was extended to the entire territory, and which he completed over the next ten years as *Hofmathematicus* for both Fredericks. The end result of this ambitious enterprise was the *Newe Landesbeschreibung der zweij Hertzogthümer Schleswig und Holstein* (The New Geographic Description of the Two Duchies, Schleswig and Holstein) of 1652, the first published, systematic atlas of an area of the German-speaking lands. Mejer produced the maps for the atlas, and Caspar Danckwerth, a doctor and later mayor of the city of Husum, wrote a very lengthy text that accompanied the cartography. The maps themselves were engraved by two pairs of brothers, the brothers Lorenzen and Petersen of Husum.

The *Newe Landesbeschreibung* represents a typical example of nationalist self-representation on the part of the royal houses of Schleswig-Holstein and Denmark. The stated purpose behind the publication of the work was not only to map the territories, but also to trace the history of the peoples who had inhabited those lands. After the rediscovery of ancient treatises, such as Tacitus's *Germania,* Humanist scholars traced the Germanic tribes who had inhabited their regions, and proudly announced themselves as their descendants.[113] The creators of the *Newe Landesbeschreibung* — the engravers, the cartographer, and the author of the written text — all used Dutch maps as models for their own work.[114]

The frontispiece of the *Newe Landesbeschreibung* depicts the authors's evident pride in his heritage (Figure 4.5). The image includes, at the very top, portraits of the two rulers who commissioned the atlas, Frederick III, King of Denmark, and Frederick III, Duke of Schleswig-Holstein-Gottorf. We see the iconic male figures of the ancient inhabitants, the representatives of the Germanic tribes who stand singly in individual niches and on an architectural plinth: "Ein Cimber," "Ein Friese," "Ein Sachse," on the left; and "Ein Jüte," "Ein Angelschwabe," "Ein Wende" (A Cimbrian, a Frisian, a Saxon on the left, and a Jute, an Anglo-Swabian, a Wend) on the right. The structure is adorned at the bottom with the oval portraits of the bishops Ansgar and Vincelin, who symbolize the early Christian presence in the land. In other words, we find a mixture of ancient pagan elements — the "Angelschwabe" with someone's head stuck on a pike — juxtaposed with Christian elements: the angel at the very top of the image, crowning the rulers; the address to God; and the depictions of the bishops, who hold croziers in defense of the faith, instead of spears.

In the dedication to the *Newe Landesbeschreibung der zweij Hertzogthümer Schleswig und Holstein* we read: "Gott, im begin der Welt, mit Maß, Gewicht und Zahl, Durch klugen Finger schuff die Sachen allzumahl . . . denn GOtt ist kein Gott der unordnung, sondern will, daß alles ordentlich zugehen und gebührlich soll unter-

4.5 Frontispiece of the *Newe Landesbeschreibung der zweij Hertzogthümer Schleswig und Holstein* by Caspar Danckwerth and Johannes Mejer (1652).

4.6 (*Opposite*) Map of the ancient world, the *Orbis Vetus*, at the time of the sons of Noah, from the *Newe Landesbeschreibung* by Danckwerth/Mejer (1652).

schieden werden" (In the beginning of the world, God created everything at once, with his clever/intelligent finger, using measure, weight and number . . . because God is not a God of disorder, but wants everything to proceed in a proper manner and with proper differentiation).[115] Thus by studying mathematics and the sciences, human beings may achieve some insight into the wisdom of God's universe. The author goes on to observe that many rulers in antiquity were versed in geometry, astronomy, and geography, such as Alexander the Great and Julius Caesar. Charlemagne even had a large collection of optical instruments and books on mathematics and in his *Kunstkammer* there was a map of the world engraved onto a silver table. As God's representatives on earth, the two rulers who are addressed in the dedication of the *Newe Landesbeschreibung* — Duke Frederick III of Schleswig-Holstein and King Frederick III of Denmark — follow in the steps of their illustrious predecessors and through their patronage are linked to the noble art of geography.

The *Newe Landesbeschreibung* begins with a map of the ancient world, the Orbis Vetus, at the time of the sons of Noah (Figure 4.6).

Scholars have debated exactly what role Olearius played in the process of publishing the atlas. It seems very likely that, as *Hofbibliothecarius* and *Hofmathematicus*, he may have supervised the project; helped arrange the engraving of the maps; or even contributed to the text accompanying the maps. Here, in this depiction, I believe we have evidence of his influence on the project. If we look at Mejer's depiction of the Caspian Sea, we see that it is almost rounded.

Other maps in the *Newe Landesbeschreibung* include a depiction of the island Helgoland (Figure 4.7). A number of different perspectives are used in the image: an oblique bird's-eye view of the island; as well as a side-view of a couple in native dress standing in a boat representing the native population. A fish and lobster in the boat represent the fruits of the sea. Between the couple, we find a huge turbot, on whose back is inscribed the title of the map, along with the date and author. This last element is reminiscent of the lionskin's function in the frontispiece to the *Persianischer Rosenthal*.

4.7 Map of the island Helgoland from the *Newe Landesbeschreibung* by Danckwerth/ Mejer (1652)

I would like to turn now to the representative work of the *Newe Landesbeschreibung*, namely the map of Schleswig and Holstein (Figure 4.8). A quick glance at the map provides some of the following information: the map is framed by scale bars that show longitude as well as latitude. Mejer's prime meridian goes through the Azores, and his calculations for the longitudes of cities were based on the astronomical tables of Tycho Brahe. Considering the rather primitive instruments at his disposal, the map is remarkably accurate.[116] Within the map,

4.8 Map of Schleswig and Holstein from the *Newe Landesbeschreibung*
by Danckwerth/Mejer (1652).

most of the white space corresponds to the bodies of water — which
are designated either with Roman letters ("Mare Cimbricum" and
"Mare Balthicum") or in ornate italics in German (*Westsee* and *Ostsee*).
In fact, most geographical terms, such as the names of cities and localities, and the title of the map, are written in German — a detail that
can be linked to the patriotic message of the work.

The decorative cartouche at the top right is adorned with strapwork and includes the title of the map in German and the date in
Latin. It is flanked by three human figures: a standing farmer; his
buxom, healthy wife seated at his side; and their child, whose face is
barely visible under her arm. A cow, long stalks of wheat, and a basket
filled with fruit underscore the agricultural bounty of the land. The
elaborate coat-of-arms of the duchy is placed below the cartouche. At

the bottom left, we find the Latin inscriptions to the patrons: here, even the typography plays a role in emphasizing the importance of the dedicatees. The titles and epithets of the two rulers are all mentioned, along with the different territories under their control. This inscription establishes the geographical purview of the rulers, that is, the names represent a kind of seal of authority indicating ownership of the map and approval for the enterprise, and thus stands as a symbol for the link between political power and modes of representation during the Early-Modern Era. The cartographer's name is included within the inscription, below the patrons' names — Mejer has allied himself with the authority figures, yet he knows his place is below his patrons. Even the legend (flanked by putti, above whom we find a compass, the symbol of the cartographic enterprise), includes symbols for "cities, churches, houses of nobles, and villages," that is, locales all essential to the administration of the land.

In this context, Harley points out:

The role of the map as a form of social proclamation is further strengthened by the systems of classification and modes of representation — the so-called "conventional" or cartographic signs which have been adopted for landscape features. It has long been one of the mapmaker's rules that the signs for towns and villages — whether depicted iconically or by abstract devices — are shown proportionally to the rank of the places concerned. Yet the resulting visual hierarchy of signs in Early-Modern maps is often a replica of the legal, feudal, and ecclesiastical stratifications. Indeed the concept of a tiered territorial society was by no means lost on contemporary mapmakers. [. . .] On other maps, towns occupy spaces on the map — even allowing for cartographic convention — far in excess of their sizes on the ground. Castle signs, too, signifying feudal rank and military might, are sometimes larger than signs for villages, despite the lesser area they occupied on the ground. Coats of arms — badges of territorial possession — were used to locate the *caput* of a lordship while the tenurially dependent settlements within the feudal order were allocated inferior signs irrespective of their population or areal size. This was particularly common on maps of German territory formerly within the Holy Roman Empire. Such maps pay considerable attention to the geography of ecclesiastic power. [. . .] But if map signs sometimes reacted to changing religious circumstances they also tended to favour the status quo, legitimising the hierarchies established on earlier maps. They were a socially conservative vocabulary.[117]

The eighteen city plans that are located in the borders, on either side of the map, reinforce the impression that the area is rich and powerful, and contains thriving metropolitan areas.

The *Newe Landesbeschreibung,* which sought to map the political and national ambitions of its patrons, suffered a political fate: as is sometimes the case with collaborative efforts, trouble arose between the authors. In this instance, Caspar Danckwerth's text had a very pro-Gottorf stance, and managed to offend the Danish line of the royal house. Despite Johannes Mejer's attempts to intercede with King Frederick, the monarch threatened to ban the sale of the work in his territories, and relatively few copies of the atlas were ever sold. Mejer's lawsuits against Danckwerth were unsuccessful and resulted in the sale of the plates to the Dutch cartographer Joan Blaeu, who incorporated Mejer's maps in his *Atlas Maior* of 1662. The plates were destroyed ten years later, when Blaeu's workshop was demolished by fire. Despite these difficulties, Mejer continued mapping the coasts of Norway and Sweden as Danish royal cartographer, producing a number of maps that were never published. Mejer eventually had to declare bankruptcy and died an embittered old man, beset by his creditors.

OLEARIUS'S *NOVA DELINEATIO PERSIAE ET CONFINIORUM* (1655)

Overview

Olearius's *Nova Delineatio Persiae et Confiniorum* of 1655 is a very dense document, containing several layers and types of information (Figure 4.9). It is so full of visual and verbal cues that a viewer may feel overwhelmed by the excess of information found therein. The document represents a kind of Baroque "horror vacui," in that there are very few empty areas on which the eye can rest. In this, one could say

4.9 Adam Olearius's map of Persia (*Nova Delineatio Persi*

finiorum, 1655) from the *Vermehrte Newe Reysebeschreibung*

that it mirrors the travel account itself, which contains such a plethora of knowledge about the country that it is not always easy to sift through. A number of readings are necessary in order to gain an understanding of the different types of subjects that are presented, and the travel account's division of topics — into chapters concerning, for example, the history of the country; the geography; the customs of its inhabitants, interspersed with a narrative of the embassy's journey — encourages a piecemeal reading of the work. That is to say, one can follow the adventures of the German travellers and skip some of the scholarly sections and return to them later, if one wishes to do so. After "reassembling" the different chapters one may reach a fuller understanding of what the author tries to accomplish in his work. This again parallels the different layers of information that are presented on the map: by looking at it all at once, it is difficult to comprehend the entire story that the author (and artist) are trying to tell. By examining individual visual elements in the map, and then linking them to the text, one can trace the different narratives extant (manifest and latent) in the work. Olearius's map of Persia adds yet another dimension to the written travel account, acting both as a type of microcosm for the entire work as well as a necessary supplement or guide.

The dimensions of the map are 38.5 cm by 54 cm, and it was made from a copperplate engraving, which permitted greater detail than woodblocks. However, it did not allow for color to be added to the block, so engraved maps were often colored by hand to increase their value. The map is framed by scale bars that, in two-degree increments, show longitude (from about 62° to 110° on the top of the map; from about 67° to 104° on the bottom of the map, implying that the cartographer is attempting to take the curvature of the earth's surface into account in a "flat" representation); as well as latitude (from about 24° to 47.5°). A grid has been superimposed on the map to facilitate the location of sites. This device relates to the ideas of the "controlling of space" that Harley sees as a necessary component of geographic expansion and the related ideas of colonialism and state control.[118] The cartographer is not so strict, however, that elements are not allowed to extend outside the boundaries of the frame: on the left-hand side, at 36° latitude, the flourishes of the italic letter "M" of Mediterraneum are allowed to escape the confines of the sea;[119] while on the right-hand side, the line connecting 106° longitude meets the line for 31° latitude, again, just outside the frame. These examples could be considered "mistakes" if one were to regard the map from the point of view of rigorous scientific standards that proclaim that all the document's information must be contained within the frames of the depiction, and that breaking the boundaries is a kind of subversion of the referent. Yet this occurs even in the most modern of maps! In a 1999 National Geographic map of the area entitled "Caspian Region: Promise and Peril," one finds a similar occurrence, namely the southernmost tip of Pakistan is allowed to cover and extend beyond the map's border.[120] However, the very center of Olearius's map — along 86° longitude — gives evidence of sloppy craftsmanship and copying. The 1655 version of the map is a reprint of the original 1647 map (with the different date provided in the cartouche), but the later map was not pieced together very carefully. Portions of place names and provinces are missing in the center, as well as half of the second "S" of the Sinus Persicus; on the bottom scale bar the numbers for 68° to 86° latitude are missing, whereas on the scale bar at the top, 90° is placed at the point where 88° should be. In other words, the later reprints of the region betray a loss of quality and craftsmanship with regard to the original 1647 map.

Within the map, most of the white space corresponds to the bodies of water — *Mediterran[eum]*, *Sinus Persicus*, *Mare Caspium sive Hyrcanum Persis Külsum*, *Pontvs Evxinvs* — which are designated either with italic or Roman letters. The explanations of the map are all written in Latin: geographical terms, names of cities, dedications to the patron, and address to the reader. This stands in direct contrast to the text of the travel account, which Olearius, as a member of the "Fruchtbringende Gesellschaft," specifically chose to write in the vernacular for the purpose of fostering the German language. Maps belonged to a different tradition, however, and were still written in Latin in order to be more "international," that is, they had a better chance of circulating as single sheets if they were in Latin.

There are two decorative cartouches adorned with strapwork: the one on the left includes the title of the map and is flanked by human figures; the cartouche on the right includes only text. The geographical elements — mountains, rivers, trees — are depicted on the entire map; so-called "mole hills" or "sugar loaves" represent mountains. The shading on the east slopes of the mountains creates a three-dimensional effect, thus simulating a light source emanating from the west. The horizontal shading (and slight stippling effects in the southern portion of the Persian Gulf) give emphasis to the coastlines and estuaries. Forested areas are represented by light or heavy concentrations of trees, for example in the province of Kirman.

The layout of the *Vermehrte Newe Reysebeschreibung* proceeds as follows: first the frontispiece or title page, then the dedications, followed by the body of the text. My reading of Olearius's cartographic text will follow the same pattern, by analyzing the corresponding features on the map.

The Title

I thus begin my reading with the title of the map, at the bottom left side of the map, which would correspond to the title page of the written travel account. Contained within an ornate strapwork cartouche, we find the title of the map, " Nova Delineatio PERSIAE ET CONFINIORVM Veteri longe accuratior. edita Anno. 1655" (Figure 4.10). The emphasis here is on novelty; the description will not simply repeat

4.10 Detail from Adam Olearius's *Nova Delineatio Persiae et Confiniorum* (1655).

the representations of older, classical authorities such as Ptolemy. The cartouche rests on a kind of architectural base in which a scale bar is contained, and above that we read: "Miliaria Germanica & Persca quae Farsang vocant." This, then, is the foundation upon which the entire enterprise is based, namely the accurate measuring of these territories. The notion of translation is addressed as well, in that the Persian term, "Farsang," is made comprehensible for a German or Western European audience — the German term, with which a reader is familiar, precedes the unfamiliar one.

Two inhabitants of the country on either side of the cartouche represent the native population. On the left, a mustachioed nobleman, wearing a cloak and *mandil* (or turban), grasps the cartouche with his right hand, and with his left holds a bowl above his hand. His legs are spread apart and his torso turns toward the written inscription of the title, thus conveying a sense of movement. His counterpart, a Persian noblewoman, stands demurely on the right side of the cartouche, her visage uncovered for the benefit of the European viewer. Her left hand rests on the cartouche and in her right she holds a flask up to her head. The figures are linked in a number of ways. We have already seen a number of iconic couples dressed in native costumes, who are meant to represent the inhabitants of a particular region, for example in the topographic city views of Braun and Hogenberg and Johannes Mejer's depiction of Schleswig–Holstein (Figures 4.3 and 4.8, pages 117 and 125). The fact that each of the Persian figures grips the strapwork serves to link them as well. Finally, there is the notion that the male protagonist expects the female to pour wine or some other liquid into the shallow bowl he is holding: this was a common topos in Persian painting. This simple gesture — the anticipation of a drink — could perhaps be construed as a gesture of welcome or hospitality for the reader, who is entering into this exotic world. Earlier we examined the significance of Early-Modern costumes and costume books when we analyzed a number of frontispieces that Olearius helped to plan. The Persian couple performs the same function as the figures on a frontispiece: in visual form, they provide the viewer with an iconic image of two "typical" inhabitants and their form of dress.

This cartographic convention has lasted to this day. In the modern (1999) National Geographic Society map mentioned earlier, "Caspian

Region: Promise and Peril" — a very Orientalist title that speaks to the riches to be found in the area, mainly in the form of natural resources, as well as to the dangers encountered there, by such factors as ethnic conflicts, nationalism, and religious fundamentalism — iconic inhabitants still grace the map, but in this case they are not found on the front of the map, or in the borders. The front of the map contains the "scientific" matter, and shows an exact map of the region along with small boxes that give information about a country's natural resources. The back is divided into three separate sections: the first provides a satellite image of the area, thus a depiction using the very latest in technology; the second gives a brief discussion of the ethnic and national types to be found in the region as well as possible factors for conflict; and the third portion gives an overview of the economic possibilities associated with the area. In the second of these sections we find a counterpart to the Early-Modern iconic couples. If we look at only the couples associated with Olearius's travel account (Figure 4.11) we find a Russian couple (a female doctor and a male fisherman) in rather small format, emphasizing the educational background of the ethnic Russian population living in the region. The couple associated

4.11 Detail from a National Geographic Map "Caspian Region: Promise and Peril" (1999).

with Iran has a larger format and corresponds to pre-established views that a typical U. S. reader might have. A forbidding-looking mullah, dressed entirely in black is seen praying, while flames from an oil well spout forth behind his shoulder. The specter of religious fundamentalism is given visual form. An Iranian woman — in native dress — can be found below the mullah, in a smaller format. Neither one is smiling, or shown to be engaged in useful activity as are a number of the other representatives in the image.

Let us return now to the Persian couple in Olearius's map. As representatives of their country, they stand not only for the entire inhabitants, but also introduce the reader to the ethnographic information included within the travel account, and are microcosms of the images of the others found within the account. Olearius devotes an entire chapter to Persian clothing in the *Vermehrte Newe Reysebeschreibung*, and infers moral character traits of the inhabitants from their clothing styles. Chapter fourteen of book five gives an overview of Persian clothing styles and begins with an illustration of different types of Persians.

Figure 4.12 depicts nine individuals divided into two groups. In the larger group we find, in the front row, a nobleman with a fur

4.12 Persian costumes from the *Vermehrte Newe Reysebeschreibung* (1656).

draped around his neck; a man holding a bow; and a married woman holding a bowl. In the back row we see a soldier holding an axe; another man with a *mandil* (perhaps a Qizilbash); a Sufi mystic with a long mustache; and another man wearing a sheepskin hat and holding a flask, from which it seems he will pour liquid into the woman's bowl. The second group, to the right, includes a woman, who is almost completely covered by a robe and whose eyes are barely visible; and a barefoot man, who may be a "Schreiber" (scribe), and whose body is cut off by the border of the engraving. The text begins with a discussion of male clothing. Olearius refers to a classical source, before questioning the manliness of his subject matter:

Was der Perser Kleidung betrifft / und wie sie sich darein stellen / beschreibet Ammianus Marcellinus zwar gar kurtz / aber sehr recht und wol / wenn er spricht: *Persae adeo dissoluti sunt, ut artuum laxitate, vagoque; incessu jactantes se, ut effaeminatos existimes, cum tamen sint celeberrimi bellatores.* Die Kleider hangen ihnen los und schludrich umb den Leib / seynd in denselben von ferne als Weiber anzusehen / gehen und wancken als wie die Gänse von einer seiten zur ander / am allermeisten ihre Weiber / und habe ich wenig Perser gesehen / welche einen gravitetischen und ansehnlichen Gang gehabt. Ich halte / daß es von ihrer art zu sitzen herkomme / denn sie alle wie die Schneider in Franckreich mit übereinander und unter sich geschlagenen Beinen auff der Erden sitzen / und also von Kindesbeinen an die Schenckel nicht gerade gewehnen. (*VNB*, 585–586)

As concerns the clothing of the Persians and how they look in it, is described briefly but very appropriately by Ammianus Marcellinus when he says: *Persae adeo dissoluti sunt, ut artuum laxitate, vagoque; incessu jactantes se, ut effaeminatos existimes, cum tamen sint celeberrimi bellatores.* Their clothes hang loosely and sloppily around their bodies. From afar they look like women; they walk and sway from side to side like geese, especially their women; and I have seen few Persians who had a solemn and imposing way of walking. I think that this derives from their way of sitting, because they all sit like the tailors of France upon the bare earth with their legs intertwined from above and below, and thus from childhood on, their thighs are not used to being straight.

Olearius also gives a possible explanation as to why they wear this type of clothing. He tells the story of the beautiful Semiramis, who was married to the general Menones. One day, *"amores impatiens,"* he wanted his wife to visit the army camp. She dressed in clothing that made it hard to tell whether she was a man or woman, and was able to get to the camp. "Der König Cyrus hat ihm hernach aus gewissen Uhrsachen solche Tracht auch gefallen lassen / und seinen Leuten zu tragen gerathen / denn man hätte in solchen Röcken ein schön und groß Ansehen / könten auch die Mängel des Leibes darunter fein verborgen seyn . . ." (King Cyrus afterwards enjoyed such clothing for certain reasons and advised his people to wear it because he thought people looked tall and imposing in such outfits, and one could hide a body's shortcomings very well under them . . . *VNB*, 586).

While the men dress like women, according to the author, the women dress like men: "Die Kleidung der Weiber seynd noch dünner als der Männer / werden auch umb den Leib nicht gebunden / sie tragen Hosen und Hembder / nach art der Männer . . ." (The clothes of the women are still thinner than those of the men; they are not tied around their bodies; they put on trousers and shirts in the manner of men . . . *VNB*, 588). In other words, the native dress of the inhabitants leads to a kind of role reversal, in that traditional, stereotypical notions about appropriate dress codes are not followed:

> Ihre Strümpffe seynd gemeiniglich von rothen und grünen Sammet / auff den Köpffen tragen sie keinen sonderlichen Zierath / lassen die Haare in viel flechten forne und hinten herunter hangen. Umb die Wangen und Kinn lassen sie eine oder zwey reigen Perlen oder Spangen rund herumbgehen / daß also das gantze Angesicht in Perlen und Spangen stehet / wie solches alles neben der andern Persischen Tracht in beygefügter Figur abgebildet ist. Ich sehe das dieses eine gar alte Orientalische Tracht ist / denn im Hohen Lied Salomonis solche auch angedeutet wird. [. . .] Die Jungfern tragen auch in den rechten Naselöchern güldene Ringe mit Edelgesteinen / gleich die oberwehnte Tartarn; Sie zieren auch ihre Finger mit

gülden Ringen / und die Arme mit silbernen breit geschlagenen Blechbändern. (*VNB*, 588)

Their stockings are usually of red and green velvet; they have no special ornaments on their heads but let their hair hang down in braids in front as well as in back. They ring their cheeks and chin with one or two rows of pearls or clasps so that their entire face is framed by pearls and jewelry, as is portrayed along with the other forms of Persian dress in the accompanying image. I can see that this is a very old oriental type of clothing because it is referred to in the Song of Salomon. [. . .] Maidens wear golden rings with precious stones in their right nostrils like the Tatars I mentioned above. They adorn their fingers with golden rings and their arms with wide silver torques.

The comment "wie . . . in beygefügter Figur abgebildet ist" (as is portrayed . . . in the accompanying image) also implies that the author is aware of the added dimension of his illustrations, that is, his prose description can inform the reader, but a pictorial representation can actually show what the words mean.

The stereotypes that a European reader would have about the Orient and of the Oriental woman as a site of mystery are addressed in the topic of female clothing — but then they are presented in an ironic form.

Die Weibes Personen / wann sie auff den Strassen gehen / lassen sich nicht untern Angesicht sehen / seynd mit langen / vom Kopff biß auff die Waden herunter hangenden weissen Tüchern bedecket / halten beym Gesichte nur einen Schlitz offen / durch welchen sie kaum sehen können. Hierunter seynd offt schöne / auch wol in schönen Kleidern heßliche Bilder verborgen. (*VNB*, 588)

Women, when they go out on the street don't let their faces be seen; they are covered with long white cloths that hang down from the head to their thighs; they leave open only a slit in front of their faces through which they are barely able to see. Under them there are often hidden beautiful images, often — one may surmise — also ugly images in beautiful clothes.

On this same topic, Olearius further contextualizes his own translation of Sa'di's *Gulistān*:

> Was mir einst mit solch einer zu Ardebil begegnet / habe ich in meinen Persischen Rosenthal bey dem 56. Sprichworte im achten Buch erzehlet. Der sinnreiche Persische Poet Schich Saadi gebrauchet ihm diese zum Gleichniß in beschreibung eines Menschen / welcher in Reden und Geberden / zwar einen guten Augenschein von sich gibt / aber wenn man sein Leben und Wercke besehen solte / wurde mans viel anders befinden. Seine Verse und Reime seynd hiervon diese: 'Viel schätzt man schön / wenn sie im Tuch verhüllet gehen. Die doch / wenn sie entblösst / als alte Mütter sehen.' (*VNB*, 588-589)

> In my Persian Valley of Roses — in the 56th Saying in the Eighth Book — I recounted what happened to me once with one of them in Ardabīl. The wise Persian poet Sheik Sa'di uses this example as a parable in the description of a human being, who makes a good impression in his speech and his gestures but would be found to be quite different if one were to examine his life and his works. His verses and rhymes concerning this fact are as follows: Many are considered beautiful when they walk about hidden by veils who would — when unwrapped — be found to look like old mothers.

Olearius concludes his chapter on Persian clothing by praising the inhabitants' cleanliness and emphasizing how the members of the upper class change their clothing right away when it becomes dirty, whereas the "gemeine Leute" (common folk) wash their clothing almost weekly. However, the author then uses this description to contrast it with what he characterizes as the "dirty" morality of the inhabitants — "in Geilheit und Unkeuschheit geben die Perser keiner Nation etwas zuvor . . ." (in lecherousness and unchastity the Persians cannot be trumped by any nation . . . *VNB*, 592) — a topic which he examines in the following chapter, entitled "Von der Perser innerlichen Natur und Sitten" (On the Persians' inner nature and customs). In short, the Persian couple depicted on the cartouche lead the interested viewer to a series of related subjects in the travel account that concern both the exterior and interior traits of the inhabitants.

The Dedicatory Cartouche

Let us turn now to the other strapwork cartouche located at the extreme right side of the Persia map (Figure 4.13). It contains a Latin inscription, written in italics, that dedicates the work to Duke Frederick III of Schleswig-Holstein, and names the author, Adam Olearius, and the engraver, Christian Lorens [Rothgiesser]. The forms of address in the dedicatory cartouche echo — in condensed form — the dedication of the travel account, which is located directly after the frontispiece and title page.[121] In the dedication to the travel account,

4.13 Dedicatory cartouche and "Candide Lector;" detail from the *Nova Delineatio Persiae et Confiniorum* (1655), from the *Vermehrte Newe Reysebeschreibung*.

the author gives the reasons for the journey, and praises his patron for his wisdom in sponsoring the mission and having the foresight to publish the work for posterity. The map's dedicatory cartouche thus reiterates the Duke's various attributes (outlined in the text), but in a shorthand form.

Let us first consider how the patron is addressed, since he occupies the position of primary importance. All the letters of the ruler's name, *FRIEDERICO*, are capitalized, and a special style of italics is used just for his name. Even the typography plays a role in emphasizing the importance of the dedicatee. The titles of the duke (*Domino . . . Haeredi Norwegiae . . . Duci . . . Comiti*) arc all mentioned, along with the different territories under his control (*Sleswicensi Holsatiae Stormariae & Delmenhorsti*). This establishes the Duke's geographical purview and serves to link the duchy with the foreign territories depicted on the map. The link is a rather fictitious one, belonging to the realm of wish-fulfillment, for the Duke's stated aim in sending the embassy to Persia was to establish a trade route with Persia and obtain exclusive rights to export silk from the area, thus squeezing out the other European competition, especially the Dutch. While this project was never realized, a real link was indeed created between these seemingly disparate areas of the world by means of the Holstein embassy and Olearius's subsequent travel account. Through knowledge and discovery, German as well as other European readers were given the opportunity to learn about Safavid Persia. Even to this day, historians of the Safavid era consult Olearius's work for an outsider's view of that society. In this sense, Gottorf, represented by its Duke, did become connected on a certain level with the Persian empire. The cartouche containing the ducal name thus represents a kind of seal of authority (indicating ownership of the map, and approval for the enterprise) and stands as a symbol for the link between political power and modes of representation during the Early-Modern Era.

Below the seven lines dedicated to the Duke we read "*dedicat Auctor M. Adam Oleari,*" thus the author inscribes his own name and his own presence on his work. Just below Olearius's name, squeezed in almost as an afterthought, we find "*Christian Lorens fecit,*" written in a smaller typeface. The engraver's position as a workman is clearly established by the placement of his name below the patron and the author. Olearius, as the inventor of the work, has a different status and a very developed sense of self. Tom Conley, who, in his work *The Self-Made Map: Cartographic Writing in Early Modern France* analyzes the intersections between literature and cartography in Early-Modern France, makes a number of observations that can apply to Olearius's situation as well. Conley, after listing David Buisseret's five reasons for the development of cartography, notes that one of the main features for the development of cartography during the Early-Modern Age

> . . . might be located in the new importance afforded to the emerging self and to the self's relation to the idea of national space. In this domain, which appears to be situated between raw perception and the creative imagination, there seems to be a correlation between mapping and the growth of a new medium — literature — in Early-Modern print culture. New modes of surveying and plotting the world influence representations of the private and public domains of the individual writer. What Erich Auerbach once called the "drama" of European literature (1984) may indeed have been, in the changes between the fifteenth and seventeenth centuries, an unforeseen theatricalization of the self, which acquired a consciousness of its autonomy through modes of positioning that are developed into both textual and gridded representations of reality. (Conley, 2)
>
> The self seems to be produced in the form of a subject that is ruled by laws of classification or by ideology, such that it can be seen not only as an "author," an "authority," an expert cosmographer or topographer, a savant, or a technician, but also as a paradoxical being divided between a representation of the conflictual relations it is producing — including the conditions of patronage and practice in which the works are crafted — and the composite nature of the simultaneously aural and visual medium of print. (Conley, 5–6)

The development of the subject and the mapping of the world can be viewed as growing pari passu in the formation of the Early-Modern Age. As stated later by Conley,

> . . . [it] coincides with the extraordinary growth of cartography in print culture. The time (1460–1640) roughly parallels that of the

coming of autobiography, thus hinting that mapping is responsible for the consciousness that leads to the production of the fashioned self. The creation of the subject is buttressed by the subject's affiliation with the mapping of the world. (Conley, 22)

While the role of autobiography in the travel account needs a separate treatment, suffice it to say that Olearius is an author who indeed marks his presence and who does not shy away from stating his own ideas, which are based on his own observations. The multiplicity of genres found in the travel account results in a multiplicity of roles that the author must play in order to present his information. To mention but a few of these roles, Olearius writes as historian, ethnographer, philosopher, naturalist, artist, geographer, traveler and tourist, merchant, and diplomat. These many roles find expression in the multiple points of view found in the text. Olearius switches constantly from the first person singular ("Ich") to an "objective" third-person observer, to the first person plural, especially when recounting adventures that relate to the entire group.

A few examples will highlight this strategy. In Shemakha, the author is bitten by a scorpion and recounts the event in the first-person singular in a rather objective manner, considering the circumstances. In the margin, we note first "Ich vom Scorpion gestochen" (I, having been stung by a scorpion), while in the text we read:

Solch Ungemach habe ich auch an mir / und zwar unter allen unsern Völckern nur alleine empfinden müssen / In dem zu Schamachie in der Rückreise ich in der nacht von einem Scorpion am Halse neben der Kehle gestochen wurde: Es lieff alsbald eine Blase eines halben Fingers lang auff / und brante als wenn Kohlen darauff gelegen. Unser Medicus aber / welcher zu meinem Glück bey mir im Gemache schlieff / legte bald Scorpion Ohl darauff / gab mir Tyriac ein und ließ mich schwitzen / wodurch sich nach dreyen Stunden die grossen Schmertzen zwar verloren / aber gleichwol über zween Tage noch ein stechen als mit einer Natel nachbliebe. Solch stechen habe ich noch etliche jahr hernach umb Herbst Zeit / und gemeinlich nach Michaelis wieder empfunden / wil nicht halten / daß etwas darzu veruhrsachet / wenn die Sonn in Scorpion getreten. (*VNB*, 495–496)

Such trouble I had to experience on my own person and, to be sure, as the only one among our company. In Shemakha on the return trip I was bitten in the neck, next to the throat by a scorpion during the night. Immediately there appeared a blister half a finger long and it burned as though there were coals upon it. Our physician who — as luck would have it — slept in my room next to me immediately put scorpion's oil upon it, gave me theriac and made me sweat whereupon after three hours the great pains subsided. However, for more than two days there remained a stabbing pain as though it were made by a needle. I have felt such a stabbing pain for several years, usually in the autumn, around Saint Michael's day. I don't want to claim that it might be caused by the Sun entering Scorpio.

At other times, when Olearius talks about the conflicts he had with the leader of the embassy, Otto Brüggemann, he reverts to an impersonal third-person narration, and refers to himself by his title as secretary of the mission.

Diese tage begab sich unser Secretarius wegen einer harten Verfolgung vom Comitat zu den Spanischen München Augustiner Ordens in ihr Kloster / woselbst er von den Patribus und Brüdern wol empfangen und 13. Tage wol gehalten worden. Er war auch willens seinen Weg durch Babilon und Alepo / selbige Orter / weil sie der alten Geschichten halber sehr berühmt / auch zu besehen / zu nehmen. Es würde aber solcher vorsatz umb gewisse Ursachen rückstellig gemachet / und der Secretarius wieder zum Comitat gebracht. (*VNB*, 519)

In these days our Secretary, being the victim of zealous persecution from inside the Committee, took refuge in the monastery of the Spanish monks of St. Augustine; there he was kindly received by the fathers and brothers and hosted well for 13 days. He also wanted to take his route through Babylon and Aleppo as these places are very famous because of ancient stories, and he wanted to see them. However, due to certain causes this resolution had to be rescinded and the Secretary had to return to the Committee.

Finally, the author makes use of the first-person plural, usually in order to refer to common adventures experienced by the members of the expedition. Sometimes "wir" is used in order to be inclusive and draw the reader into the narrative and make him/her feel closer to the events. This is especially true for the chapter "Von der Perser Ehestand / von vielheit der Frawen / und was es bißweilen geschadet" (On the marital life of the Persian, on the great number of wives, and how it sometimes did harm), in which the "we" acquires an almost voyeuristic feel: "Nach dem wir in der Perser Haußhaltung gekommen / Küche und Keller besehen / und was ihre Gewerbe etwas zu gewin[n]en / wollen wir uns auch zu ihren Cammern nahen / und ihren Ehestand betrachten" (After we entered the household of the Persians, looked at the kitchen and the cellars, and their means of earning by different trades we want to approach their bedrooms and examine their married life, *VNB*, 602).

Candide Lector

In the map, we see that the presence of the author is further emphasized in a direct address to the reader, located just below and to the left of the dedicatory cartouche, at the very bottom border of the map. The very position of the text — in the bottom right-hand corner of the map — marks it as a kind of signature, as the locus that corresponds to where an artist would sign his name. As mentioned above, Olearius considered himself as fulfilling a number of roles — author of the text, sketch artist, cartographer/geographer, historian — and of blurring the boundaries between these different functions. For example, when writing the history of Holstein, he uses a cartographic metaphor to indicate the fact that he can only sketch out the historical events for the reader, who then has to consult other sources in order to gain a fuller understanding of the subject matter:

Ich habe dieses als ein Compendium geschrieben / in welchem ich nach Art der Mathematicorum, so die Landkarten machen / im engen Begriff viel Städte nur mit Puncten andeuten / meist nur den Einhalt der Geschichten ohne vielen Umbständen melden / und gleichsam als durch Bäche zum großen Meer führen / und dem

Leser zu weitleufftigeren und vollständigern Autoren den Weg weisen wollen. Zu dem behuff habe ich die loca der citirten Autorum mit Fleiß darzu setzen wollen.[122]

I have written this as a compendium following the method of mathematicians who construct maps. In a narrow space they indicate many cities only by dots. Thus I wanted to report the content of stories without much embellishment. Leading through little brooks to the great sea I wanted to direct the reader towards authors who write more at length and with more depth. For that purpose I wished to give complete references for the authors I quoted.

Perhaps the most visually striking instance of Olearius's "production of self" concerns the only representation of the author as artist in the travel account. In the depiction of the city of Derbent — located at the very boundary of the Persian empire on the west coast of the Caspian — Olearius depicts himself as sketching the view of the city (Figure 4.14). Our author can be found in the lower right-hand corner of the image, dressed in a travel cloak, holding a sketchpad and drawing utensils and accompanied by a small dog sitting behind him. A Persian man standing beside him points toward the city with one hand and toward the sketchpad with the other. Olearius observes the viewer

4.14 View of Derbent with portrayal of Adam Olearius,
from the *Vermehrte Newe Reysebeschreibung* (1656).

from his vantage point seated in a cemetery in the foreground; the middleground contains the depiction of the city itself, above which looms Mount Barmach in the background. This self-depiction of the author — one of only two or three in the entire account — occurs just a few pages after the official artist of the Holstein embassy has passed away.[123] Olearius makes a special point of remarking that he drew the sketch of the city himself: "Ich habe die Stadt gar eigentlich abgerissen / und mit hieher setzen wollen" (I drew the city with my own hands and wanted to insert it here, *VNB*, 719), in other words, the mantle of artist is passed on to the author, who asserts himself and his new status in pictorial form.

Other, previous instances of this kind of self-representation were not unknown to the author. In one of the maps from the *Newe Landesbeschreibung,* the geographer Johannes Mejer depicts himself at work, albeit in the bottom left-hand corner (Figure 4.15). In this case, Mejer's face is not presented to the viewer. A hat obscures the specific character traits of the individual, and the image opts instead to emphasize the professional activity of the geographer.

Now that we have analyzed the placement of the Latin text, we can analyze its content. The text reads as follows:

Candide Lector
Harum Provinciarum, urbium, montium et fluviorum cum iteribus cum modernis nominibus insigniorum situm prout illae partim â Persis, partim propria observatione exhibet haec Tabula, quâ adhibitâ res ibidem locorum gestae, praesertim Alexandri mag. lucidiores existent.

4.15 Detail of map of Flensborg with depiction of Johannes Mejer, from the *Newe Landesbeschreibung* by Danckwerth/Mejer (1652).

Illustrious Reader,

This map shows the location of these significant provinces, cities, mountains and rivers with roads and modern names, that is, as they derived partly from the Persians and partly from my own observation, to which are attached also the places where great events took place especially the more illustrious ones of Alexander the Great.

Olearius inserts himself into the text by "talking" directly to his "Lector" or reader — not the viewer or spectator — and presupposes that a reader of the text will be using the map to gain a deeper understanding of the narrative. That is to say, the "Nova Delineatio Persiae" is not thought of as an independent entity, to be sold as a single sheet, the map is conceived of as a kind of text that is meant to be read. The address emphasizes the fact that both old and new can be found on the map: the most modern names along with the most important classical sites from the age of Alexander. Olearius asserts that his new information (the location of the sites) is based on information received from the Persians as well as from his own observations.

THE CASPIAN SEA

The Caspian Described in Olearius's Text

On Olearius's map of Persia, the Caspian Sea is referred to as "MARE CASPIVM Sive HYRCANVM Persis KÜLSUM." The naming of the object thus presents the first question to be considered, that is, the designation of the sea creates as much confusion as its correct depiction.[124] The author begins by noting that:

Dieses Meer hat von unterschiedlichen Landes Leuten und Völckern auch unterschiedliche Namen. Die Uhralten haben es Mare Chosar . . . genandt . . . Die Mauri Bohar Corsun, gleich sie auch den Arabischen Meerbusen titulieren. Die Perser Külsum, welcher Nahm auch dem rothen Meer zugeeignet wird . . . In gemein aber wird es von den Scribenten Hyrcanum und Caspium nach den daran gelegenen Landschafften und Völckern genennet / wie auch von der in Schirwan gelegenen Stadt Bakuje, Mare de

Baku. Bey den Russen heist es Gualenskoi more. (*VNB*, 405)

This sea has been given different names by different peoples. The ancients called it . . . Mare Chosar . . . The Moors called it Bohar Corsun, a name they also give to the Arabian Gulf. The Persians call it Külsum, a name also given to the Red Sea . . . In general, howeverer, writers call it Hyrcanian or Caspian after the names given to the surrounding territories and peoples, as it is also called Mare de Baku after the city of Baku in Schirwan. The Russians call it Gualenskoi more.

After mentioning these different possibilities, Olearius goes on to discuss the question whether the Caspian is in fact a lake. Olearius lists all the writers before him, who had assumed that the Caspian Sea was connected to other bodies of water, but he agrees with Aristotle and Herodotus, who say that it is an independent body of water. He quotes their statements:

"Hyrcanum mare & Caspium ab extero mari sejuncta sunt, & circumquaq; alcolas habent." Dieser aber: "Mare Caspium per se est, nec ullo cum alio commiscetur." Es ist ein eigen Meer / welches keine Gemeinschafft hat mit dem grossen Meere / ist allenthalben mit Ufer umbschlossen / und mag wol recht mare mediterraneum genandt werden. Es haben auch solches bekräfftiget die Kilaner so an der Westen seiten dieses Meeres wohnen und andere Perser / die ich mit fleiß darumb befraget. (*VNB*, 407)

"The Hyrcanian and the Caspian Sea are separate from the outer sea, and have shorelines everywhere surrounding them." The latter, however, says: "The Caspian Sea is itself a sea and does not mix with another anywhere." It is a sea all by itself which does not have anything in common with the big sea, it is everywhere surrounded by a shore and could rightly be called mare mediterraneum. The Gilanians who live on the Western side of this sea and other Persians whom I assiduously asked about it, have confirmed this fact.

In one significant passage, Olearius discusses the shape and size of the

Caspian Sea and underlines the fact that the sea is longer from north to south rather than from east to west, as had been thought by his contemporaries. Since this question is important for later discussions concerning both the history of the sea's representation and the influence of Islamic geography on Olearius's map, the entire text is quoted here:

Die länge der Caspischen See wird in gemein von den Scribenten auff 15. die breite aber / da sie am grössen / auff 8. TageReisen / geschätzet / wenn man nemblich / wie sie sagen / ohne Hülffe des Windes mit rudern unverhindert darüber fahren solte. Wenn ich aber ihre Gräntzen nach dem am Ufer gelegnen Städten und Ortern / wie ich dieselbige nicht alleine im Catalogo longitudinum & latitudinum, so ich von den Persern bekommen / und ebenmässig in den fragmentis Astronomicis Johannis Gravii befindlich / sondern auch zum theil selbst erforschet / legen wil / so wird die länge der See nicht wie bißher in den gemeinen Landtaffeln angedeutet worden / von Osten nach Westen / sondern von Norden nach Süden / oder von Mitternacht nach Mittag / die breite aber von Osten nach Westen / oder von Morgen gegen Abend sich erstrecken. Die länge vom ostio maris oder Eingange des Meeres unter Astrachan biß nach Ferabath wird auff 8. Grad aequatoris, und also 120. deutscher Meilen / die breite aber von der Landschafft Chuaresm biß an das Cyrcassische Gebirge / bey 6. Grad aequatoris und also 90. Meilen seyn.

Es haben etliche meiner guten Freunde von der Universitet Leipzig / nach dem sie in meiner ersten Edition die Persischen Langkarte [sic] gesehen / mir zugeschrieben und verweisen wollen / daß ich die Persische See also geleget; Es wäre wider aller Geographorum bißher gehabte meynung / weil ich aber / wie gedacht / der Sachen bessern Nachricht bekommen / darff ich mich an Meynung der andern nicht kehren. Es heisset: Errante uno, errant omnes. Wenn Dionysius Alexandrinus aus Irrthumb die See also geleget / haben andere derer keiner sie selbst gesehen / ihm gefolget. (*VNB*, 407)

Writers estimate the length of the Caspian Sea to be that of a journey of 15 days, the maximum width, however, to be that of 8 days were one to row across it, as they say without being aided by the wind. I measure its limits, however, according to the cities and other places that I found in the catalogue of longitudes and latitudes that I received from the Persians, and which are also to be found in the "Astronomical Fragments" of Johannes Gravius, and some of which I reconnoitered myself. In that case the length of the sea extends not from east to west — as has so far been indicated in common maps — but from north to south, or from midnight to midday. Its width, however extends from east to west, or from morning to evening. The length from the ostio maris or beginning of the sea below Astrachan until Ferabath is about 8 degrees of latitude, that is 120 German miles; the breadth, however, is from the territory of Khwarizm until the Circassian mountains about 6 degrees of latitude that is 90 miles.

Some of my good friends of the University of Leipzig have written to me and reproved me that in my first edition I saw the Persian map in such manner and that I put the Persian Sea in those dimensions. They said that it was against the opinion held by all geographers so far. Since I, however, have better information about such matters, I must not worry about the opinion of others. It is said: If one person makes a mistake, all others do too. When Dionysius of Alexandria erred by positioning the Sea in such a manner, others, who did not see it with their own eyes, followed him.

The dimensions that Olearius gives for the sea — 120 German miles long and 90 miles wide — bear repeating, since we will return to these proportions in the third section. The shape of the sea is now radically different from previous representations, and the author who has traveled to the area, sticks to his calculations despite the criticism he receives from colleagues and friends.

Olearius goes on to describe the physical characteristics of the sea, e.g., whether it has a tide or not; the number of tributaries flowing into it; the salinity of the waters; the fact that there are few good harbors. He also observes that no one had yet been in the center of the Caspian Sea. The Schleswig delegation had planned for some of their delegation to explore the center of the Caspian Sea while the others were at the Shah's court, but because their vessel was shipwrecked during a storm, they were not able to follow through on this plan.[125] Olearius also denies the reports that water on top is "schwartz als Pech und

Theer" (black as pitch and tar), as Petrus Petraeus contends in his *Muscovitische Chronica* of 1620. Nor does the sea contain islands with pretty cities and villages on them, as others have stated, only "Ensil bey Ferabath, so der schönen Viehweide halber etliche Hirten Hütten hat" (Ensil near Ferabath which has some shepherds' huts since the pasture there is very nice, *VNB*, 411).

Regarding the fauna in the sea, he rejects eyewitness accounts that there are enormous snakes in the sea, as Curtius Rufus had claimed. Nor is there a "runder fisch ohne Kopff und anderen Gliedern / so bey anderthalb ellen groß . . . auß welchem sie Thraan schmeltzen zum Lampen brennen und Camehle Salben im gantzen Lande herumb verkauffen wollen" (round fish without head and other limbs about one and a half ells long . . . from which they melt the fat which they want to sell in the entire country for the lighting of lamps and the salving of camels, *VNB*, 411). That is not necessary, as Olearius was told by his Persian informants, "weil in dieser Gegend sehr viel Nefta fällt, welches sie zu solchem Nutzen gebrauchen können" (because much naphta is falling in this region which they can use for that purpose, *VNB*, 411). However, there are some enormous fish, which can capsize boats with their tails, "so daß sich kein Fischer über 4. Faden tieff in die See waget" (so that no fisherman dares to go out to sea where it is more than four fathoms deep, *VNB*, 411). Besides outlining the different types of fish to be found in the waters — "schöne große Lachse, Störe, Karpen über 2 Ellen lang / eine art von Hering / eine grosse art Brassen . . ." (beautiful large salmon, sturgeon, carp more than two ells long, a type of herring, a large type of bass . . ., *VNB*, 412) — he points to an enormous source of income for the Shah, who rents out the mouths of rivers going into or out of the Caspian Sea for fishing. From September to April, certain parts of the beach are closed to the public, and only people who have paid are permitted to fish there. However, it is a risky business since the rents are very high and some years there are not enough fish to make the expense worthwhile. Olearius personally knows a man who lost 2,000 Thalers one year (*VNB*, 412).

Especially interesting in the context of the Caspian Sea discussions is his treatment of the question where the waters of the Caspian Sea flow when they leave the *mare mediterraneo*. Here Olearius's scientific reticence is notable. "Etliche meinen" one reads — and he quotes without attribution the opinion of the scholar Athanasius Kircher (1601–80) — "daß die Erde so wol als der Himmel ihre Inteligentsias Engel oder Geister habe / welche in demselben die bewegungen thäten / und die wasser aus den Tieffen also aufführeten" (Some think that the earth, as well as the heavens have their intelligent angels or spirits which move inside them and thus bring the waters out of their depth, *VNB*, 408). There are others who believe that the earth, like a living creature, has a body and soul by whose motion all parts of the earth were made alive and made to move in their turn: "Daher giengen die Wasser durch eine natürliche Krafft durch die verborgene Adern der Erden / und stiegen an das Gebirge / gleich wie in dem Menschen das Geblüte von der Leber zum Hertzen und durch die venam cavam sich auffwerths und zum Häupte begebe" (Therefore the waters were driven by a natural power through the hidden veins of the earth and rose up into the mountains, just as in a human being the blood rises from the liver to the heart and moves upwards and to the head through the vena cava, *VNB*, 408). This is a reference from another scientific debate of the seventeenth century, and it has not yet been resolved to the point where Olearius wants to take a stand. Harvey's discovery of the circulation of blood, published in his book *De motu cordis et sanguinis* (1628), had by no means been accepted in Germany when Olearius wrote his book. Many luminaries of the medical as well as the theological establishment were not ready to give up the beautiful theories of a fire that burned in the human heart, and the "ignis spissus coelestis" that brought about new life — traditions derived from Galen's medicine. Olearius would be on uncertain ground here, and thus, in order to avoid both subscribing to the theory of the Jesuit Kircher or the much-maligned foreigner Harvey, he only quotes "etliche und etliche" (some of them and others). Julius Caesar Scaliger's theories about the saline qualities of water are safe science, so Olearius discusses them at length and contributes his own observations about astrolabes.

These few quotes give a good impression of Olearius's way of writing. He first lists the main features of a subject under discussion, then quotes the classical and contemporary authorities in order to elicit different opinions, as well as record other traditions and myths. These he either confirms or denies on the basis of his own observations and/or other eyewitness accounts. He states clearly that some erroneous interpretations arise from the fact that the original writer had not seen the place, and that others in turn had copied him without checking the facts. Olearius's appeal to a wide public is explained in this discussion of the Caspian Sea. His work is of interest to the professional man: the fisherman, the merchant, and the sailor. Our author also appeals to the erudite and educated of all Western nations who, after all, have read the same books as he. As has already been mentioned, the most radical claim Olearius makes in his chapter on the Caspian Sea concerns its shape, and it is precisely this tradition — how the sea and Persia itself have been depicted — which will be discussed in the next section.

The Depiction of the Caspian Sea
in Early-Modern Europe

We will now focus on the depiction of the Caspian Sea as it developed in Western Europe during the Early-Modern Era, that is, from approximately 1500 to 1725. We shall begin by examining maps that resulted from the presence of Italian merchants in Persia during the Renaissance; then look at Sebastian Münster's Ptolemaic maps of the area; and discuss how the Caspian Sea was represented during the golden age of Dutch cartography by such figures as Abraham Ortelius, Gerardus Mercator, and the firm of Henricus Hondius and Jan Jansson. Also we will see how Johannes Mejer's portrayal of the area in his map of the world owes an obvious debt to Olearius. We conclude with Johann Baptist Homann's map of Persia from the early-eighteenth century, which almost succeeds in showing the Caspian Sea in its true shape. By following the progress of the Caspian Sea's shape over little more than two centuries, we can see not only how geographic knowledge evolved, but also how this type of visual representation in the cartographic literature both reflected and brought about changing perceptions of the world.

Alfons Gabriel provides the single best overview regarding the topic of European travelers to Persia, and gives valuable insights about the mapping of the country by these visitors. Some of the earliest Europeans to the area hailed from Italy, the most famous of whom was the Venetian Marco Polo. Polo was a merchant by trade, and his observations concerning the shape of the country at the end of the thirteenth century did not lead to an improved depiction of the area.[126] As Gabriel notes:

> Die Reise Marco Polos hatte nicht den Einfluß auf die Erdkunde, den man hätte erwarten können. Die Hauptursache lag in dem damals hoffnungslosen Darniederliegen der geographischen Wissenschaft. Die Kartenzeichner machten kaum einen Versuch, die übernommenen bildlichen Darstellungen der Länder durch den Stoff, der durch neuere Reisende gesammelt worden war, zu verbessern. [. . .] Erst auf der . . . Carta Catalana aus dem Jahr 1375 finden sich die Entdeckungen Marco Polos einverleibt. In späteren Zeiten war der Einfluß von Marco Polos Werk auf die Kartographie fast schädlich. Die Geographen trugen die Namen, die bei dem Venezianer erwähnt sind, oft in verstümmelter Form in die ptolemäischen Karten ein, ohne jedoch die Grundfehler dieser Karten zu verbessern. Marco Polo, der keine entsprechende Vorbildung besaß, hatte astronomische Beobachtungen nicht machen können, und das Ergebnis dieser zusammengewürfelten Karten war ein völliges Durcheinander. (Gabriel, 39)

The journey of Marco Polo did not have the influence on geography that one might have expected. The main reason lay in the utter depression of the geographic sciences at that time. The designers of maps hardly made an attempt to improve the traditional pictorial representations of countries by using material which had been collected by more recent travellers. [. . .] It is only . . . in the Carta Catalana from the year 1375 that the discoveries of Marco Polo are incorporated. In later times the influence of Marco Polo's work upon the cartographers was almost harmful. The geographers entered the names mentioned by the Venetian into the Ptolemaic charts, often in a garbled form; however they did not correct the basic mistakes of these maps. Marco Polo, who had no corresponding education, had been unable to make astronomical observations, and the result of these thrown-together maps was complete chaos.

A number of missionaries who traveled in Persia — such as Giovanni di Monte Corvino (ca. 1300), the founder of the Catholic Church in China — recorded their observations about the land and the people. But it was merchants from the Italian city states, not only from Venice, but Pisa and Genoa as well, who most furthered the cause of the geographic description of Persia and the Caspian Sea during this time period. It seems that the Genoese in particular were responsible for mapping the coastline and advancing the cartographic knowledge of the Sea. The Genoese, who even had a consulate in the important city of Tabriz, exported silk from Gilan (in northeastern Persia) over the Caspian Sea, using the Volga and the Don to transport their wares to Italy.

> Den Genueser Händlern ist es wahrscheinlich zu danken, daß die auf Ptolemaeus zurückgehende, von Westen nach Osten gestreckte Gestalt des Kaspisees auf den Landkarten im 14. Jahrhundert aufgegeben wurde. [. . .] Es gibt Karten aus dem 14. Jahrhundert, auf denen, wahrscheinlich nach Angabe der Genueser, eine ganze Reihe Punkte an der Küste des Kaspischen Meeres verzeichnet sind, über die früher jede Kunde fehlte. Auf der Catalanischen Karte von 1375 beginnt die Küstenaufnahme bei der Halbinsel Manghischlak und erstreckt sich über die ganze West- und Südküste, die mit dem 'Golf von Mazanderan' schließt. (Gabriel, 34–35)

> We probably owe it to the Genoese merchants that the shape of the Caspian Sea going back to Ptolemy, namely as a west-east extension, was discontinued on fourteenth-century maps. [. . .] On maps from the fourteenth century a series of points are noted at the coast of the Caspian Sea which are probably based on the data provided by the Genoese, and about which previously nothing was known. On the Catalan map of 1375 the description of the coastline begins at the peninsula of Mangyslak and stretches along the entire western and southern coast which ends in the 'Gulf of Mazandaran.'

The cartographic activities of the Genoese and other Italians resulted in a few maps that depicted the Caspian more or less correctly. Fra Mauro's world map of 1459 portrays the Sea with an incorrect orientation and a protuberance in what should be the upper northeast region (Figure 4.16).[127] A remarkably accurate representation of the Sea can be found on an anonymous circular world map, probably published in Venice around 1485 (Figure 4.17).[128] To my knowledge, this map is the most precise European depiction of the Caspian Sea before the early-eighteenth century, and includes not only the correct orientation, but even shows that it is longer from north to south than from west to east. However it does not seem to have had an effect on later depictions of the area. The Ptolemaic canon, which held that the Sea had an elliptical shape, stretching from west to east, held sway in all of Europe — both southern and northern — from the early Renaissance until the late-seventeenth and early-eighteenth centuries.

4.16 World map by Fra Mauro (1459).

4.17 Anonymous Venetian Map (ca. 1485).

Let us now turn to the work of Sebastian Münster, the cartographer/publisher who was most responsible for disseminating this Ptolemaic vision of the world in Renaissance Europe. Münster is best known as the editor of Ptolemy's *Geographia* (1540) and the *Cosmographia universalis* (1544). As was noted earlier, Münster helped establish the ancient Greek author's works as canonical for the sixteenth century. Conley notes that:

> His *Cosmographia universalis* attempted to summarize all classical and medieval sources about the world, incorporated information gathered since the turn of the sixteenth century, and, no less, solicited individuals for items pertaining to all the local areas of Europe

and other continents. Its initial size, 659 pages and 520 woodcuts qualified the project as encyclopedic. It expanded progressively (1545, 1546, 1548, and 1550) to a bulk of over 1,200 pages. Twenty-seven editions were published from 1553 to 1628.[129]

As these many editions suggest, Münster's works were very popular: they contained the authoritative versions of the earth's representation, and included updates as new information about an area was received, leading to ever-growing works that would contain the old as well as the new, side by side. Figure 4.18 shows Ptolemy's "Tabula Asiae VII" which includes a representation of the entire Caspian Sea. This shape of the body of water — as an oval, stretching from west to east — would remain fundamentally unchanged in Europe throughout the sixteenth century, until Olearius proposed his radically new depiction during the mid-seventeenth century. And even then, it would take almost another half century until cartographers would begin to depict

4.18 Tabula Asiae VII of Ptolemy's *Geographia* in the edition
by Sebastian Münster (Basel, 1540).

the Sea longer from north to south rather than west to east. Münster's representation of the Caspian Sea is reproduced in a smaller format and incorporated into his *Cosmographia*, but the main difference in the later work is the predominance given to the textual description of the country. The portrayal of the country includes geographic information; the history of the ancient kings of Persia, and the conquests of Alexander the Great; burial practices; religious customs; natural resources and economic activity; and customs concerning marriage and parenting. In other words, it can be considered the forerunner of Olearius's travel account, which also seeks to be encyclopedic. The Caspian Sea, in which one finds both treasures and giant snakes, is truly a land of "Promise and Peril," as the editors at the National Geographic Society still maintain. Various general characteristics of the Caspian Sea are described as follows:

> . . . am Caspischen Meere / so doch diß Meere süsser Wasser hat dann kein ander Meere / unnd viel Edelgestein darauß kommen / besunder Cristallen unnd Jaspen / wiewol man darneben auch schreibt / daß es trefflich grosse Schlangen zeucht: den Nammen hat es von den Caspischen Bergen die daran stossen / und etlich Porten dardurch gehn in andere Länder. [. . .] Die Hauptstatt dieses Landts hat vor zeiten auch Hyrcania geheissen / und das Caspisch Meere wird auch genen[n]t hurcanisch meere / von diesem Landt daran es stoßt. Man schreibt daß diß caspisch Meere bey diesem Landt trefflich unrühig und ungestüm ist / und werden wenig inseln darinn gefunden. Aber sein Wasser ist vast süß / un[d] das von dieser ursach willen / daß gerings umb viel fliessender Wasser dareyn fallen / und ihm sein gesaltzene art nemmen / wie Plinius schreibt. Diß Meere wird gemacht auß Flüsse die dareyn kom[m]en / un[d] hoch uber die Felsen hineyn fallen / daß an dem Gestad dieses Meers ein weiter Weg ist under den abfallenden Wässern für zu gehn. Daher kompt es auch daß die Persier unnd Medier im Sommer da erkühlung suchen wider grosse Hitz.[130]

> . . . at the Caspian Sea which contains fresh water as no other sea does; and from which come many jewels, especially crystals and jaspers; people also write that it produces enormous snakes; it has its

name from the Caspian mountains which are on its borders and some gates through them lead into other countries. The capital of this country was formerly called Hyrcania and the Caspian Sea is also called the Hyrcanian Sea because it borders on this land. People write that this Caspian Sea near the Caspian territory is especially restless and stormy, and thus one finds few islands in it. But its waters are very fresh and the reason for that is because many water courses end in it and take away its salty taste, as Pliny writes. This sea is composed of rivers which flow into it and cascade down from the mountains into it so that at the edge of the sea there is a broad road under the cascades. That is why the Persians and Medians look for refreshment there against the great heat.

Sebastian Münster's work heralds a more modern description of Persia, which is indeed Orientalist in that it describes and judges the deviations from the European norm. A few examples of his approach will be mentioned here.

Münster observes that the Persians take their kings from one reigning family, a practice that was common in Europe as well. It is quite barbarous, though, that any insult to the King results in the deprivation of limbs and the destruction of the body itself: "Sie haben ihre König gemacht von einem Geschlecht / unnd welcher dem König ungehorsam war / dem schlug man das Haupt ab / unnd hiew ihm die Arm ab / unnd warff ihn auff Feld" (They select their king from a single family line and whoever did not obey the king had his head chopped off and his arm chopped off and was thrown out onto the field, Münster, 1356). As a European used to an abundance of water in all of its forms, Münster describes the respect of the ecologically-minded Persians for their rivers and streams, which is different from the usages of Europeans: "Es haben die Persier auch ein Brauch gehabt / daß sie sich haben geweschen in den Flüssen / haben nicht dareyn gebruntzt oder gespewt / haben auch kein todten Leichnam dareyn geworffen / sonder das Wasser verehret alß ein Heylig ding" (The Persians had another custom, namely that they washed in the rivers; they did not pee or spit into them, they also did not throw dead bodies into them but they venerated water as though it were sacred, Münster, 1356). The education of Persian children had also been a matter of interest to the European world since Herodotus and Thucydides, and the author points out that Persian men do not acknowlege their children until they are five years old, because infant mortality was so high: "damit dem Vatter kein beschwärd uber den Halß käme / wann sie in den Fünff jaren sturben" (So that the father would not feel depressed if they died in those five years, Münster, 1356). The tough training of a Persian warrior was already a matter of marvel to antique sources, and toughness also bred cruelty. It was proverbial in ancient Rome that some people have hearts as cold as those of the "Hyrcanian Tigers:"

> Von dem Fünfften jar an biß zu dem 24. lahrt man die Kinder reit- en unnd schiessen / man übt sie auch zu lauffen / unnd gewehnet sie zu leiden Hitz unnd Kelte / und zu watten durch die strengen Wasser / item zu schlaffen im Harnisch unnd nassen Kleydern. Unnd so sie sich geübt hatten / gab man ihnen zu essen hart Brot / ein knollen Saltz / unnd gebraten oder gesotten Fleisch / unnd Wasser zu trincken. (Münster, 1356)

> From the fifth year until they are 24 the children are taught to ride and to shoot; they are also trained to run and to suffer heat and cold; to wade through wild waters, to sleep in their armor and in wet clothes. And when they had finished their exercises they were given hard bread, a lump of salt, and baked or steamed meat; and water to drink.

Münster skillfully interweaves ancient source material with mod- ern accounts in order to delight and amaze his readers. His final judg- ment about the Persian male, although it may sound objective, is one of disdain: "Sie reden nicht viel / sonder sind geneigter zu thun / dann zu reden. Sie hangen nach der Unreinigkeit oder Geilheit des Leibs / sind mässig in der Speiß / unnd halten selten was sie zusagen / dann so viel es ihnen nutzt" (They do not speak much and are more apt to act than to speak. They like the uncleanness or lust of the body; they are measured in their eating habits; they seldom keep to what they promise unless it is to their advantage, Münster, 1360). A laconic group of people who are frugal in their habits, rarely keep their word unless it is to their advantage and are also oversexed. They are indeed different from the Europeans according to Münster.

Münster's basic model — of presenting the area, including the Sea as an oval stretching west to east — as well as an accompanying narrative describing the area, would be followed by succeeding generations of cartographers, including two of the most important figures in Early-Modern cartographic history: Gerardus Mercator and Abraham Ortelius. While it is not our aim here to examine in detail the influence of these last two authors on cartography, their work had a far-reaching impact on the discipline, whose effects still resonate into the present. Mercator (1512–1594) is best known for the cartographic projection that he used in his world map of 1569, in which he magnifies the true size of Europe so that it seems to occupy a greater area than it actually does.[131] He also coined the term "atlas" in his compilation *Atlas, Sive Cosmographicae Meditationes de Fabrica Mundi et fabricati Figura*, the complete version of which was published in 1595, a year after his death. Ortelius, a friend as well as a competitor of Mercator, first made use of the atlas form and solicited maps and material from around Europe for his celebrated *Theatrum Orbis Terrarum* (1570), which became a work consisting of a number of different parts that were constantly updated. He combined image and text on a single sheet, with the map on one side of the paper, and a narrative on the reverse side. As Conley writes:

> Instead of placing maps and figures within the flux of discourse, the material process of production accords equal but separate space to image and to text. Of primary interest are the maps — each printed on a single sheet, which is folded and monted on an *onglet*. The full folio page displays the map. On its reverse side is printed the descriptive text pertaining to the map. On the upper side, then, is the image of the area, while on the inverse side is situated the quasi-ekphrastic material that animates, follows, or diverges from the map. Textual limits are imposed by the format of the atlas. In the first edition, Ortelius furnishes a brief description of the area to be seen following and leaves the opposite page blank. The accompanying text cannot be copious. Restricted by the physical plan of the book, the discourse of analogy cannot compete with the cartographic evidence

printed on the reverse side of the page. When Ortelius commissions individuals to procure material that he can edit into a single work, he produces a serial creation, a book of others, that acquires an identity less through an innate design than in the way it fashions received information. An ordering in which an individual authors his or her creation gives way to another order, in which there reigns a system of variation that serves to distinguish different areas of the enterprise. Ortelius's innovation in the science of cartography is that he attends less to the "big picture" of the world than to putting together an illustrated summary of a possibly infinite number of fragmentary parts. (Conley, 204–205)

With regard to the shape of the Caspian, the maps of Mercator (Figure 4.19) and Ortelius (Figure 4.20) do not deviate substantially from those of Münster. However, their representations of the area are more "scientific," in that they include scale bars, and graticules. Most fundamentally, since they are copperplate engravings, they can show a great deal more detail than the woodblock images from the *Geographia*.

The plates of Mercator's *Atlas* were acquired by the Hondius family in Amsterdam. Henricus Hondius, along with his brother-in-law

4.19 Map of Persia by Gerard Mercator (1606).

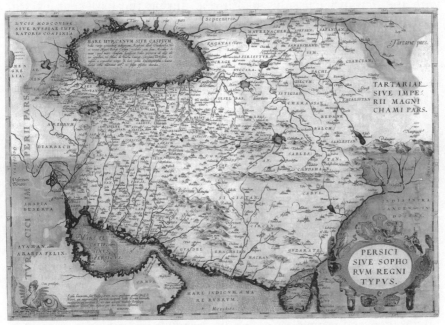

4.20 Map of Persia by Abraham Ortelius (1574).

Jan Jansson continued publishing Mercator's maps, and added new ones to the ever-growing atlas, which eventually expanded to six volumes. Thus, certain maps which had originally been part of Mercator's atlas continued to be reproduced for several decades — sometimes without any or only minor emendations. The map of Persia is one such example, which, due to the relative paucity of new material about the area, stayed almost unchanged from one edition to the next. This is true in particular of the shape of the Caspian Sea. The depiction of the Persian Gulf actually did undergo significant changes in its appearance over time, due to the mapping efforts of European merchants who traded around Hormuz and along the southern Persian coast. In 1607 Jodocus Hondius, the patriarch of the family, published an *Atlas minor,* which made geographic information even more accessible to a wider audience. These "pocket atlases" went through a number of editions. In a 1651 edition by Hondius and Jansson, reference is made in the narrative to earlier editions by Münster, and some information is even borrowed from descriptions Münster had written over a hundred years before. It is interesting to note that Jansson sets the Persians against the Turks in his text. After the horrific experiences with the Turkish invasions in Europe during the past century, the image of the enemy is set against that of the "good" foreigner. The Persians are described in the following manner:

> Die Brüder und Eltern gehen uber die massen freundlich mit einander umb / halten den Adel sehr hoch / und werden fürnemblich / auch in diesem Stück von den Türcken unterscheyden als welche von keinem Unterscheyd des Geblüts und Herkommens jegtes wissen. Alle frembdlinge werden freundlich von ihnen auffgenommen und empfangen : bekommen jedoch ihre / der Persianer / Weiber als welche gemeiniglich sehr schön sind / niergent zu sehen / dieweil sie nemlich umb der selbigen willen leichtlich eyfern / und ihnen doch nichts destoweniger all gebührliche Ehr erzeigen / da hergegen die Türcken ihre Weiber für Mancipia oder leibeygene Sclaven halten.[132]

> Brothers and parents are extremely friendly with each other. They honor the nobility and in that also are distinct from the Turks, who do not know of a distinction by blood or family. All foreigners are received in a friendly manner; however, they never get to see the Persians' wives who are generally very beautiful; because they are easily jealous, and yet show them all due respect, whereas the Turks keep their women like mancipia or slaves.

The basic concerns in the Hondius/Jansson text remain the same as in the *Cosmography*: Persian men may take many wives, and the country is known for its silk, pearls, jewels, and spices. The updated information includes the observation that the Persians are courteous and hospitable toward foreigners, and "zu diesen jetzigen Zeiten" are more cultured and peaceful than the Turks, Tatars, and Saracens.

Finally, the works of the Blaeu family should be mentioned among the most important cartographic family firms of the seventeenth century. Willem Janszoon Blaeu, who had studied under Tycho Brahe, published his first atlas in 1631. "After the death of their father in 1638, Joan and his brother Cornelis took over the business, and the atlas began to increase rapidly in size; by 1655 it contained six volumes, and by 1667 eleven volumes. [. . .] It also took a new title, *Geographia Blavania*."[133] The mid-seventeenth century editions of both the Hondius/Jansson and Blaeu maps of Persia were the definitive, standard ones for Europe at the time of Olearius's voyage, against which his own map would come to be measured.

Olearius's new map of Persia (from the first edition of the travel account in 1647) was first incorporated in Johannes Mejer's map of the ancient world (the *Orbis Vetus*) in the *Newe Landesbeschreibung* of 1651. Figure 4.6, p. 123 shows the Caspian Sea in a more rounded form that is reminiscent of the shape found in Olearius's "Nova Delineatio Persiae." This then is the first world map in which Olearius's representation of the sea is reproduced, but it would take another half century before this new version would begin to be accepted outside the area of Schleswig-Holstein. Thanks to the mapping efforts of a number of French cartographers (e.g. Nicolas Sanson), new information regarding the shape and extent of the Sea slowly began to find its way onto maps. By the early-eighteenth century, Adrianus Reland's map begins to depict the form of the Caspian correctly (Figure 4.21) and Johann Baptist Homann's map (ca. 1720–1725) (Figure 4.22) already depicts the form of the country and the Sea very accurately. This new and improved representation is truly the result of an international effort, and Homann's title underlines this fact, by acknowledging the work of its predecessors, Olearius, Jean Baptiste Tavernier, and Adrianus Reland. Homann's map, while already more accurate than its precursors still contains a number of images in the body of the map that depict the inhabitants of the represented lands. The accompanying page of this map contains sixteen cityscapes of Persian cities, with those of Derbent, Kashan, and Isfahan taken directly from Olearius's travel account. In the bottom left-hand corner of the map, the figures surrounding the cartouche include Persians (two noblemen, with armed servants, and a seated scholar or merchant); symbols of the land's riches (silk and coins); as well as examples of fauna (a lion and a tiger that frame a quote by Ovid between them: "Armeniae Tygres iracundique Leones.") In the top right corner of the map, figures of Tatars are seen engaged in various activities (a man riding horseback, and a woman with child outside a tent).

Homann's map — which stands on the brink of the Enlight-

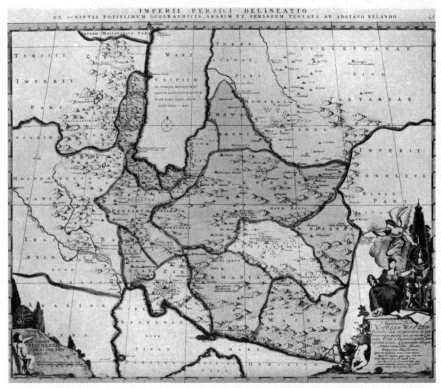

4.21 Map of Persia by Adrianus Reland (1705).

enment and combines the visual traditions of the Early-Modern Age, while pointing the way toward scientific, objective cartographic representation — will thus conclude this overview of the development of the representation of Persia and the Caspian Sea. If we recall the *Rudimentum novitiorum* from 1475 (Figure 4.1, page 114), we can appreciate the strides that cartography took within little more than two centuries in Western Europe. Olearius's map of Persia, with its rounded Caspian Sea, can be considered a milestone in this trajectory. The next section will analyze how Olearius created his new and improved map.

OLEARIUS AND ISLAMIC CARTOGRAPHY

At this stage we need to investigate what kinds of sources Olearius may have consulted in creating his "Nova Delineatio Persiae," a map which not only depicts all of the Caspian Sea, but also the entire territory of Persia. The author constantly reiterates the claim that his

4.22 Map of Persia by Johann Baptist Homann (ca. 1720).

map is based on his own observations, but how can this be true, when he only traveled along half of the Sea's west coast and in a very small portion of the empire itself? Olearius realizes that this is a problem, together with the fact that he spent a relatively short time in the country. He therefore assures the reader that his information is based on information received from Europeans he befriended in Isfahan, mainly monks, who had a thorough knowledge of the country. In addition, his main informant is his friend and houseguest (and native Persian), Hakwirdi, the secretary of the Persian embassy, who defected and remained in Gottorf. Finally, Olearius also refers to the authorities, both classical and contemporary, whom he has consulted in writing his work, and he lists them in an extensive bibliography at the beginning of the *Vermehrte Newe Beschreibung*. With regard to the geographical coordinates and shape of the Caspian Sea in his new map of Persia, the author writes that he consulted Persian and Arabic sources (for example in the "Candide Lector" passage cited earlier; and in the introduction). Where his own observations accorded with those sources, he used those same sources for the areas where he was not able to travel himself. Nowhere, however, does he note exactly which Islamic sources or texts he used. Although he mentions certain Arabic geographers by name, and refers to the "Catalogo der Perser und Araber" he does not provide any details about which geographic tables or maps he consulted. This is a rather curious omission, since he is otherwise scrupulous in citing his European sources. We will explore the various possibilities concerning this topic, so that the contribution of the Islamic tradition on Olearius's map may be more fully appreciated.

Some Characteristics of Islamic Cartography

One of the best sources to consult for an overview of Islamic cartography are the articles on "Khārita" and "Djughrāfiyā" in the *Encyclopaedia of Islam*, as well as the monumental *History of Cartography*, in particular Volume 2, Book 1 on "Cartography in the Traditional Islamic and South Asian Societies."[134] The latter work contains very thorough sections on Islamic cartography and the Greek heritage, foreign geographical influences, questions relating to prime meridians, marine charting, and Ottoman cartography. Two of the most influential medieval cartographers — Abū Zayd Aḥmad ibn Sahl al-Balkhī (d. 934) and Abū 'Abdallāh al-Idrīsī (d. 1166?) — each have a single chapter devoted to their work. This very rich tradition and history yields four groupings that bear on Olearius's geographic texts.

The first section concerns the influence of Ptolemy on the early Islamic cartographers, especially at the time of Caliph al-Ma'mūn (r. 813–833). The Caliph surrounded himself with scholars, whose "study of Indian, Iranian, and Greek geographical science . . . resulted in completely revolutionizing Arab geographical thought. Such concepts as that the Earth was round and not flat, and that it occupied the central position in the Universe, were introduced to them for the first time properly and systematically."[135] Other characteristics of this early period included the notion of the inhabitable world being divided into seven horizontal bands called *climata* or *aqālīm*, (a geographical model derived probably from Persia). The influence of Ptolemy's *Geographia* can be seen in the importance placed on Islamic tables of longitude and latitude. However, "one thing not taken up by Arab scholars was Ptolemy's chapter on the construction of geographical map projections."[136] This failure to take into account the curvature of the earth's surface would affect future Arab cartography, and may account for the "flat" appearance in relatively late maps from the Islamic world.

The second group concerns the geographer al-Balkhī and his school, which emphasized regional maps that were specifically concerned with describing the Islamic world. They also produced round world maps in which the "Encircling Ocean" surrounded the known world, and that usually have south at the top, probably to emphasize the importance of Mecca. These maps included physical representations of landmasses, and hence no longer subscribed to the system of "climes," which was an improvement on the previous geographers. Followers from this school included al-Iṣṭakhrī (ca. 951), Ibn Ḥawqal (ca. 977) and al-Muqaddasī (ca. 985), who "present for the first time the concept of a country as defined in geographical terms, and even go so far as to delimit the boundaries of the four main kingdoms of the world" ("Djughrāfiyā," 578). Figure 4.23 depicts a world map by

4.23 World map by al-Iṣṭakhrī (1193).

4.24 World map by al-Idrīsī (1456).

al-Iṣṭakhrī, from about 1193. In the lower left-hand quadrant, the schematic, circular Caspian Sea is landlocked, colored blue, and has a kind of stem attached to it, representing a river, most likely.

Third, al-Idrīsī (d. 1166?), born in Ceuta, Morocco, was a prince of the Ḥammūdid dynasty originally from Málaga. His most important work was written at the Norman court of Roger II in Palermo, who had invited him there originally for political purposes. Al-Idrīsī created a world map engraved on a silver disk (which no longer exists), and wrote a geographical compendium, the *Nuzhat al-mushtāq* also known as the "Book of Roger."[137] Although al-Idrīsī followed the cartographic tradition of Ptolemy, his world map (Figure 4.24) represents a significant advance over the previous Islamic cartographers of the

Ptolemaic school. The map shows south at the top, is surrounded by the "Encircling Ocean," and is divided into seven climes, which are represented by means of curved lines. The map is dominated by Africa, which occupies the top half of the depiction. The area that interests us in particular, the Caspian Sea, is represented rather accurately in the bottom left-hand quadrant, as a landlocked Sea, longer from north to south than from east to west.

Fourth, the period from the twelfth to the sixteenth century is characterized as one of decline for Arab geography. "The process was chequered and with some exceptions like the works of al-Idrīsī and Abū al-Fidā' the general standard of works produced was low compared to those of the earlier period" ("Djughrāfiyā," 584). Cartographers were generally content to consolidate information published in earlier studies instead of continually striving to update older learning. In the field of astronomy, however, the work of the Timurid ruler Ulugh Beg (d. 1449) stands out, especially his *Zīj-i jadid-i Sultani*, which incorporated astronomical data acquired at the observatory of Samarkand and which sought to update the Ptolemaic tables. Ulugh Beg used the star catalog of a certain Abū al-Ḥusayn al-Ṣufī (d. 983), whose work had been translated by the cosmographer Aḥmad al-Ṭūsī (ca. 1180), author of the *Kitāb 'Ajā'ib al-makhlūqāt* (written 1180). One more cartographer should be mentioned, Ḥamd Allāh al-Mustawfī Qazvīnī (d. 1340) who attempted to adapt a rectangular grid system, or graticules, onto a world map in his *Nuzhat al-qulūb* (Diversion for the hearts). The small squares which were formed contained place names that indicated their geographical position, a system that may have been derived from China.[138]

OLEARIUS AND THE CASPIAN

It is not clear what kinds of maps Olearius himself acquired or saw on his trip to Persia, but he notes that while in Shemakha, he received information about geographical coordinates from a certain "Moheb Ali." This Mullah Muhibb 'Ali was his teacher and became his friend in the months they were together. Fifty years later the mullah recounted to Engelbert Kaempfer, the German traveller who visited him in Shemakha, that Olearius "had had a good brain and was a good man but that he had not yet quite picked up the elements of Arabic" (cited in Lohmeier, "Nachwort," 21). Olearius also obtained regional maps of Persia — perhaps from the Balkhī school — but again, it is not clear what maps he may have consulted. As we have seen from the two examples above, it is likely that the maps he did make use of were older, more traditional maps from the classical age of Islamic cartography, that had not been updated in the seventeenth century. The fact that the Islamic world did not make use of the printing press until the eighteenth century — and manuscripts are rarer than printed works — also helps to explain why today there are relatively few maps available from the time when Olearius visited the Safavid empire. Rudi Matthee comments on this situation when he writes:

> Numerous examples of Iranian curiosity and inquisitiveness notwithstanding, therefore, it may be said that Safavid society did little to explore the underlying dynamics of European society and culture and that, while the manifestations of European technology were admired, artifacts other than weapons remained curiosities rather than objects to be scrutinized and disassembled for the purpose of unlocking the secrets of Western inventiveness and technological achievement. The rarity of maps, those quintessential tools of early modern Western exploration, is perhaps emblematic in this regard.[139]

Olearius thus may have seen examples of al-Idrīsī's world map, in which the Caspian Sea was longer north to south than from west to east, but he probably did not have access to recent Persian maps of the land. Firstly, up-to-date Persian maps were either extremely rare, or may not even have existed. Secondly, the tradition of cartographic representation was very different both within the Islamic world (as the maps above by al-Idrīsī and al-Iṣṭakhrī demonstrate), and vis-à-vis cartography in Early-Modern Europe. It is thus unclear exactly what impact such a representation would have had upon the German author's cartographic production. Rudi Matthee also observes that "especially in later times traditional Islamic cartography had lost all of its practical relevance and served to illustrate texts rather than to guide explorers, it seems that Safavid familiarity with modern mapmaking was at best rudimentary."[140] In a case such as this, where it is difficult to compare the visual record, we can use textual documentation to trace possible sources for Olearius's shape of the Caspian Sea, and examine how it is described in Arabic texts that Olearius could have encountered.

Let us recall what Olearius says concerning the shape of the sea: "Die länge vom *ostio maris* oder Eingange des Meeres unter Astrachan biß nach Ferabath wird auff 8. Grad *aequatoris*, und also 120. deutscher Meilen / die breite aber von der Landschafft *Chuaresm* biß an das Cyrcassische Gebirge / bey 6. Grad *aequatoris* und also 90. Meilen seyn" (The length from the beginning of the sea below Astrakhan until Ferabath measures 8 degrees of latitude and therefore 120 German miles; the width however from the territory of Khwarizm until the Circassian mountains measures about 6 degrees longitude and therefore 90 miles, *VNB*, 407). This proportion — 120 German miles in length by 90 miles width — is already prefigured in fundamental Islamic geographical texts by the authors al-Mas'ūdī and Ḥamd Allāh Mustawfī from the tenth and fourteenth centuries respectively. These are standard works that would have been known to Persian scholars (such as the mullah in Shemakha and Olearius's friend Hakwirdi), so it is possible that they could have made Olearius aware of these texts, in which the Sea's shape was already an oblong shape stretching from north to south.

In the first of these texts, the *Book of Notification* (*Kitab al-tanbīh*) by the traveler and author al-Mas'ūdī (896–956) we read in a French translation:

La troisième mer ou mer des Khazars.

La mer el-Khazari est la mer des Khazars, de Bab el-Abwab (Derbend), d'Arménie, d'Aderbaïdjân, de Moukan, de Djîl (Guilan), de Deïlem, d'Abaskoun qui est le port de Djordjân, de Tabaristan, de Kharezm et d'autres contrées qu'habitent des peuples non arabes établis autour de cette mer. Sa longueur est de 800 milles et sa largeur de 600 milles et de plus que cela, selon quelques-uns. Sa forme est celle d'un boudin. [FN 1: "L'éditeur des *Prairies d'or* a lu (t. I, p. 263): 'elle représente à peu près un ovale dans sa longueur.'] Elle est quelquefois appelée la mer de Khoraçân parce qu'elle baigne le pays de Kharezm, dans le territoire du Khoraçân. Beaucoup de Turcs Gouzz vivent dans des steppes qui s'étendent sur ses bords. C'est sur elle aussi que se trouve le lieu appelé Bakouh, où il y a des mines de naphte, dans le royaume de Chirwân, du côté de Bab el-Abwab. On y exploite le naphte blanc. Là sont des atmeh, c'est-à-dire des sources de feu qui sourdent de terre. En face des mines de naphte se trouvent des îles où jaillissent de fortes sources de feu visibles dans la nuit à de très grandes distances.[141]

Third sea or sea of the Khazars.

The sea el-Khazari is the sea of the Khazars, of Bab el-Abwab (Derbent), of Armenia, Azerbaijan, Moukan, Djîl (Jilan), of Deïlem, of Abaskoun, which is the port of Jurjan, Tabaristan, Khwarizm and other regions inhabited by other non-Arab peoples, who settled around this sea. Its length is 800 miles and its width is 600 miles or more than that, according to some. Its shape is that of a sausage. [FN 1: "the editor of the *Prairies d'or* reads (vol. I, p. 263): 'it is approximately oval-shaped in its length.'] It is sometimes called the sea of Khorasan because it bathes the country of Khwarizm, in the territory of Khorasan. Many Gouzz Turks live in steppes that extend to its shores. It is here that one finds the place called Baku, where the naphtha mines are, in the kingdom of Shirvan, on the side of Bab el-Abwab. White naphtha is won here. There atmeh, or springs of fire, come out of the earth. Opposite the naphtha mines are islands where strong wells of fire spout out, visible in the night from very great distances.

There exist a number of parallels between the work of this author and Olearius, which may have predisposed the German kindly to the work of the Islamic author. In the introduction to a modern English translation of Mas'ūdī's *Meadows of Gold*, we read:

When he was nineteen, Mas'udi travelled widely in Persia, visiting the Zoroastrian fire temples of Nishapur and Istakhr and examining Pahlavi books still in possession of the Zoroastrian community. [. . .] Sometime in the 930s, Mas'udi travelled in the Caspian area, collecting information about the Caucasus and the peoples who lived beyond them — Khazars, Slavs, and Bulgars. He made a number of original observations in these regions and was able to correct certain false geographical notions inherited from antiquity. [. . .] At the very beginning of the *Meadows of Gold,* Mas'udi makes the point that a man who stays at home and relies on information that happens to come his way cannot pretend to the same authority as the man who has travelled widely and seen things with his own eyes. Unlike most of his contemporaries, Mas'udi tried to visit the places and countries about which he wrote, and this points to the most original feature of the *Meadows of Gold* — the placing of historical events in a geographical context. This is most noticeable in the early chapters of the book, which contain long excurses on the geographical features of the known world, both within and without the borders of Islam.

This interest in the non-Islamic world is another characteristic that distinguishes Mas'udi from other Muslim historians. One of the major motives of his travels seems to have been to gather as much information as possible about the peoples who lived beyond the borders of Islam, in particular about their religious beliefs, which he recounts with a notable lack of distortion.[142]

What I would like to underline in al-Mas'ūdī's passage about the Caspian Sea — besides its sausage-shaped form! — are the proportions of the body of water: 800 miles in length by 600 miles in width.

The other writer, Ḥamd Allāh Mustawfī who writes in the fourteenth century, describes the Caspian in the following manner:

The Sea of Khazar (the Caspian) . . . forms part of none of the Seven Seas, nor of the Circumambient Ocean (described above). It takes its name from the city of Khazar, which lies on the bank of the river Itil (Volga), and Ptolemy calls it the Sea of Arqaniya (Arcania). You may travel all round it without having . . . to cross any other water, except only the rivers which flow into it, for this Sea (as already said) is in communication with no other sea. Some call it the Sea of Jurjan, others the Sea of Jilan. The common folk name it the Sea of Qulzum, but this is a vulgar error, and the Sea of Qulzum (the Red Sea) has already been described. [. . .] The bottom of the Caspian is formed of mud, for which reason its waters are dark and turbid, not clear, as are the waters of most other seas, which same have a sandy bottom that is visible from the upper surface. In the Caspian too no pearls or gems are found, as is the case in many other seas, but it has some 200 islands of which the most famous is Abaskun (or Abashkun), which, at the present day has disappeared beneath the waters. And the reason is this: that formerly the Oxus flowed out into the Eastern lake (the Aral) which lies over against the lands of Gog and Magog, but since the time of the irruption of the Mongols it has changed its course, and now passes to the Caspian; hence this sea, by reason that it has no outlet to any other sea, at first began to overflow the dry land on its shores, but now at last the inflow and decrease (by evaporation) have come to equal one another (and so the level is stationary). Other islands here are that of the Serpents, which same are venomless, and the Isle of the Jinn with the Island of the Black Mountain; also the Islands of Ruy and of the Wild-sheep. [. . .] The Island of Allah Akbar, which lies off Baku, is now inhabited, and it has become the chief harbour of the Caspian. The other islands of this sea will be found described in books of cosmogony. Many great rivers flow into the Caspian, such as the Itil (Volga), the Jayhunj (Oxus), the Kur and the Aras, the Shahrud, the Safid-rud and others. The length of the Caspian is 260 leagues, and its breadth 200 leagues, the circumference amounting to near a thousand leagues. In this sea the waves run very high and are more dangerous than in any other; but there is no ebb or flow of the tide. [. . .] In the Caspian Sea is a great whirlpool, which, from afar, draws ships to itself, causing them to founder.[143]

Again, the proportions of the Caspian Sea are of particular interest here: 260 leagues long, and 200 leagues wide.

If we now summarize the results of the three writers' measurements we come up with the following chart for the dimensions of the Caspian Sea:

The Shape of the Caspian

	Olearius	Mas'ūdī	Mustawfī
Length	120 German miles	800 "milles"	260 leagues
Width	90 German miles	600 "milles"	200 leagues

If we discount the fact that different standards of measurement are used ("Meilen, milles, leagues") and then find a common denominator of 1,800 for the three proportions, we arrrive at the following results:

	Olearius	Mas'ūdī	Mustawfī
Length	2,400	2,400	2,340
Width	1,800	1,800	1,800

In other words, Olearius's proportions for the Caspian Sea are exactly the same as al-Mas'ūdī's and very close to those of Ḥamd Allāh Mustawfī. While this does not necessarily prove that Olearius consulted these specific sources, it does indicate that proportions similar to his were already known in the Islamic world beginning in the tenth century.

Detlef Haberland, in his modern edition of Olearius's *Vermehrte Newe Beschreibung,* briefly addresses the issue of the Baroque author's cartographic achievements, and remarks:

> Seine neue Festlegung der Lage des Kaspischen Meeres ist insofern folgenreich, als sie mit ihrer neuen Längen- und Breitengradbestimmung natürlich auch die Ausdehnung und Lage Persiens in den Karten berührt. [. . .] Es ist deutlich, in welchem Maße die Persienkarte des Olearius alle vorherigen übertrifft und wie er recht eigentlich als Pionier auf dem Wege zu einem geographisch richtigen Persienbild gelten kann.[144]

> His new determination of the Caspian Sea is insofar of consequence as the new determination of longitude and latitude has bearing upon the size and position of Persia on maps. [. . .] It is quite obvious to what degree Olearius's map of Persia surpasses all previous ones and that he really must be considered the pioneer on the road toward a geographically correct picture of Persia.

He also contends that: "Von den Gelehrten der frühen Neuzeit hingegen überhaupt nicht zur Kenntnis genommen wurde die arabische Geographie" (Scholars of the Early-Modern Era, however, did not take Arabic geography into consideration at all).[145] This statement is not entirely correct. Some transmission of Islamic cartographic materials to Europe did in fact occur, and Olearius was involved in this intellectual transaction. The process occurred primarily through his use of the geographic tables by Ulugh Beg and Naṣīr al-Dīn al-Ṭūsī, whose works had been translated into Latin by the Oxford Orientalist John Greaves (1602–1652). Greaves, whom Olearius refers to as "Johannis Gravius," had collected Islamic manuscripts during a scientific expedition to the Middle East from 1637 to 1640, approximately the same time as Olearius's journey to Persia. During his travels to Istanbul, Alexandria, and Cairo, Greaves took measurements of the pyramids, and bought works written in Greek, Arabic, and Persian, including copies of the astronomical tables of Naṣīr al-Dīn al-Ṭūsī, as well as "five Persian manuscripts of the Samarqand Tables" by Ulugh Beg.[146] Upon his return to England, where he became professor of astronomy at Oxford, he published works on *Pyramidographia, or a Discourse of the Pyramids in Egypt* (1646); *Elementa Linguae Persicae* (1649); and a *Description of the Grand Seignor's Seraglio* (1650).[147] It is his translations into Latin of the tables of Ulugh Beg and al-Ṭūsī — the *Binae Tabulae . . .* (1652) — that interest us most in our discussion concerning the influence of Islamic science on Olearius's map of

4.25 Page from John Greaves's *Binae Tabulae Georgraphicae* (1652).

Persia. Figure 4.25 reproduces a page from Greaves's *Binae Tabulae* and shows how the author included the original Arabic on one side of the page and the Latin translation on the other. Olearius makes a point of citing Greaves as an authority when he discusses the creation of his map:

> Wenn ich aber ihre Gräntzen nach dem am Ufer gelegenen Städten und Ortern / wie ich dieselbige nicht alleine im *Catalogo longitudinum & latitudinum,* so ich von den Persern bekommen / und ebenmässig in den *fragmentis Astronomicis Johannis Gravii* befindlich / sondern auch zum theil selbst erforschet / legen wil / so wird die länge der See nicht wie bißher in den gemeinen Landtaffeln angedeutet worden / von Osten nach Westen / sondern von Norden nach Süden / oder von Mitternacht nach Mittag / die breite aber von Osten nach Westen / oder von Morgen gegen Abend sich erstrecken. (*VNB,* 407)

I measure its limits, however, according to the cities and other places that I found in the catalogue of longitudes and latitudes that I received from the Persians, and which are also to be found in the *Astronomical Fragments* of Johannes Gravius, and some of which I reconnoitered myself. In that case the length of the sea extends not from east to west — as has so far been indicated in common maps — but from north to south, or from midnight to midday. Its width, however extends from east to west, or from morning to evening.

At a number of points in the travel account, Olearius provides his own observations concerning a city's location — giving the longitude and latitude — and then compares his figures to those of the "Perser und Araber."[148] For example, his figures for the city of Rasht (which he terms "Rescht" and the Arabs "Husum," see *VNB,* 701) can give a sense of his methodology:

Rasht:	*Latitude*	*Longitude*
according to Olearius	37° 32'	85° 10' (?)
according to the "Araber"	37°	85° 10'

Olearius expresses it in the following way: "Die Araber nennen sie in ihrem *Catalogo Urbium, Husum,* wie obgedacht / und setzen sie secundum *Longitudinem* 85. grad 10. min. *Latitud.* 37. grad. Diese aber habe ich durch genawe observirmng [sic] 32. min. höher / und also 37. grad 32. min. befunden" (The Arabs call it Husum in their Catalogue of Cities, as mentioned before, and they give its position as 85 degrees and 10 minutes longitude and 37 degrees latitude. By close observation, however, I have found it to be situated 32 minutes higher and therefore at 37 degrees and 32 minutes, *VNB,* 701).

However, since only about fifteen cities are referred to in the text of the *Vermehrte Newe Beschreibung,* the sampling there is not large enough to serve as a basis for comparison. Nevertheless, if we turn our attention to the geographic coordinates — the longitude and latitude — of the cities located on the "Nova Delineatio Persiae" it may be easier to come to some conclusions regarding Olearius's Islamic sources. In my dissertation, I compiled a listing of geographical coordinates for a number of cities found on Olearius's map of Persia.[149] Most of these coordinates were obtained by estimating the longitude and latitude and by examining the city's position on the map. Subsequently these coordinates were tabulated and compared with the geographic coordinates taken from Greaves's translation of al-Ṭūsī's and Ulugh Beg's tables. Coordinates taken from other Ulugh Beg and al-Ṭūsī tables were also included, since there were many variants of these figures that changed over time, due to either scribal errors or other reasons. These last two versions, along with coordinates from the tables of al-Kāshī and in the *Āʾīn-i Akbarī,* were included in the appendix, in order to provide other possible sources that Olearius might have consulted.[150]

For example, if we look at the coordinates for the city "Sawa," we find that Olearius has located it at 35° N latitude and 85° W longitude:

City	Olearius	al-Ṭūsī	al-Ṭūsī	Ulug Begh	Ulug Begh	al-Kāshī	*Āʾīn-i Akbarī*
	(from VNB)	(Greaves)	(Kennedy)	(Greaves)	(Kennedy)		
Sawa	35° 00' M	36° 00'	36° 00'	36° 00'	35° 00'	36° 00'	36° 15'
Sawa	85° 00' M	85° 00'	85° 00'	85° 00'	85° 00'	85° 00'	85° 00'

By examining the different coordinates in the table listed above, we see that Olearius and all the Islamic geographers listed arrive at 85° W longitude; but only the latitude provided by Ulugh Beg, from Kennedy's compilation, gives the same latitude at Olearius, 35° N. This figure of 35° N latitude (i.e., the only one that agrees with Olearius's results) implies that Olearius may well have had access to a geographical table by Ulugh Beg, since he uses the same figure to plot that city on the map of Persia. A comparison of all the data reveals the following result: most of the coordinates that agree with Olearius's map are those of Ulugh Beg, be it the Kennedy version or the Greaves version. While this does not positively prove that Olearius used Ulugh Beg, it does strongly suggest that the German author made use of an Ulugh Beg table in plotting the cities on his map. This, then, may be the Islamic connection that Olearius hints at in his address to the reader, the Candide Lector, located in the corner of the "Nova Delineatio Persiae."

V

Conclusion

In analyzing the works of Adam Olearius, I have been arguing for the necessity of examining image and text as a kind of intertwined dialogue. Adam Olearius's visual text (frontispieces, cartography) and written text (travel account and translation of Persian literature) have to be viewed against each other. In order to better understand the relationships within one of his visual representations we need to know what kind of written representation is being referred to. Similarly, in order to make the reader comprehend the prose descriptions, say, in the travel account, the author refers to accompanying illustrations in order to make visible what he is trying to express with words. This process may point to the fact that neither form of representation — visual or verbal — is able to convey properly by itself what it wishes to denote: each needs the other form in order to represent the "reality" experienced by the author more fully. Olearius, who is also a clever salesman, realizes that the value of his work, the travel account, will be greatly enhanced by the inclusion of a great number of engravings. Doubtlessly, the success of his book was in no small part due to the many new illustrations that accompanied the text, most of which were "drawn from life," and were new representations of an area that was relatively unknown to the Early-Modern European reading public.

The notion of a dialogue, or interplay, between the visual and the textual is the leitmotif that links the different chapters of this study.

As shown, the Baroque frontispiece can be seen as a kind of portal or gateway to the written description that follows. The imagery and allegorical figures found on the frontispiece are learned signifiers belonging to a visual world that reflects and prefigures the verbal description that forms the body of the work. These images are a type of visual shorthand for the written works they introduce, and, in making use of recondite symbolism, represent a microcosm of the discursive narrative that follows.

Olearius makes full use of the interpretative possibilities of the genre, and creates frontispieces that introduce works associated with travel accounts, panegyrics, belles lettres, and marriage celebrations, as well as historical and religious works.

The full potential of the genre comes to play, however, in the frontispiece to the *Persianischer Rosenthal*. In this translation of Sa'di's *Gulistān*, Olearius designs a brilliant visual program in the opening illustration, which includes a number of Persians engaged in various activities. As becomes clear after examining the text, each image in the frontispiece actually stands for a different chapter of Sa'di's text. Stated another way, the (visual) figures represent an entire (written) visual table of contents that can be deciphered only after the reader has confronted the text that follows. Olearius, as a member of a German language academy, is interested in fostering the development of the vernacular, and expresses his nascent nationalist feelings in the introduction that accompanies his text. Olearius translates for his European audience both the literature of the Persian poet, as well as the visual code of the land he has visited; the medium of the frontispiece allows him to combine both these aims.

The analysis of Olearius's map of Persia opens up other possibilities for the interaction between the visual and the textual. The cartographic discourse depicts a different type of journey, a condensed version of the author's voyage, but one which includes a number of subtexts within its pictorial boundaries. The "Nova Delineatio Persiae" is a good example of the rapid advances made in the field of mapmaking from the late-fifteenth century to the mid-seventeenth century in Europe. The traces of the author within the map, particularly his position with regard to his patron and his reader, exhibit signs of the hidden power relationships that can be found in all maps.

Olearius's map also plays a role in the depiction of the exotic "other," who is represented visually and typologically categorized, be it within the map itself, or in the boundary areas, in the margins of the representational space.

Finally, an analysis of the shape of the Caspian Sea and the location of certain cities sheds some light on the kinds of Islamic sources available to Olearius at the time he created his map of Persia. Since there is no documentation from the author detailing which maps or geographical tables he used in placing the cities on his map, one can only guess which works he used. Olearius's admiration for John Greaves's works, and the fact that Greaves's opinion is frequently quoted throughout the travel account, suggest that the German author made frequent use of the Oxford Orientalist's translations of Islamic geographical tables. A careful analysis of the city coordinates of the map — derived both from the text and the locations of the cities on the map itself — reveal a certain debt to the zīj-i of the Timurid Ulugh Beg.

By reading some of the different visual and textual elements in the "Nova Delineatio Persiae" we may discern the subtexts that are to be found beneath the surface of the engraved image. The signs and symbols, the scratches and numbers, on the exterior are all part of a larger story, involving questions of patronage, authorship, naming, and unattributed borrowing from different cultures and traditions. Olearius's map of Persia marks a transition from the classical/medieval era with its debt to Ptolemy, and through its use of Islamic knowledge and his eyewitness observation, points the way to a more correct representation of the area. What all these modes of representation — maps, frontispieces, and literary works — indicate is that the encounter between the German Baroque author and his subject matter, Persia, is one that is fundamentally determined by the visual/textual nexus.

*　　　*　　　*

It would have been of value to be able to compare the Persian reaction to the Holstein embassy with Olearius's account, but unfortunately there is hardly any Persian material — be it visual or verbal — that relates to the visit of the Germans. As Rudi Matthee notes:

The contrast in the relevance and prestige accorded to Muslim and Western envoys, respectively, is tellingly reflected in the respective amounts of space and attention devoted in the *Zayl-i tarikh-i 'Abbasi* to a diplomatic mission from the Mughal ruler, Shah Jahan, in 1047 [A.H.]/1637 and the commercial Holstein mission that visited Isfahan in the same year. Whereas the visit of Safdar Khan, the Indian envoy, is narrated in considerable detail in an account that covers several pages, the embassy representing the Duke of Holstein receives the cursory comment of "a visit by Westerners."[151]

Although examples of Persian painting from around this time-period do portray Europeans (as well as the influence of European painting styles),[152] to my knowledge, no Persian depictions of the Holsteiners exist. Considering this lack of comparative material, I shall do the next best thing and conclude this study by juxtaposing two separate moments of encounter between the cultures: the first depicts the Europeans' encounter with the Persian ruler and the second records the reception of the Persian embassy in Holstein.

While each of these images can be "read" on the surface, and understood as a moment of official meeting between representatives of two cultures, the accompanying textual narrative is necessary in order to recognize what is depicted in the image. The pertinent texts also may allow the viewer/reader to understand what elements are not included in the image; and what images that are represented should not be there.

The first image we will consider portrays the highpoint of the *Vermehrte Newe Beschreibung* in terms of Oriental drama, namely Shah Safi's audience for the Holstein embassy in his royal palace, the Chihil Sutun (Figure 5.1). As Olearius observes: "Es gab eine lustige perspectiv" (There was a charming perspective, *VNB*, 509). The gaze of the viewer is raised, as if s/he were in a private box at the theater, commanding the entire scene. At the center of attention in a closed space is the Shah's "Diwanchanè" (*divan-khana*, the "Richthauß," or house of judgment), a kind of stage raised above the main courtyard by three steps. It is equipped with red velvet curtains that can be raised or lowered by means of ropes and that control the spectacle "forne mit rothen Cattunen Gardienen / so man mit Stricken auff und nieder

5.1 Shah Safi's banquet for the Holstein embassy
from the *Vermehrte Newe Reysebeschreibung* (1656).

lassen kunte" (in front with red cotton curtains which one could raise
or lower with the help of ropes).[153]

The foreground, partitioned into three sections by two walls, contains, on the left, the monarch's horses: "Des Königes Pferde bey 50.
Stück / mit köstlichen Decken . . . etliche gesattelte schöne Arabische
Pferde / die Sattel und Zeuge waren mit klarem Golde überzogen /
und mit Edelgesteinen besetzet . . . grosse güldene Schalen [waren]
gesetzt / aus welchen man den Pferden zu trincken gab" (The King's
horses, about 50 of them with precious covers . . . some beautiful sad-
dled Arabian horses; saddles and cloths were covered with red gold
and decorated with precious stones . . . big golden bowls were set up
from which one gave the horses to drink, *VNB*, 509). The right-hand
side depicts thirteen, gorgeously dressed dancers, whose faces are
uncovered, seated next to the lesser members of the German
embassy.[154] Of note in this scene is the woman alongside the right wall,
who seems to be flirting coquettishly with a German looking in her
direction, thus establishing a kind of contact between the two cultures.
The center foreground includes servants, guards, dogs, and wrestlers,

located between the two small walls.

If one extends the axes of these walls, the eye is led to the alcove in which the Shah is to be found: "Saß der König auff der Erden . . . war ein Herr von 27. Jahren / wolgestalt / weiß und frisch von Angesichte / hatte wie die Perser fast all / eine erhabene habicht Nase / und einen kleinen schwartzen Knebel-Bart / jedoch nicht wie die andern Perser herunterhangend" (The King sat on the ground . . . he was a gentleman of 27 years, with a good figure and a white and fresh face; like almost all the Persians he had a proud nose like a hawk's beak and a little twisted black moustache, however, it did not hang down as with most Persians, *VNB*, 509). The monarch's true nature is laid bare to the viewer in the emblematic portrait on the following page, which points to the dual nature of the Oriental despot. The Latin motto tells the reader: "You see me from the outside, as a pleasant young man in years, but on the murderous interior I am a tyrant." In the travel account, a number of verbal descriptions of the Shah and of his rule also characterize him as a bloodthirsty monarch — this trait is not something that can be distinguished by a viewer, however. In the banquet scene, only the generous, "exterior" side of Safi is visible.

Exotic excess is everywhere: European paintings and costly tapestries hang from the walls; the fountain at the monarch's feet contains "allerhand Blumen / Citronen / Pomerantzen / Granaten / Apffel und andere Früchte" (all kinds of flowers, lemons, pomegranates, apples, and other fruit, *VNB*, 509). The table settings are all gilded but unadorned, "außgenommen des Königes Trinckgeschirr nemblich die Surahi und *Piali*, Weinflasche und Schale / welche mit Turkois und Rubinen überall versezet waren" (except for the King's drinking vessels, namely the surahi and piali, the wine bottle and bowl, which were studded everywhere with turquois and ruby, *VNB*, 511). The diners listen to the musicians perform, albeit a music that is not entirely to their liking: "Die Instrumente in der Königlichen Music waren Handpaucken / Pfeiffen / heimliche Schalmeyen / Lauten und Geigen / darein sang der Handpaucker in unsern Ohren gar einen jämmerlichen Thon" (The instruments in the royal music were hand drums, flutes, shawns, lutes, and violins; and the one who played the small drums also sang a quite pathetic melody, *VNB*, 512). While eating and drinking the good wine of Shiraz the delegates seem to enjoy themselves, comparing the wrestlers at the Shah's court to those at home:

> Es wurde bey niessung der Früchte vom guten Schirasserwein etliche mahl herumb getruncken / mitlerweile trat einer auff und machte aus Gauckeltasche allerhand behende und lustige Possen [. . .] Die obgedachte Täntzerinnen sprungen auff eine seltzame manier lustig herumb. Item etliche wolgeübte Ringer liessen ihre Kunst und Behendigkeit gleich denen zu Kaßwin mit feinen Handgriffen sehen. (*VNB*, 511–512)

> While eating the fruit we drank a few rounds of the good Shiraz wine; in the meantime one person performed all kinds of nimble and entertaining tricks [. . .] the above-mentioned female dancers moved around gracefully in a strange manner. Some well-trained wrestlers showed their art and agility — like those in Qazvīn — with deft moves..

This scene of Eastern opulence and decadence corresponds to a seventeenth-century (or even a twenty-first century) Westerner's conception of an Oriental court — it is a necessary representation, necessary for the simple fact that it confirms and repeats the stereotypical elements of the Oriental "stage." The reader/viewer is comforted by the fact that in spite of Olearius's "scientific" observations and attempts to correct long-held views regarding Persia, the fundamental picture still corresponds to established views.

The description of the drawing so far does not present any major surprises. However, there is one interesting detail that is not readily apparent from the engraving: a Persian spy is located in a hidden room behind the German ambassadors! On the right-hand side of the "Diwanchanè" (*divan-khana*), his face is barely visible, peering from behind a curtain (Figure 5.2).[155] The Shah had positioned him there, so that he could find out what the Holsteiners were really saying among themselves and what they thought about the Persians. The official interpreter used by the Germans was a Portuguese monk, who conversed with his charges in Latin and Portuguese, so it seems that the Persian spy could only understand the Portuguese part of their

5.2 Detail from Shah Safi's banquet for the Holstein embassy from the *Vermehrte Newe Reysebeschreibung* (1656).

conversation. The spy can be seen hiding behind the Holstein dignitaries in the engraving. His presence speaks to the issues of translation, and what can or cannot be conveyed when two cultures meet; as well as the problem of mistrust between peoples, or, perhaps more correctly, the ruler's attempt to control information when dealing with foreigners. These types of issues can only be resolved when the verbal narrative is available; the image alone does not make it possible. However, once the spy has been identified in the text, the reader is able to examine the engraving more closely and then perhaps ponder the implications of the Shah's action. In short, the visual and the verbal interact in this instance, in order to provide a visual and narrative account of the embassy's reception by the Shah.

The second image we will examine is a drawing by Jürgen Ovens that shows the Persian embassy in Gottorf, at the moment when Duke Frederick III receives Imam Quli Sultan the Persian ambassador (Figure 5.3).[156] This work is a study for a painting that was never completed, perhaps because the mission to Persia was ultimately unsuccessful. The scene takes place outdoors in a type of square in front of a building that frames the left border of the image. The two cultures are represented schematically as being divided into two separate groups: the Holsteiners occupy the left-hand side of the depiction, while the Persians are on the right. As the legend below the picture explains, the courtiers and soldiers of Gottorf stand in the left foreground, surrounding the Duke, who is seated on a dais under a silken canopy, holding a staff of office in his right hand. The Persian ambassador is seated on a chair at a lower level than the German ruler, in the

5.3 Duke Frederick III receives the Persian ambassador,
pen-and-ink drawing by Jürgen Ovens (ca. 1665).

right middleground. His right hand at his breast, and wearing a turban
with a feather sticking out of it, Imam Quli Sultan seems to interact
with Duke Frederick. His Persian servants, distinguished by their tur-
bans, stand behind him. One of them, the secretary of the embassy is
seen bowing down, holding a cushion before him on which rests a letter from the Shah. The silhouettes of what seem to be two camels are
barely recognizable in the center of the portrayal, but none of the verbal accounts speak of camels. Thus an Orientalist element has been
introduced by the artist, and added for "color." The viewer is asked to
associate the subject matter with the iconographic elements it is supposed to be linked with — as in the frontispieces in which we find allegories of the continents.

What does this image tell us? Since this representation is a sketch,
we must examine the verbal narrative which can provide us with some
more details of the encounter. This meeting was so significant for the
Northern German area that we have at least four texts that we can consult: Olearius's description in the travel account; his entry in the

Holsteinische Chronik (1674), a chronicle about the most notable events that occurred in the Northern Lands, especially Holstein, from 1448 to 1663; a letter recounting the event *Relation, Oder Eigentliche Erzehlungen auß Gottorff* . . . (Relation or Actual Report from Gottorf . . .) — author and provenance unknown, from a private collection; and a report in the *Theatrum Europeum,* another compilation of notable events that took place primarily in Europe.[157] This relative plethora of accounts stands in stark contrast to the lack of Persian sources, and indicates that the event was much more important for the Germans than it was for the Persians. Each of the accounts underlines different types of information, and by piecing together the versions, it is possible to get a sense of the true story. A few main points will be examined here.

The *Theatrum Europeum,* which is concerned with important European events, gives relatively short shrift to the encounter. It provides a detailed listing of the presents that were brought from Persia for Duke Frederick and seems overly preoccupied by the number of salutes fired by the musketeers and cannon fired in honor of the Persian ambassador. The *Relation* provides a rather detailed description of the ambassador's arrival, describes his retinue and comments on the fact that he seemed to be enjoying himself: "zimlich lustig unnd frölich . . . in Geberden als Gespräch," (rather in a good mood and happy . . . in gestures as well as in conversation)[158] as he talks with the Duke. The text makes a point of noting that the conversation between the ruler and the ambassador takes place via two interpreters. In other words, each country has its own interpreter, so that it does not have to rely on the words — that can be changed or manipulated — of the other. Shah Safi, who knows about such things, probably insisted on this after his experiences with the Holsteiners in Isfahan:

> [. . .] welches doch durch einen Interpreten oder Dolmetscher geschehen müssen: Derowegen dann Ihre Fürstlichen Gn[aden] einen Griechen / so mit ihnen Persianisch unnd Türckisch reden kundte bey sich stehend hatten: Imgleichen hatte der Persianische Gesandte auch einen Dolmetscher bey sich / der auff Deutsch reden unnd alles außlegen kundte / was die eigentliche Discursen.[159]

[. . .] which had to happen through an interpreter or intermediary: Therefore His Ducal Highness had a Greek standing next to him who could speak Persian and Turkish with them. In the same way the Persian ambassador also had an interpreter standing at his side who could speak German and could explain the scope of the discussion.

Olearius's description of events in the *Vermehrte Newe Beschreibung* focuses on the letter that the Shah had sent to the Duke, and provides a detailed description of the written document, a document that he would be particularly interested in as Court Librarian: "Auff schön von Seide und Cattun gemachtes Papier geschrieben / nach ihrer Canceley art mit hohen prächtigen Worten" (written upon paper made handsomely out of silk and cotton with great and magnificent words in the style of their Chancery, *VNB*, 763). He also is interested in the fate of his counterpart, the *Secretarius* of the Persian mission, Hakwirdi. Olearius details the cruelty of the Persian ambassador and explains that six members of his retinue defected and did not return to Isfahan with him. Hakwirdi's presence in Gottorf would become especially important for Olearius, for the purpose of learning Persian and having a reliable, cultured informant living in his house in order to check his information as he wrote his travel account and translation. The German author emphasizes the fact that Hakwirdi eventually converted to Christianity: "Als er sahe / wie es mit der Christlichen Religion bewand / auff was Fundament sie sich gründete / und hergegen betrachtete wie der Mahumedische Glaube / welcher mit so vielen Handgreifflichen Lügen versetzet / nicht auff den rechten Weg zur Seligkeit führen würde . . ." (When he saw what was the special story behind the Christian religion, upon which precepts it was based, and then contemplated how the Muslim faith, which contains such palpable lies, would not lead him on the road to eternal bliss . . . *VNB*, 764).

Finally, in the *Holsteinische Chronik*, which repeats most of the information noted above, Olearius mentions the Persian ambassador's wife. When the ambassador arrives in Gottorf, he is accompanied by one of his wives, a Tatar whom he purchased in Astrakhan during the voyage. At the very beginning of this work I related an anecdote concerning the unfulfilled expectations of the Persian populace of Qazvīn, who had expected to see German virgins descending from the palanquins that transported the Holstein embassy. I conclude with a similar episode: the Holsteiners were just as eager to get a glimpse of what they expected would be a Persian woman. Imam Quli Sultan, however, dashed their hopes when he ordered her coach to pull up next to his residence and had two tent walls attached from the wagon to the door, so that his wife would be able to walk into her lodgings without being seen by the public.[160] Jürgen Ovens's image, in which the Duke meets the Persian ambassador, is also notable by the absence of the wife/female, the exotic other, who must remain hidden from the Western gaze (be it a male or a female gaze). This mysterious, exotic element, the Tatar wife who represents the lands in-between (Persia/Germany) does not allow herself to be controlled, however. Like the material that resides in-between the visual and the written, she is in-between as well, she exists in the gap between what can be verbalized and what can be seen.

As Olearius reports with evident satisfaction: Imam Quli Sultan ". . . gab auch nicht zu / daß so lange er sich in Holstein auffhielt / sie von jemand / ausser seinem Verschnittenen Cammerdiener mit seinem Willen gesehen würde. Sie aber ließ sich doch Ihm unwissend offt durchs Fenster sehen." (. . . as long as he was in Holstein, he did not allow her to be seen by anyone else besides his eunuch servant. However, she often allowed herself to be seen through the window without his knowledge.)[161]

Notes

1. This episode is described in Adam Olearius, *Vermehrte Newe Beschreibung der Muscowitischen und Persischen Reyse* (The Expanded, New Description of the Muscovite and Persian Journey) facsimile reprint of the 1656 edition, afterword by Dieter Lohmeier, *Deutsche Neudrucke 21* (Tübingen: Max Niemeyer, 1971), 480–1. Quotations will refer to this edition and all subsequent references to this text will be abbreviated as "*VNB*." I follow the seventeenth-century orthography established in the Lohmeier edition, although to facilitate reading I replace initial "v" and "j" with "u" and "i" respectively. All translations of the text, unless noted, are my own. This second edition of the voyage uses information from subsequent trips to Russia, and is considerably longer than the first edition, Adam Olearius, *Offt begehrte Beschreibung Der Newen ORIENTALischen REJSE* (The Oft Requested Description of the New Oriental Journey), Schleswig: zur Glocken, 1647. A modern scholarly translation into English by Samuel Baron is limited to the Russian section of the journey. See his *Travels of Olearius in Seventeenth-Century Russia* (Stanford: Stanford University Press, 1967).
2. Edward Said, *Orientalism* (New York: Vintage, 1979), 73.
3. Said, 63.
4. The story of Alexander the Great and his exploits, including the Persian campaign, were also transmitted in the Renaissance through new editions of the works of Arrian, Diodorus Siculus, and Plutarch. Johann Freinsheim, in Strasbourg, published an edition of Curtius's *Historiae*, as well as a reconstruction of the lost Books I and II in 1648 and 1670. See Quintus Rufus Curtius, *De rebus Alexandri regis Macedonum*, Johann Freinsheim ed. (Argentorati: Dolhopff & Zetzner, 1670).

5. Thomas Herbert, *A Relation of Some Yeares Travaile* (London: 1634).

6. Herodotus, *The Histories*, with an introduction and notes by Andrew Robert Burn, (Hammondsworth, England: Penguin Books, 1972), 97. [I,135] Rudi Matthee observes a similar phenomenon with the Persians of the Safavid Empire, who also had a "sense of superiority . . . [and were] convinced that their realm was the epicenter of the world." Rudi Matthee, "Between Aloofness and Fascination: Safavid Views of the West," *Iranian Studies* 31, no. 2, Spring (1998), 240.

7. Herodotus, *Histories*, 17.

8. In the sixteenth-century *Pannonicum Bellum* by Pietro Bizzarri, one of Olearius's sources, the Spartans are the models for German imperial forces fighting against the Ottoman invaders under Suleyman the Magnificent. Bizzarri, *Pannonicum Bellum* (1573), 134.

9. Laurence Lockhart, "European Contacts with Persia," in *The Cambridge History of Iran*, ed. Peter Jackson (Cambridge: Cambridge University Press, 1986), 373–74.

10. Alfons Gabriel, *Die Erforschung Persiens: Die Entwicklung der abendländischen Kenntnis der Geographie Persiens* (Wien: A. Holzhausen, 1952), especially 56 ff. Subsequent references to Gabriel's work will be abbreviated as "Gabriel" in the text.

11. Engelbert Kaempfer, *Am Hofe des persischen Grosskönigs, 1684–1685*, (At the Court of the Persian Great King, 1684–1685) [Translation of *Amoenitates exoticae* (1712) by Walther Hinz] (Tübingen: H. Erdmann, 1977).

12. Raphaël Du Mans, *Estat de la Perse en 1660*, edited by Charles Schefer (Paris: E. Leroux, 1890).

13. For a more detailed account of the journey, see Dieter Lohmeier, "Nachwort" to Adam Olearius, *Vermehrte Newe Beschreibung der Muscowitischen und Persischen Reyse* (Schleswig 1656), Tübingen: Max Niemeyer, 1971, 9–28.

14. Johann Albrecht von Mandelsloh (1616–1644), a member of the embassy, who later travelled to the East Indies, was sensitive to this fact: "Wir waren Fremde und wollten alles mit Pochen haben, wollten den Leuten ihr[e] natur verändern." (We were strangers and wanted to have everything by insistence, we wanted to change the nature of the people.) Cited in Lohmeier, "Nachwort," 23.

15. Lohmeier also notes: "Besonders hart ist sein Urteil über die Moslems, die 'Kinder des Unglaubens' in denen er den Teufel am Werk sieht. In seinem Ballett *Von Unbeständigkeit der Weltlichen Dinge und von Herrligkeit und Lobe der Tugend*....[1650] läßt er daher einen Türken, einen Araber, einen Inder und einen Mohren ihren Mangel an Tugend feststellen . . . und die Verschleierung der Orientalinnen als Verbergen der Schande erklären." (His judgment concerning the Muslims, "the Children of Unbelief," in whom he sees the devil at work, is especially harsh. In his ballet *Concerning the Changeability of Worldly Things, and the Glory and Praise of Virtue* ...[1650] he has a Turk, an Arab, an Indian, and a Moor declare their lack of virtue . . . and has the veiling of oriental women

explained as the Hiding of Shame.) Lohmeier, "Nachwort," 52–53.

16. "Die eine faßte auff den Platz einen Topff / fast einer Ellen hoch / sprang eine weile darumb herumb / und ehe man sichs versahe / hatte sie sich darüber geschwungen / und den Topff zwischen die Beine gefasset/ sprung und überschlug sich..." (One of them [standing] in the free space took hold of a vase, which was almost a cubit high; she jumped around it for a while, and before we were expecting it she jumped over it, took the vase between her legs and made a somersault . . .) (*VNB*, 531).

17. "[Und hat] den Plunder mit einem Schermesser abgeschnitten / und dem Könige vortragen lassen / mit bitte / er möchte ihm den Kopff schencken / ohne welchem er dem Könige keine / ohne 'Sijk' [Olearius: 'membrum virile'] aber gute und bessere Dienste leisten könte..." ([And] he cut off the worthless thing with a razor and had it taken before the king, begging him to grant him his head without which he could not [serve], but without a *Sijk* [Olearius: *membrum virile*] he could give good and better service . . .) (*VNB*, 532).

18. After the first edition was published in 1647, enlarged editions appear in 1656, 1661, 1663, 1671, and 1696. Regarding the various editions of the travel account, see Lohmeier, "Nachwort," 63–77 and John Emerson, "Adam Olearius and the Literature of the Schleswig-Holstein Missions to Russia and Iran, 1633–1639," in *Études safavides* ed. Jean Calmard (Paris: Institut français de recherche en Iran, 1993).

19. A history of this globe is provided in Ernst Schlee, *Der Gottorfer Globus Herzog Friedrichs III.* (Heide in Holstein: Westholsteinische Verlagsanstalt Boyens & Co., 1991) and Felix Lühning, *Der Gottorfer Globus und das Globushaus im 'Newen Werck,'* ed. Heinz Spielmann and Jan Drees, vol. 4, *Gottorf im Glanz des Barock: Kunst und Kultur am Schleswiger Hof, 1544–1713* (Schleswig: Neumann, 1997).

20. In this context see especially Mogens Bencard, "Idee und Enstehung der Kunstkammer," in *Gottorf im Glanz des Barock: Kunst und Kultur am Schleswiger Hof, 1544–1713*, ed. Heinz Spielmann and Jan Drees, (Schleswig: Wachholtz, 1997), 261–268.

21. Adam Olearius, *Gottorffische Kunst-Cammer / Worinnen Allerhand ungemeine Sachen / So theils die Natur / theils künstliche Hände hervor gebracht und bereitet. Von diesem Aus allen vier Theilen der Welt zusammen getragen. Jetzo beschrieben / Durch Adam Olearium, Bibliothecarium und Antiquarium auff der Fürstl. Residentz Gottorf* (Schleswig: Holwein, 1666), (The Gottorf Cabinet of Curiosities, in which there are to be found all kinds of unusual objects that either nature or skilled hands have produced and prepared. Brought together from all four parts of the world by himself. Now described by Adam Olearius, the Librarian and Antiquarian of the Ducal Residence in Gottorf), 3a-b. Subsequent quotations from the *Gottorffische Kunstkammer* are cited in the text with the abbreviation "*GK*."

22. In accordance with my Early-Modern subject matter, I use the terms "frontispiece" and "title page" interchangeably in my text. In other words, the

division between frontispiece (which includes primarily visual elements) and title page (containing only text) occurs after the time period under discussion.

23. See José Montesinos, *Estudios sobre Lope de Vega* (Madrid: Anaya, 1969), xiv.

24. Margery Corbett and Ronald Lightbown provide a very helpful overview of the history and development of the frontispiece genre in their study *The Comely Frontispiece: The Emblematic Title-Page in England, 1550–1660* (London: Routledge, 1979). My discussion of the frontispiece genre follows the survey provided in Corbett and Lightbown's work; subsequent quotations from *The Comely Frontispiece* are cited in the text with the abbreviation *CF*. Marion Kintzinger's *Chronos und Historia: Studien zur Titelblattikonographie historiographischer Werke vom 16. bis zum 18. Jahrhundert* (Wiesbaden: Harrassowitz, 1995) analyzes title-pages in German Baroque historical texts.

25. Rodney Shirley, "The Decorative Cartographic Title-Page," *Map Collector*, no. 41 (Winter, 1987), 4.

26. For a more complete outline of emblematics, as well as the history and theory associated with the genre, see especially Arthur Henkel and Albrecht Schöne's *Emblemata: Handbuch zur Sinnbildkunst des XVI. und XVII. Jahrhunderts*, Ergänzte Neuausgabe, 2nd ed., [1st ed. 1967] (Stuttgart: J. B. Metzler, 1976). Subsequent quotations from *Emblemata* are cited in the text with the abbreviation *H/S*. Regarding the emblematic tradition in Holland, see Karel Porteman, *Inleiding tot de Nederlandse emblemataliteratuur* (Groningen: Walters–Noordhoff, 1977). Daniel S. Russell gives an overview of the French emblem in *The Emblem and Device in France* (Lexington, KY: French Forum, 1985); and Aquilino Sánchez Pérez, *La literatura emblemática española: (siglos XVI y XVII)* (Madrid: Sociedad General Española de Librería, 1977) discusses its background in Spain.

27. "It was a great nobleman, Ambrogio Visconti of Milan, who in the early 1520s first hit on the idea of the genre. But apparently the only use he made of his invention was to suggest it to the celebrated jurist Andrea Alciati (1492–1550) and to another Milanese jurist Aurelio Albrezi, who both realised it in poems. The author of its popularity was in fact Alciati . . ." (*CF*, 15).

28. Bohuslaus Balbinus, *Verisimilia*, [1st ed. 1678], p. 234 of 1710 edition. Quoted in *H/S*, XII.

29. An edition of the *Anthologia Graeca* was also published by Alciatus. Cf. *H/S*, XI.

30. The passage in the original reads: "In dem Versuch, die Bibel, die Natur, die Geschichte, die Kunst als einen Kosmos von Signaturen, die Welt als Mundus symbolicus zu begreifen" (*H/S*, XVI). Emblems also played an important role in Baroque drama, in both Reformation and Counter-Reformation circles. See in this context Albrecht Schöne, *Emblematik und Drama im Zeitalter des Barock* (München: Beck, 1964); as well as Peter Daly, who observes: "We are justified in labelling images in dramatic texts 'emblematic' only if their formal and structural qualities, or their meaning, actively invite comparison with emblems, in other words, only if the dramatic image could be translated into the emblem of an emblem-book," *Literature in the Light of the Emblem* (Toronto: University of

Toronto Press, 1979), 135.

31. During the Renaissance, the work of compiling systematic encyclopedic accounts of classical gods and myths was begun in the fourteenth century by Boccaccio, in his *Genealogia Deorum*. Editions of Ovid's *Metamorphoses* also whetted the appetite for a complete knowledge of classical mythology. Roelof van Straten observes that "A variation of the *Metamorphoses* is the *Ovide Moralisé*, an anonymous early fourteenth-century work, in which the Ovidian stories are interpreted as Christian parables," Roelof van Straten, *An Introduction to Iconography*, trans. Patricia de Man (Amsterdam: Gordon and Breach, 1994), 88.

32. Ripa's work "is a remarkably full repertory of allegorical images of man's emotional, moral, intellectual and physical nature and of the external adjuncts of his existence, wealth, poverty, dominion, glory, the political forms of his societies. It represents his qualities and properties, virtues and vices" (*CF,* 32).

33. Van Straten, "*An Introduction,*" 29.

34. "Olearius" means "of or belonging to oil" or "oil-grinder or oil-seller."

35. Regarding the background of August John and Christian Rothgießer and their work for the court at Gottorf, see Ernst Schlee, "August John, ein Künstler in Gottorfer Diensten," *Nordelbingen: Beiträge zur Kunst- und Kulturgeschichte* 51 (1982): 77–125; Ernst Schlee, "Kupferstecher im Umkreis des Gottorfer Hofes," in *Von allerhand Figuren und Abbildungen: Kupferstecher des 17. Jahrhunderts im Umkreis des Gottorfer Hofes*, ed. Holger Borzikowsky (Husum: Husum Druck- und Verlagsgesellschaft, 1981), 7–55; and the *Dansk Kunstnerleksikon*, s.v. "Andreas Rothgiesser" and "Christian Rothgiesser."

36. Regarding the artistic activities at the Gottorf court, see Holger Borzikowsky, ed., *Von allerhand Figuren und Abbildungen: Kupferstecher des 17. Jahrhunderts im Umkreis des Gottorfer Hofes* (Husum: Husum Druck- und Verlagsgesellschaft, 1981), which contains a number of articles devoted primarily to the engravings; and the sumptuous exhibition catalogue by Heinz Spielmann and Jan Drees, eds., *Gottorf im Glanz des Barock. Kunst und Kultur am Schleswiger Hof, 1544–1713*, 4 vols. (Neumünster: Wachholtz, 1997), which includes studies of engravings, paintings and sculpture produced at the Gottorf court. See also the articles on John and Rothgießer in F. Hollstein, *German Engravings, Etchings and Woodcuts, ca. 1400–1700* (Amsterdam: M. Hertzberger, 1954).

37. For a discussion of the ballet and its function see Wolfgang J. Müller, "Bildwelt und Weltbild im barocken Kupferstich," in *Von allerhand Figuren und Abbildungen: Kupferstecher des 17. Jahrhunderts im Umkreis des Gottorfer Hofes*, ed. Holger Borzikowsky (Husum: Husum Druck- und Verlagsgesellschaft, 1981), 116–119; and Ingrid Höpel, "Gottorfer Feste – Anlässe zur Repräsentation," in *Gottorf im Glanz des Barock: Kunst und Kultur am Schleswiger Hof, 1544–1713. Kataloge der Ausstellung zum 50-jährigen Bestehen des Schleswig-Holsteinischen Landesmuseums auf Schloß Gottorf und zum 400. Geburtstag Herzog Friedrichs III.*, ed. Heinz Spielmann and Jan Drees (1997), 239–241. In footnote 15 to her article, Höpel notes Mara Wade's contention that

the bride's mother, Maria Elisabeth von Schleswig-Holstein-Gottorf, may have written the text and designed the frontispiece of the ballet.

38. Höpel makes this observation in "Gottorfer Feste," 239.

39. Quoted in Höpel, "Gottorfer Feste," footnote 16, [*Von Unbeständigkeit der Weltlichen Dinge*, Bl. A1v (2)].

40. The origin of the motto and its adoption by Duke Frederick III is discussed in Müller, "Bildwelt," 113–116.

41. Müller, 115.

42. The engraving was done by August John. See also Schlee, "Kupferstecher," 40; and Dieter Lohmeier, "Die Gründung der Universität Kiel," in *Gottorf im Glanz des Barock. Kunst und Kultur am Schleswiger Hof, 1544–1713*, ed. Heinz Spielmann and Jan Drees (Neumünster: Wachholtz, 1997), 376–380, where he gives a brief overview of the history of the university's founding. Regarding the choice of Frangipani, Lohmeier notes: "Sein zweifelhaftes Verdienst ist es, den Bericht mit soviel hochtrabender lateinischer Rhetorik aufgeputzt zu haben, daß die sachliche Information zuweilen nur mühsam zu finden ist. Olearius hatte sich von der Festschrift als Verleger einen ähnlichen Verkaufserfolg erhofft wie von seiner eigenen Reisebeschreibung, wurde aber enttäuscht, und es soll ihn später gereut haben, auf einen Schwätzer wie Torquatus hereingefallen zu sein" (It is his dubious contribution to have dressed up the report with so much pretentious Latin rhetoric that factual information can sometimes be found only with difficulty. Olearius had hoped that as publisher he would have a similar success with the commemorative volume as he had had with his own travel account; however, he was disappointed; and he is said to have regretted that he had let himself be duped by a windbag like Torquatus), 378.

43. Paul Fleming, *Teütsche Poemata*, (Lübeck: Jauch, 1646).

44. Cited in Dieter Lohmeier's catalogue notes in *Von allerhand Figuren und Abbildungen: Kupferstecher des 17. Jahrhunderts im Umkreis des Gottorfer Hofes* (Concerning all Kinds of Figures and Illustrations: Copper Engravers of the Seventeenth century associated with the Court of Gottorf), ed. Holger Borzikowsky (Husum: Husum Druck- und Verlagsgesellschaft, 1981), 177. In the same work, see Lohmeier's article on "Adam Olearius und die Gottorfer Kupferstecher," especially 64–65.

45. For a fuller account of Mandelsloh's travels and the publishing history of his journeys, see Johann Albrecht von Mandelsloh, *Journal und Observation: 1637–1640*, Margrete Refslund-Klemann ed. (Kobenhavn: A. F. Host, 1942). Regarding the title page, see also Hollstein, "Rothgießer," 127-128.

46. In this context, see the emblem "Gloria mit Flügel" that depicts another such winged sphere in Henkel/Schöne, *Emblemata*, 24.

47. This "Hassanist" is also described and depicted in the text; Johann Albrecht von Mandesloh, *Des HochEdelgebornen Johan Albrechts von Mandelslo Morgenländische Reyse-Beschreibung* (Schleßwig: Johan Holwein, 1658), 107.

48. Dorothy Alexander, introduction to *The German Single-Leaf Woodcut,*

1600–1700: A Pictorial Catalogue, preface by Walter L. Strauss, vol. 1, (New York: Abaris Books 1997), 17.

49. As Alexander observes: "Albrecht Dürer (1471–1528), Hans Burgkmair the Elder (1473–1531), Albrecht Altdorfer (1497–1543), and Lucas Cranach the Elder and the Younger, who all made illustrations; Hans Sachs (1494–1576), the poet laureate Conrad Celtis (1459–1508), and later Michael Moscherosch (1601–69) all authored texts that accompanied *Flugblätter*." Alexander, *Woodcut*, 18.

50. Alexander, 19.

51. Regarding this topic see the *Reallexikon der deutschen Kunst*, s.v. "Vier Erdteile."

52. Hugh Honour, "Science and Exoticism: The European Artist and the Non-European World before Johan Maurits," in *Johan Maurits van Nassau-Siegen 1604–1679: A Humanist Prince in Europe and Brazil*, ed. E. van den Boogaart (The Hague: Johan Maurits van Nassau Stichting, 1979), 269–296; quoted in Peter Mason, *Infelicities: Representations of the Exotic* (Baltimore and London: The Johns Hopkins University Press, 1998), 16.

53. For a fuller discussion concerning these terms and their relationship to the exotic, see Peter Mason, *Infelicities*, especially 2–5.

54. The etymology of the term is pertinent here, as Dieter Vogellehner notes: "Das awestisch/altiranische Wort 'Paradies' bedeutet 'umfriedeter Garten'" (The Avestic/Old Iranian word 'Paradise' means 'fenced-in garden.') Dieter Vogellehner, introduction to *Der Garten von Eichstätt: Das große Herbarium des Basilius Besler von 1613* [Originally *L'Herbier des quatre saisons*, Mazenod Editio, Paris, 1987] (München: Schirmer/ Mosel Verlag, 1988), 1.

55. Vogellehner, *Der Garten*, 2.

56. According to Ernst Schlee: "Es ist also wohl an eine Parkarchitektur gedacht" (One probably has to imagine the architectural design of a park.) See Ernst Schlee, "August John, ein Künstler in Gottorfer Diensten," *Nordelbingen: Beiträge zur Kunst- und Kulturgeschichte* 51 (1982), 108-109.

57. Schlee, "August John," 108.

58. Adam Olearius, *The Voyages & Travels of the Ambassadors*, trans. John Davies (London: Thomas Dring and John Starkey, 1662).

59. Adam Olearius, *Beschrijvingh Van de Nieuwe Parciaensche oste Orientaelsche Reyse, welck door gelegentheyt van een Holsteynische Ambassade, aen den Koningh in Persien gheschiet is . . .*(Description of the new Persian and Oriental journey, which occurred as a result of the Holstein embassy to the King of Persia . . .), trans. Dirck van Wageninge (Utrecht: Lambert Roeck, 1651).

60. Below the simulated busts the title seems to be inscribed on a flat stone and reads: "De Nieuwe | Par Sianz | Reyse oste een Oost- | indische voyagie te | lant eerst int Hoogh- | duyts beschreven door | M Admy Oleary, ende | nu in Neer duyts over | geset door D.V. Wa- | geninge met | Copere fy- | guren" (The new Persian journey, and overland voyage to the East Indies, described for the first time in High German by M. Adam Olearius, and now translated into

Low German by D. V. Wageninge, with copper figures).

61. Adam Olearius, *Persianischer Rosenthal. In welchem viel lustige Historien / scharff-sinnige Reden und nützliche Regeln. Vor 400. Jahren von einem Sinnreichen Poeten SCHICH SAADI in Persischer Sprach beschrieben. Jetzo aber von ADAMO OLEARIO, Mit zuziehung eines alten Persianers Namens HAKWIRDI übersetzet / in Hochdeutscher Sprache heraus gegeben / und mit vielen Kupfferstücken gezieret . . . Schleßwig In der Fürstl. Druckerey gedruckt durch Johann Holwein. Bey Johann Nauman Buchhändelern in Hamburg. Im Jahr / 1654* (Persian Valley of Roses in which [there are] many entertaining stories, clever speeches and useful rules. Described four hundred years ago by a wise poet Sheik Saʻdi in the Persian language. Now, however, translated by Adam Olearius with the help of an old Persian named Hakwirdi, edited in the High German language and decorated with many copper plates . . . Schleswig in the Ducal Printing Shop, printed by Johann Holwein. Sold at Johann Naumann's, bookdealer in Hamburg. In the year 1654. Schleswig: Johann Holwein, 1654). Subsequent quotations from the Persianischer Rosenthal are cited in the text with the abbreviation "*PR.*"

62. In his "Noten und Abhandlungen zu besserem Verständnis des 'West-östlichen Divans'" Goethe praises the "Geradsinn des trefflichen Olearius . . . er gibt uns höchst erfreuliche und belehrende Reiseberichte, die um so schätzbarer sind, als er nur wenige Jahre nach della Valle und kurz nach dem Tode Abbas' des Großen nach Persien kam und bei seiner Rückkehr die Deutschen mit Saadi, dem Trefflichen, durch eine tüchtige und erfreuliche Übersetzung bekannt machte. Ungern brechen wir ab, weil wir auch diesem Manne für das Gute, das wir ihm schuldig sind, gründlichen Dank abzutragen wünschten." (In his "Notes and Treatises towards a better understanding of the West-Eastern Divan" Goethe praises the "straightforwardness of the splendid Olearius . . . he gives us most pleasant and instructive travel reports, which are all the more valuable as he arrived in Persia only a few years after della Valle and shortly after the death of Abbas the Great, and upon his return acquainted the Germans with Saʻdi, the Splendid, by means of a competent and enjoyable translation. We break off reluctantly because we wish to give heartfelt thanks to this man, too, for the good we owe him.") Johann Wolfgang von Goethe, "Noten und Abhandlungen zu besserem Verständnis des 'West-östlichen Divans,'" in *Werke, Hamburger Ausgabe in 14 Bänden*, textkritisch durchgesehen und kommentiert von Erich Trunz (München: DTV/Beck, 1988), 243.

63. Naime Omar Bishr, "Das *Persianische Rosenthal* von Adam Olearius und Saʻdis *Gulestan*: Eine geistesgeschichtliche Untersuchung" (Dissertation, Rutgers University, 1974), 229. Subsequent quotations from this work are cited in the text with the abbreviation "Bishr." "Dzingizchans Enkel" mentioned above, is Hülegü Khan, the "Mongol ruler in Iran who founded the Il-Khan dynasty and, as part of a Mongol program of subduing the Islāmic world, seized and sacked Baghdad, the religious and cultural capital of Islām. Some historians consider that he did more than anyone else to destroy medieval Iranian culture."

Encyclopaedia Britannica, fifteenth ed., s.v. "Hülegü."

64. For additional biographical information on the author, see also *The Encyclopaedia Britannica,* fifteenth ed., s.v. "Sa'di;" and *The Encyclopaedia of Islam,* new ed., s.v. "Sa'di."

65. "Quintus Ennius (239–169 B.C.E.), epic poet, dramatist and satirist . . . the most influential of the early Latin poets, rightly called the father of Roman literature. His epic *Annales,* a narrative poem telling the story of Rome from the wanderings of Aeneas to the poet's own day, was the national epic until it was eclipsed by Virgil's *Aeneid.*" *Encyclopaedia Britannica,* fifteenth ed., s.v. "Quintus Ennius."

66. See for example Herder's *Ideen zur Philosophie der Geschichte der Menschheit* (1784–1791) and Voltaire's *Essai sur les moeurs* (1756).

67. The ceremony is described in Adam Olearius, *Vermehrte Newe Beschreibung,* 764 and in his *Holsteinische Chronik,* 94–95.

68. Influences for Opitz's *Buch von der deutschen Poeterey* include Horace's *Ars poetica;* the works of Scaliger and Heinsius; and of the French Pléiade poets, in particular Pierre de Ronsard and Joachim Du Bellay. The most important "Sprachgesellschaften" in Germany were the "Fruchtbringende Gesellschaft" (Weimar, 1617–1680); the "Pegnitzschäfer" (Nürnberg, ca. 1644); the "Teutschgesinnte Genossenschaft" (Hamburg, 1642); and the "Elbschwanenorden" (Lübeck, 1658–1667).

69. A member of the high nobility, Du Ryer (1580–1660) was entrusted with a number of important diplomatic missions while ambassador to Egypt and Constantinople. See Faramarz Behzad, *Adam Olearius' "Persianischer Rosenthal" Untersuchungen zur Übersetzung von Saadis "Golestan" im 17. Jahrhundert* (Göttingen: Vandenhoeck & Ruprecht, 1970), 26. Subsequent references to this work will be abbreviated in the text as "Behzad."

70. "Weil die Perser keine Druckerey im Lande haben / auch umb gewisse Uhrsachen / (darvon ich an einem andern Ort gesaget habe) haben wollen / und sich nur mit den geschriebenen Büchern behelffen müssen . . ." (Because the Persians have no printing presses in the country and for certain reasons — of which I spoke in another context — don't want to have them, and thus have to make do with hand written books . . . *PR,* B3r).

71. Behzad provides a helpful overview of Gentius's life and his contribution to the field of early Orientalist studies: "Der in Dahme (an der Ostsee) geborene Georgius Gentius (1618–1687), der — nach seinem Studium vor allem in Halle — 1635 einige Zeit in Schleswig als Hofmeister tätig war, widmete sich dem Studium orientalischer Sprachen . . . 1641 [reiste er] mit einem türkischen Gesandten in die Türkei . . . Nach einem siebenjährigen Aufenthalt — inzwischen hatte er auch eine Reise nach Persien unternommen — kam er 1659 nach Amsterdam zurück. Vom Kurfürsten Johann Georg II. von Sachsen, dem er später seine 'Golestan'-Übersetzung widmete, erhielt er ein jährliches Gehalt . . . Die 'Golestan'-Übersetzung, die Gentius zweisprachig (Edition des

'Golestan' und lateinische Übersetzung) herausgegeben hat, ist seine einzige veröffentlichte Übertragung aus dem Persischen. Im Manuskript soll er eine Übersetzung des 'Bustan' ('Musladini Sa 'di Pomarium Politicum, persisch und Lateinisch mit vielen Noten') hinterlassen haben. Gentius schreibt in seiner Vorrede, er werde, wenn seine 'Golestan'-Übersetzung bei den Lesern Gefallen finde, das Werk Saadis in Kürze auch ins Deutsche und ins Französische übersetzen. Dieser Vorsatz wird jedoch nicht verwirklicht. Eine zweite Auflage seiner lateinischen Übersetzung erscheint 1673, und zwar in kleinerem Format und ohne den persischen Text." [George Gentius, 1618–1687, was born in Dahme on the Baltic Sea, and studied primarily in Halle. In 1635 he spent some time in Schleswig as court tutor and dedicated himself to the study of oriental languages. In 1641 [he travelled] with a Turkish ambassador to Turkey . . . After a stay of seven years — in the meantime he had also undertaken a trip to Persia — he returned to Amsterdam in 1659. He received a yearly stipend from the Elector John George II of Saxony to whom he later dedicated his translation of the 'Golestan.' . . . The 'Golestan' translation which Gentius published in a bilingual edition (edition of the 'Golestan' and a Latin translation) is his only published translation from the Persian. He is said to have left a translation of the 'Bustan' ('Musladini Sa'di Pomarium Politicum in Persian and Latin with numerous notes'). Gentius writes in his foreword that he intends in the near future to translate the works of Sa'di into German and French provided they pleased the readers. This intention, however, was not realized. A second edition of his Latin translation appeared in 1673 in a smaller format and without the Persian text. Behzad, 27–28].

72. The meaning of "sharp," in the sense of cleverness, comes across clearly in the Spanish term *agudeza*.

73. Julius Wilhelm Zincgref: *Teutscher Nation Klugaußgesprochene Weißheit / Das ist: . . . Lehrreiche Sprüche / geschwinde Anschläg / artige Hoffreden / denckwürdige Schertzfragen / Antworten / Gleichnüsse / vnd was dem allen gleichförmig / von Griechen Apophthegmata genandt ist / . . . Auß allerhand Schrifften zusammen getragen . . .* (The German nation's wittily-expressed wisdom, that is . . . Educational sayings, quick replies, polite courtly speeches, clever riddles, answers, similes, and all that which was commonly called apophthegmata by the Greeks . . . collected from all kinds of writing, Amsterdam, 1653), 6a. Quoted in Behzad, 52.

74. *Mr. Du Refuge Kluger Hofmann: Das ist / Nachsinnige Vorstellung deß untadelichen Hoflebens / mit vielen lehrreichen Sprüchen und denkwürdigen Exempeln gezieret; . . . Gedolmetscht . . . Durch Ein Mitglied der hochlöblichen Fruchtbringenden Gesellschafft . . .* (Mr. Du Refuge's Prudent Courtier: That is, a thoughtful presentation of impeccable courtly life decorated with many educational sayings and memorable examples . . . translated . . . by a member of the illustrious Fruitbearing Society . . . Frankfurt and Hamburg, 1655). See Behzad, 117.

75. *PR*, G2r–v. The English translation is taken from the table of contents of Sa'di's

The Rose Garden (Gulistân), trans. Omar Ali-Shah (Reno, Nevada: Tractus, 1997), 5.

76. See Paul Sprachman, "'Le beau garçon sans merci:' The Homoerotic Tale in Arabic and Persian," in *Homoeroticism in Classical Arabic Literature*, edited by J.W. Wright and Everett K. Rowson (New York: Columbia University Press, 1997), especially 201-203.

77. See the *Encyclopaedia of Islam*, new edition, s.v. "Luḳmān."

78. See in this context Parviz Tanavoli, *Lion Rugs: The Lion in the Art and Culture of Iran* (Basel: Werner Druck AG, 1985). To my knowledge, this is the only general study (written in English) on lion imagery in Persian art. Subsequent quotations from *Lion Rugs* are abbreviated in the text as "Tanavoli."

79. *Encyclopaedia Britannica*, 15th ed., s.v. "Mithraism." Parviz Tanavoli notes that: "Despite the many centuries that separate our era from the time when Mithraism flourished, the name Mithra (*Mehr*) continues to be a part of the Persian language and to maintain the ancient meanings of 'friendship' and 'covenant' as well as 'sun'" (Tanavoli, 12).

80. James Hall, "Lion," in *The Illustrated Dictionary of Symbols in Eastern and Western Art* (New York: Harper Collins, 1994), 33.

81. *Encyclopedia of Islam*, s.v. "Al-Asad."

82. Tanavoli notes that: "During the Safavid period the metal standards and their lions were generally much simpler than those used today in Iran. The Safavid lions were flat and had rings at their feet to hold the green and black banners" (Tanavoli, 26).

83. Lion tombstones were in use long before the Safavid era. "The oldest known funeral lion (3.56 m. long) can still be seen in Hamadan, the ancient city of Ecbatana. Once a guardian of the city gates, and originally conceived as a monument to a companion of Alexander the Great, this lion now rests in a square and serves as a symbol of that ancient city. Local girls and women consider it a talisman, and those desiring a husband or a child wash the lion's paws with syrup or honey on *chahar-shanbeh suri* (the last Tuesday evening of the year), a ritual that is Mithraic in origin" (Tanavoli, 29).

84. "Ibn Ibri (died 685 A.H.) tells the following story of how the combination of the lion and sun came about: 'Keykhosrow fell madly in love with the daughter of the king of Georgia and took her for his wife. She so affected him that he wanted to have her portrait engraved on his silver coins. But as figural representation was not in accordance with Islam, and in truth was considered to be against it, the persistence of the shah led some of his courtiers (said to be astrologers) to suggest that the figure of the lion be drawn and on top of it the sun with a female face. Thus if anyone were to ask, it could be answered that this was the horoscope of the shah since the sun was in the sign of Leo when he was born. The ruler happily followed their advice'" (Tanavoli, 36–38). Ibn Ibri, *Tarikh i-Mokhtasar Aldowal*, edited by Al eb-Antone Alyasu'i (Beirut, 1890), 447 (in Arabic), quoted [and translated from the Arabic] by Tanavoli, 36–38.

85. The German traveler Engelbert Kaempfer, who traveled through Iran from 1683 to 1685, writes: "The lion motif, which was carved in stone, is also found in many of the ancient buildings of Iran. From ancient times this symbol has had a connection with the Iranian monarch, but most often it is shown in conjunction with the sun. In most depictions the lion holds the sun in its open mouth" (cited in Tanavoli, 21). [E. Kaempfer, *Am Hofe des Persischen Gross-königs (1684–85)*, Leipzig, 1937, 199–200.]

Jean Chardin, who went to Iran twice in the period 1664 to 1677, talks about a painting of a lion and sun above the entrance of the Ashraf Palace in Mazandaran and considers it a sign of sovereignty. Jean Chardin, *Voyages du Chevalier Chardin en Perse* (Paris, 1811), vol. III, p. 277 (cited in Tanavoli, 21). In addition, Chardin "refers to banners bearing the lion and sun emblem on Imam Ali's sword, Zu'l-Faqar. In Safavid times the metal standard and cloth banner were also carried not only by groups of mourners during Moharram but also by soldiers during war" (cited in Tanavoli, 39).

86. See Apoc. 5:5, quoted in the *Encyclopaedia of Islam*, s.v. "Al-Asad."

87. Olearius's source is the *Rerum gestarum libri* by the Roman historian Ammianus Marcellinus (330–395 A.D.). "Shah Sapor" is Shapur II of Persia (308–379 A.D.), the tenth king of the Sassanian Empire.

88. The artists who engraved Olearius's frontispieces — especially August John and Christian Rothgiesser — either studied in the Netherlands, or had extensive contact with Dutch and Flemish artists.

89. Jay Richard Judson and Carl van de Velde, *Book Illustrations and Title-Pages*, vol. 2, *Corpus Rubenianum Ludwig Burchard*, (London and Philadelphia: Miller / Heyden, 1978), 65. My discussion of Rubens's frontispieces is based on Judson's article and catalogue notes; subsequent quotations from his work are abbreviated in the text as "Judson."

90. Two examples of this type of borrowing include: "In *Het Paradys der Wellusticheyt* . . . the designer introduces trees that enframe and reinforce the personifications to the right and left as found in Rubens's 1620 *De Contemplatione Divina*. The change to the freer and more illusionistic style of Rubens becomes even stronger in the 1630s and there are numerous borrowings from the master. In the frontispiece engraved by C. Galle for the 1632 *Missale S. Monasteriensis Ecclesiae*, the title is printed on a piece of drapery held at the top corners by an angel — an illusionistic device employed by Rubens as early as 1620 for Thomas a Jesu's *De Contemplatione Divina*" (Judson, 67).

91. "This is the earliest preserved grisaille design by Rubens made specifically for a title page. The modello, in the same direction as the engraving, was closely followed by the engraver, who very likely made a working drawing, now lost, before cutting the plate. However, Rubens himself made a change in the oil sketch. The angel in the upper left holding the open book has two faces, one frontal and the other in profile. The latter was used by Galle in the engraving. The lion in the upper right and the eagle on the opposite side also appear in two oil sketches"

(Judson, 252).

92. To conclude with the interpretation of the frontispiece: "Truth places a chain with sixty-five medallions made of beautiful and precious stones around St. Luke's neck. The Holy Spirit descends just above St. Luke's head to the left while an angel holding an open book, symbol of St. Matthew, stands dressed as hermit-monks flank the title below. St. Augustine is on the left and holds a book in his right hand and a burning heart pierced by an arrow in his left. This is an often used attribute for St. Augustine in seventeenth-century Flemish art. The tradition of representing him as a hermit-monk goes back to the Middle Ages. . . . On the right of the title, Rubens has placed a large figure covered with ample drapery and with three Greek crosses decorating the area around his neck. He holds a book in his left hand and points to an open page with the other. . . . By placing St. Augustine on one side of the title and St. Athanasius on the other, Rubens has deliberately juxtaposed a Latin Church Father with a Greek one. Emperor Ferdinand II's coat-of-arms, with the crown and the double eagle, is in the bottom center of the title page" (Judson, 250).

93. Willem Floor's article, "Fact or Fiction: The Most Perilous Journeys of Jan Jansz. Struys," in *Études Safavides*, ed. Jean Calmard (Paris: Institut français de recherche en Iran, 1993), 57–68, investigates the question concerning whether Struys's travel account was based on eyewitness experience, or whether it was fabricated, as other critics believe. Floor's study does not deal with Struys's alleged first and second voyages, in East Asia, Africa, and the Mediterranean, but is concerned with the author's adventures in the third book, which take place in Muscovy, the Caspian Sea, and Persia. The critic comes to the conclusion that Struys's observations about these regions are basically correct, and thus fundamentally sound. Floor notes certain places where Struys follows and copies Olearius's travel account. He also compares English and French translations of the text with the Dutch original and concludes that the German translation is the more faithful one.

94. The English and French titles are the following: John Struys, *The Perillous and most Unhappy Voyages of John Struys . . .*, trans. John Morrison (London: Samuel Smith, 1683); and Jan Struys, *Les Voyages de Jean Struys en Moscovie, en Tartarie, aux Indes, et en d'autres pays etrangers*, trans. Monsieur Glanius (Amstredam [sic]: LaVeuve Iacob van Meurs, 1681). Citations in the text refer to the English translation.

95. This image is located in Struys, *Voyages*, 272.

96. The English translation of Struys's text reads: "The Man having as was said permission to punish her at his own Discretion had already provided a Wooden Cross, upon which, with the help of his Servants, he bound her fast, being mother naked, and with his own hands, flea'd her whilst yet living. I stood my self all the while at the Door with a great company of Men, Women and Children, and heard her cry out most bitterly. Yet none thought that his cruelty was of so high a nature till we saw the Carcase, thrown out into the street where it lay an hour

or two, and afterwards by his order was dragged into the Fields, to be devoured of the Eagles, and other Birds of prey: but he not satisfied herewith took the Skin and nailed it upon the Wall for a Monument and Warning to his other Wives, which were 12 in number, who never saw it but trembled, as indeed I myself did, so often as I went by the House, or passed by that way" (Struys, 270–71).

97. In his travel account, Olearius mentions that flaying was an accepted punishment in Persian society: "Die Verbrecher werden hart gestrafft / denn weil es ein hart Volck / daß sehr zur Mißhandelung geneiget / un[d] gelinde Straff nicht groß achte[t] / muß man mit ihnen nach der schärffe verfahren. Die arten aber zu straffen seynd mancherley / welche sie offt nach ihren Einfällen selbst erdencken. Nasen / Ohren / Hände und Füsse abschneiden / Kopff abhawen / nieder sebeln / daß Fell über die Ohren ziehen ist das geringste und gemeineste / und bey den Persern gar ein alter Gebrauch gewesen / wie aus dem *Marcellino* erhellet: Wer ein Weibesbild mit Gewalt schwächet / muß / wann das Weib dreymahl einen Eyd darauff thut / des Instruments / womit er gesündiget / verlüstig seyn" (Criminals are punished harshly because they are a harsh people and much inclined towards ill-treatment and do not pay sufficient heed to light punishment; therefore one has to treat them with strictness. The types of punishment, which they often invent themselves, differ. Cutting off of noses, ears, of hands and feet, decapitation, killing by saber strokes, and flaying is the least and most common, and is an old custom with the Persians as one can read in Marcellinus; whoever rapes a woman, if she swears to it three times, must lose the instrument with which he has sinned, *VNB*, 674).

98. Struys, 207 ff.

99. See Walther Benjamin's notion of the "emblematic corpse" in his *Ursprung des deutschen Trauerspiels* (Frankfurt am Main: Suhrkamp, 1963).

100. The version of the Persia map used in my analysis is taken from the *Vermehrte Newe Reysebeschreibung* (1656).

101. Reimer Witt, *Die Anfänge von Kartographie und Topographie Schleswig-Holsteins, 1475–1652* (Heide in Holstein: Westholsteinische Verlagsanstalt Boyens & Co., 1982), 7.

102. J. B. Harley, "The Map and the Development of the History of Cartography" in *The History of Cartography*, ed. J. B. Harley and David Woodward (Chicago: University of Chicago Press, 1987), 3.

103. J. B. Harley, "Maps, Knowledge, and Power," in *The Iconography of Landscape: Essays on the Symbolic Representation, Design and Use of Past Environments*, ed. Denis Cosgrove and Stephen Daniels (Cambridge: Cambridge University Press, 1988), 278. Harley refers specifically to W. J. T. Mitchell, ed., *The Language of Images* (Chicago: Chicago University Press, 1980).

104. Svetlana Alpers, *The Art of Describing: Dutch Art in the Seventeenth Century* (Chicago: University of Chicago Press, 1983), 136.

105. "Die Karte gilt als die älteste gedruckte überhaupt" (This map is considered to be the absolutely oldest printed map), Reimer Witt, *Die Anfänge*, 8. Examples

from my discussion of Renaissance and Baroque cartography of the Schleswig-Holstein region are taken from Witt's very helpful overview.

106. Anthony Grafton, *New Worlds, Ancient Texts: The Power of Tradition and the Shock of Discovery* (Cambridge, MA: Harvard University Press, 1995), 49.

107. Grafton, *New Worlds*, 54.

108. Georg Braun and Franz Hogenberg, *Theatrum urbibus orbis terrarum* (Coloniae Agrippinae: 1606).

109. This map is based on the 1631 map by Henricus Hondius, "Ducatus Holsatia nova tabula."

110. J. B. Harley, "Deconstructing the Map," in *Human Geography: An Essential Anthology*, ed. John Agnew, David Livingstone, and Alisdair Rogers (London: Blackwell, 1989), 438–439.

111. Harley, "Maps, Knowledge, Power," 281–282.

112. Schlee, "Kupferstecher," 26.

113. See Christian Degn, Introduction to the *Newe Landesbeschreibung der zweij Hertzogthümer Schleswig und Holstein, 1652* (Hamburg: Otto Heinevetter, 1963), 4.

114. An example of this type of juxtaposition of text with cartography can be found in Volume IV of Joan Blaeu's *Novus Atlas* (1645), where, along with his own maps of England, Blaeu includes the 460-page text of William Camden's *Brittania* (1586). Also, a map of the Northern part of Gottorf includes a depiction of a stone arch, a detail that has been adapted from a Dutch engraving by Jan van de Velde. The engravers borrowed a number of other figures, primarily from Dutch sources: for example, figures in a 1650 map of "Wagrien" are taken from a 1634 map of Nottinghamshire by Joan Blaeu; and the soldier's camp at the bottom of a map of Rendsburg is taken from Jacques Callot's series of engravings that depict the "Misères et malheurs de la guerre" (1633). See Rudolf Zöllner, "Zum Kartenschmuck der Mejer-Landkarten in Danckwerths Neue Landesbeschreibung von 1652," (Concerning the ornamentation of the Mejer maps in Danckwerth's *New Description of the Territory of the Two Duchies of Schleswig and Holstein* of 1652) in *Von allerhand Figuren und Abbildungen: Kupferstecher des 17. Jahrhunderts im Umkreis des Gottorfer Hofes*, ed. Holger Borzikowsky (Husum: Husum Druck- und Verlagsgesellschaft, 1981), esp. 99–101; and his catalogue notes in *Von allerhand Figuren*, 168.

115. Caspar Danckwerth and Johannes Mejer, *Newe Landesbeschreibung der zweij Hertzogthümer Schleswig und Holstein* (Husum, 1652), iiir.

116. Christian Degn comments on Mejer's achievement when he writes: "Schier unglaublich erscheint es, daß Mejer in so kurzer Zeit und mit den primitiven Mitteln, die ihm zur Verfügung standen, ein so großes Areal hat vermessen können, noch dazu mit bewundernswerter Genauigkeit. [. . .] Das mathematisch-exakte Grundgerüst für seine Karten, das Gradnetz, gewann Mejer dadurch, daß er für viele Orte die Polhöhe bestimmte. Diese seine Breitenberechnungen kommen den tatsächlichen Werten sehr nahe; da er die

Lichtbrechung durch die Erdatmosphäre nicht berücksichtigt hat, liegen sie im ganzen etwa anderthalb Bogenminuten zu nördlich (4 Bogenminuten = 7,4 km sind eine deutsche Meile).

Viel schwieriger war die Berechnung der geographischen Länge. Hierfür legte Mejer die von Tycho Brahe für Uranienburg vorausberechneten Mondfinsternis-Tabellen zugrunde. Aus der Zeitdifferenz, die sich ihm bei der Beobachtung der Mondfinsternisse von 1641, 1645, 1646 und 1649 ergab, leitete er die geographische Länge von Husum ab. Als Null-meridian wählte er, wie damals üblich, den durch die Azoren verlaufenden Mittagskreis. Im übrigen hat er 'aus der distantz auf Erden' die geographische Länge bestimmt. Die Genauigkeit wie bei den Breitenmessungen konnte er dabei nicht erzielen. [. . .] Er hat dann, im Rahmen des Gradnetzes, 'alles mit mathematischen Instrumenten von Kirche zu Kirche durchgehends gemessen'; viele Strecken hat er abgeschritten, abgefahren oder auch nur–aber mit wahrer Könnerschaft geschätzt. Bei seinen Kompaßpeilungen ließ er die Mißweisung außer acht."
(It seems incredible that Mejer in such a short time and with the primitive means at his disposal should have surveyed such a large area, and with such an admirable exactitude. [. . .] He achieved the mathematically exact basis for his maps, the network of parallels and meridians by determining the position of the pole for many locations. These calculations of latitude come very close to the actual values; since he has not accounted for the refraction of light through the earth's atmosphere they are in all about one and a half minutes too far north [4 minutes = 7,4 km = one German mile].

The calculation of the geographical longitude was much more difficult. For that Mejer used the tables of lunar eclipses established by Tycho Brahe for Uranienburg. From the time differences he noted when observing the lunar eclipses of 1641, 1645, 1646, and 1649, he deduced the geographic longitude of Husum. For the zero meridian he chose, as was usual at that time, the meridian which runs through the Azores. He determined the geographic longitude "from the distance on earth." He was not able to achieve the same exactitude as he did when measuring the degrees of latitude. [. . .] He then measured within the framework of parallels and meridians "everything with mathematical instruments from church to church"; many distances he walked, he drove or estimated — however with true expertise. When he took bearings with a compass he did not consider the declination.) Degn, "Introduction," 2.

117. Harley, "Maps, Knowledge, Power," 292-93.
118. Harley, "Maps, Knowledge, Power," 279.
119. The italics are reminiscent of the lettering used to name bodies of water in Abraham Ortelius's *Theatrum Orbis Terrarum* of 1579.
120. Conceivably the border could have been extended to enclose the entire country within the frame, but then perhaps there would not have been room for the magazine's advertisement in the bottom right-hand corner that gives the toll free number, mailing address and Web site for consumers who wish to purchase

more of the *National Geographic Society*'s maps.

121. Olearius dedicated the first edition of his work, the *Offt Begehrte Beschreibung*, to Duke Frederick III. The second edition, the *Vermehrte Newe Reysebeschreibung*, is dedicated to his friend, J. A. Kielman, who helped Olearius secure a permanent position at the Gottorf court.

122. Introduction to *Holsteinische Chronik*, 0.

123. "Unterwegs starb unser Mahler Dieterich Nieman von Buxdehude / welcher / nach dem er eine lange Zeit mit dem quartan Fieber behafftet gewesen / endlich den Durchlauff bekam / und inner vier Tagen darvon seinen Geist auffgab / und zwar auff einem Karn in bösem Wetter. Wir liessen ihn den 22. dieses vor der Stadt Schamachie auff der Armener Kirchhoff mit gebührlichen Ceremonien begraben. Er war ein frommer / stiller Gottfürchtiger und in der mahler Kunst wolerfahrner Mensche / daß er auch seiner Kunst halber vom Könige in Persien / auff etliche Jahr zu dienen begehret wurde / weil er aber sahe / wie es dem Uhrmacher Rudolff Stadler ergangen / wolte er nicht bleiben. Areb Chan beklagte ihn auch sehr / dann er von ihm / wie obgedacht / etliche schöne Stücken Gemählete bekommen / und die Person selbst gerne gehabt hätte." (During the journey our painter Dieterich Nieman from Buxtehude died; for a long time he had suffered from an intermittent fever, finally contracted diarrhea and within four days breathed his last, and that on a cart in bad weather. We had him buried with the proper ceremonies in the Armenian cemetery outside the city of Shemakha on the 22nd of this month. He was a pious, quiet, godfearing man and well-versed in the art of painting; thus because of his ability he was asked by the King of Persia to serve him for a few years. But when he saw how the clockmaker Rudolff Stadler had fared, he did not want to stay. Areb Chan also mourned him deeply because he had received some beautiful paintings from him and he would have liked to host the painter himself. *VNB*, 713).

124. Regarding the multiple names of this sea, cf. Xavier de Planhol's useful entry, "Caspian Sea," in the *Encyclopaedia Iranica*, especially page 52, where he notes that there were more than thirty-seven different designations for this sea in Islamic geographical texts.

125. "Es waren unsere Gesandten willens und entschlossen / daß unser Schiff und Schlupe / wenn sie wären behalten worden/ die Zeit über / so wir beym Könige in Persien gewesen / diese See die länge und breite hätte durchfahren / und von dero Gelegenheit gute Kundschafft einziehen sollen / welches auch leicht hätte geschehen können / wenn nicht durch den Schiffbruch solch Vornehmen zu Wasser gemachet worden. Es wird diese See von Persern / Tartern und Russen des Sommers über besegelt / welche / weil sie schlechte und übel verwahrte Schiffe haben / und fast nicht als nur vor Winde gehen können / sich niemahls durch die Mitte wagen / sondern nur neben dem Lande bleiben / da sie anckern können" (It had been our ambassadors's decision and intention that our ship and our sloop — if they had survived — should

cross this Sea in its length and width during the time that they spent with the King of Persia, and thus should get reliable information. This would have been relatively easy if our plans had not collapsed because of the shipwreck. Persians, Tatars, and Russians sail upon this sea during the summer. Since their ships are bad and badly maintained and can basically only run before the wind, they do not dare to cross in the middle of the sea but stay close to land where they can throw anchor. *VNB*, 410).

126. Concerning Marco Polo's travels, see the recent work by John Larner, *Marco Polo and the Discovery of the World* (New Haven: Yale University Press, 1999).

127. This map has a south orientation. Cf. Leo Bagrow, *History of Cartography*, revised and enlarged by R. A. Skelton, ed. (Cambridge, MA: Harvard University Press, 1966), 72–73.

128. This map from about 1485 is a copper-plate engraving, with a diameter of ca. 175 mm. Cf. Erich Woldan, "A Circular, Copper-Engraved, Medieval World Map," *Imago Mundi* 11 (1954): 12–16; and Rodney W. Shirley, *The Mapping of the World: Early Printed World Maps, 1472–1700* (London: Holland Press, 1987).

129. Conley, 202. See also Robert W. Karrow, *Mapmakers of the Sixteenth Century and Their Maps: Bio-Bibliographies of the Cartographers of Abraham Ortelius, 1570* (Chicago: Speculum Orbis Press, 1993), 410 and ff.

130. Sebastian Münster, *Cosmographey: das ist / Beschreibung Aller Länder / Herrschafften und fürnemesten Stetten des gantzen Erdbodens / sampt ihren Gelegenheiten / Eygenschafften / Religion / Gebräuchen / Geschichten und Handtierungen* (Cosmography, that is the Description of all countries and governments and most important places on the entire earth together with their locations, qualities, religion, customs, history, and actions, 1598), 1357–1359. Subsequent references to this work will be abbreviated as "Münster."

131. In this context, *see* Harley, "Deconstructing the Map," and "Maps, Knowledge, Power."

132. Jan Jansson, *Atlas Minor*, 325.

133. Bagrow, *History of Cartography*, 181.

134. J. Brian Harley and David Woodward, eds., *The History of Cartography*, vol. 2, bk. 1, *Cartography in the Traditional Islamic and South Asian Societies* (Chicago: University of Chicago Press, 1992).

135. *Encyclopaedia of Islam*, s.v. "Djughrāfiyā," 578.

136. Gerald R. Tibbets, "The Beginnings of a Cartographic Tradition," in *Cartography in the Traditional Islamic and South Asian Societies*, ed. J. Brian Harley and David Woodward (Chicago: Chicago University Press, 1992), 94.

137. See S. Maqbul Ahmad, "Cartography of al-Sharīf al-Idrīsī," in *The History of Cartography*, ed. J. Brian Harley and David Woodward (Chicago: University of Chicago Press, 1992), 156.

138. Cf. the *Encyclopaedia of Islam*, s.v. "Khārita," 1081.

139. Matthee, 239. Concerning Jean Chardin (1643–1713), another famous traveler

to Persia, Matthee writes: "Chardin's claim [*Voyages*, 2:352] that the Iranians knew nothing about geography is patently false — he himself contradicts this assertion when he describes how the army commander (*sardar*) Rustam Beg, showed him maps of Azerbaijan that he had recently drawn," Matthee, "Safavid Views," 239. In the chapter on "Persian Science in Safavid Times" in the *Cambridge History of Iran* (Cambridge: Cambridge University Press, 1986) 6: 581, H. J. J. Winter also points out that "Persia was a place of exchanges in ideas rather than a focus of original discovery." Regarding cartography during Safavid times, we read that "Most *zîjât* listed the geographical coordinates of cities, since apparent celestial positions are affected by the geographical position of the observer, and these appeared inscribed in the *umm* of astrolabes. But there is a dearth of information on cartography. After the maps of the Arab al-Idrîsî in . . . twelfth century Norman Sicily, which superseded the medieval monastic maps and persisted in their influence for four hundred years, no maps appear from the Islamic world until the rise of Ottoman Turkey as a maritime power. The impetus to the study of cartography which was provided in Turkey by her maritime exploits, and the enthusiastic translation of European geographies into Turkish, appear to have aroused no parallel activity in Persia" (Winter, "Persian Science," 594–95).

140. Matthee, "Safavid Views," 239.

141. From al-Mas'ûdî, *Le livre de l'avertissement et de la revision*, translated by B. Carra de Vaux (Paris: Société Asiatique, 1896), 90.

142. We also read that: "Mas'udi was born in Baghdad about 896 A.D., during the Caliphate of Mu'tadid and died in Egypt some time around the year 956. Besides the *Meadows of Gold* and the *Tanbih*, Mas'udi wrote some thirty-four works of varying length on a wide variety of subjects — jurisprudence, comparative religion, polemics, philosophy, political theory, astronomy, medicine, and history . . . [He] breaks up his narrative with all sorts of digressions, anecdotes, jokes, and poems. Most Arabic historical writing is impersonal. [. . .] Mas'udi's use of the first person is unusual and as one reads one gradually forms an idea of the sort of man he was — curious, warm-hearted, tolerant, vain, a man who disliked lawyers. He writes fluent, unmannered Arabic and uses a wide vocabulary. Although he was interested in the sciences of his day, he was no pedant." Mas'udi, *The Meadows of Gold; The Abbasids*, trans. and ed. by Paul Lunde and Caroline Stone (London: Kegan Paul, 1989), 13–17.

143. From Hamd-Allah Mustawfi, *The Geographical Part of the Nuzhat-al-Qulub by Hamd-Allah Mustawfi of Qazwin in 740 (1340)*, trans. Guy Le Strange (Leyden: E. J. Brill, 1919), 231–32.

144. Olearius, Adam, *Moskowitische und persische Reise: die holsteinische Gesandtschaft beim Schah, 1633-1639*, edited by Detlef Haberland (Stuttgart: Thienemann, Edition Erdmann, 1986), 37.

145. Haberland, 36.

146. Winter, "Persian Science," 591.

147. Greaves also befriended the celebrated Orientalists of Persian and Arabic, James Golius in Leyden and Edward Pococke at Oxford. For a complete listing of Greaves's publications, see the *Dictionary of National Biography*, s.v. "Greaves," 481–482.

148. At times he also comments on the calculations of other Europeans, whom he mentions by name.

149. See Elio Brancaforte, "Reading Word and Image: Representations of Safavid Persia in the Maps and Frontispieces of Adam Olearius (ca. 1650)," (Dissertation, Harvard University, 2001), Appendix B, 259-265. The information gleaned from this list can help ascertain what Islamic geographical tables Olearius might have consulted in the production of his *"Nova Delineatio Persiae."*

150. All coordinates, besides the ones from Olearius and from Greaves's translation, are derived from the compilation of Islamic coordinates in Edward S. Kennedy and Mary Kennedy, *Geographical Coordinates of Localities from Islamic Sources* (Frankfurt am Main: Institut für Geschichte der Arabisch-Islamischen Wissenschaften an der J. W. Goethe-Universität, 1987).

151. Rudi Matthee, "Safavid Views," 227.

152. See, for example, Sheily Canby's article on "Farangi Saz: The Impact of Europe on Safavid Painting," in *Silk and Stone: The Art of Asia, Third Hali Annual* (London: 1996), 46–59.

153. *VNB*, 509. The theatricality of this scene should be emphasized. Also, the author notes that European paintings, perhaps historical works, hang "zur lincken an der Wand" (on the left wall, *VNB*, 509). This implies that Olearius is making use of this particular illustration in conjunction with the text in order to create a representation of the event.

154. "Funffzehen der fürnembsten unsers Comitats wurden auff selbigem Saal zu sitzen genötiget / die Pagen aber und andere Völcker ausserhalb des Gemaches / neben 13. köstlich außgepuzten Tänzerinnen / so mit offenen Angesichtern auff Tapeten sassen. Diese sollen nicht / wie etliche der unserigen vermeinten / und auffgezeichnet hatten / des Königes bestelte Tänzerinnen / sondern gemeine / aber die fürnembsten Huren der Stadt gewesen seyn / welche dem Könige jährlichen Tribut geben und auffwarten müssen" (Fifteen of the most illustrious of our Embassy were asked to sit in the same hall, the pages, however, and other people were sitting outside the room, together with 13 marvellously decked-out dancers, who sat on carpets with their faces unveiled. These were not, as some of our people surmised, the King's dancers, but were common whores of the city, however they were the most elegant ones who have to pay a yearly tribute to the King and serve him, *VNB*, 509).

155. "In dem dieses alles vorgieng / hatten sie hinter den Gesandten in einer Thür / so in ein absonderlich Gemach gieng / und mit einer Gardin oder Decke behänget war / einen Perser / welcher der Portugalischen und Italienischen Sprache kündig / verstecket / umb zu hören / was doch die Gesandten unter

sich und mit ihrem Dolmetsch redeten / und was ihr judicium von den Persern. Dann unser Dolmetsch war ein Portugalischer Augustiner Münch Nahmens Pater Joseph *â Rosario* (sonst ein frommer / verständiger / williger und freundlicher Mann / seines Alters von 40. Jahren) welcher durch 24. jährige conversation unter den Persern / dero Natur / Humor / Leben und Thun wol erlernet hatte / und daher uns gute Dienste leisten kunte. Dieser redete mit dem Gesandten Crusius in Lateinischer / und mit Herrn Brügman in Portugesischer Sprache. Was Brügmans meynung von ein und andern / sonderlich von der Europeischen Schilderey / und Persischen art zu sitzen und zu essen hatte dem König nicht allerdinges wolgefallen . . ." (While this was going on they had hidden behind the ambassadors (in a door which led to a secret chamber and was covered with a curtain or cloth) a Persian man who knew Portuguese and Italian in order to hear what the ambassadors discussed among themselves and with their translator, and what they thought of the Persians. Our translator was a Portuguese Augustine monk named Father Joseph a Rosario (otherwise a pious, intelligent, willing and friendly man, 40 years of age) who had gotten to know the nature, humor, lifestyle and activities of the Persians after 24 years of conversing with them; and therefore he was able to give us good service. He spoke with Ambassador Crusius in Latin and with Mr. Brüggemann in Portuguese. The King did not like, however, what Brüggemann had to say about the one or other [custom], especially about the European paintings and the Persian way of sitting and eating, *VNB*, 512).

156. Regarding the life and work of Jürgen Ovens, see Harry Schmidt, *Jürgen Ovens: Sein Leben und seine Werke* (Kiel: H. Schmidt, 1922).

157. See Adam Olearius, *Kurtzer Begriff einer Holsteinischen Chronik* (Short Review of a Holstein Chronicle; Schleswig: Schultze, 1674), 92–95; *Theatrum Europeum*, 4: 68–69.

158. *Relation*, 3.

159. *Relation*, 3–4.

160. He had already experienced this situation in the city of Narva — in present-day Estonia — when a crowd had gathered in front of the inn at which he was staying, in order to catch a glimpse of his wife (*VNB*, 760).

161. Olearius, *Holsteinische Chronik*, 93.

Bibliography

"Orient und orientalische Literaturen." In *Reallexikon der deutschen Literaturgeschichte,* edited by Werner Kohlschmidt and Wolfgang Mohr, 816–869. Berlin: Walter de Gruyter, 1965.

Ackerman, Phyllis. "Standards, Banners and Badges." In *A Survey of Persian Art: From Prehistoric Times to the Present,* edited by Arthur Upham Pope, 2766–2782. London: Oxford University Press, 1967.

Adams, Percy G. *Travel Literature and the Evolution of the Novel.* Lexington: University Press of Kentucky, 1983.

Ahmad, S. Maqbul. "Cartography of al-Sharīf al-Idrīsī." In *The History of Cartography,* edited by J. Brian Harley and David Woodward, 156–174. Chicago: University of Chicago Press, 1992.

Akerman, James. "Atlas: Birth of a Title." In *The Mercator Atlas of Europe: Facsimile of the Maps by Gerardus Mercator Contained in the Atlas of Europe, circa 1570–1572,* edited by Marcel Watelet, 14–30. Pleasant Hill, OR: Walking Tree Press, 1998.

Alciati, Andrea. *Emblematum Liber [1531].* Hildesheim: Olms, 1977.

Alexander, Dorothy. Introduction to *The German Single-Leaf Woodcut, 1600–1700: A Pictorial Catalogue.* Preface by Walter L. Strauss. New York: Abaris Books, 1977.

Alpers, Svetlana. *The Art of Describing: Dutch Art in the Seventeenth Century.* Chicago: University of Chicago Press, 1983.

Augustin, Bernd. "Safawidische Metallarbeiten." In *Gottorf im Glanz des Barock. Kunst und Kultur am Schleswiger Hof, 1544–1713,* edited by Heinz Spielmann and Jan Drees, 122–131. Schleswig: Wachholtz, 1997.

Babaie, Sussan. "Shah 'Abbas II, The Conquest of Qandahar, The Chihil Sutun, and its Wall Paintings." *Muqarnas* 11 (1994): 125–142.

Babinger, Franz. "Orient und deutsche Literatur." In *Deutsche Philologie im Aufriss*, edited by Wolfgang Stammler, 565–588. Berlin: Erich Schmidt, 1962.

Bagrow, Leo. *History of Cartography*. Revised and enlarged by R. A. Skelton, ed. Cambridge, MA: Harvard University Press, 1966.

Bagrow, Leo. *A History of Russian Cartography up to 1800*. Edited by Henry W. Castner. Wolfe Island, Ontario: The Walker Press, 1975.

Balke, Diethelm. "Orient und orientalische Literaturen." In *Reallexikon der deutschen Literaturgeschichte*, edited by Werner Kohlschmidt and Wolfgang Mohr, 816–868. Berlin: Walter de Gruyter, 1965.

Baron, Samuel. *The Travels of Olearius in Seventeenth-Century Russia*. Translated by Samuel Baron. Stanford: Stanford University Press, 1967.

Behzad, Faramarz. *Adam Olearius' "Persianischer Rosenthal." Untersuchungen zur Übersetzung von Saadis "Golestan" im 17. Jahrhundert*. Göttingen: Vandenhoeck & Ruprecht, 1970.

Bencard, Mogens. "Idee und Enstehung der Kunstkammer." In *Gottorf im Glanz des Barock. Kunst und Kultur am Schleswiger Hof, 1544–1713*, edited by Heinz Spielmann and Jan Drees, 261–268. Schleswig: Wachholtz, 1997.

Benjamin, Walter. *Ursprung des deutschen Trauerspiels*. Frankfurt am Main: Suhrkamp, 1963.

Berger, Günter, and Stephan Kohl, eds. *Fremderfahrung in Texten des Spätmittelalters und der frühen Neuzeit*. Vol. 7, *LIR Literatur, Imagination, Realität*. Trier: Wissenschaftlicher Verlag Trier, 1993.

Besler, Basilius. *Hortus Eystettensis [1613]. Der Garten von Eichstätt. Das Grosse Herbarium des Basilius Besler von 1613*. Introduction by Dieter Vogellehner. München: Schirmer-Mosel, 1988.

Bhabha, Homi, ed. *Nation and Narration*. London: Routledge, 1990.

Bishr, Naime Omar. "Das *Persianische Rosenthal* von Adam Olearius und Sa'dis *Gulestan*: Eine geistesgeschichtliche Untersuchung." Dissertation. Rutgers University, 1974.

Bizzarri, Pietro. *Pannonicum Bellum*. Basilea, 1573.

Blaeu, Joan, and Willem Janszoon Blaeu. *Novus Atlas, Das ist Welt-beschreibung Mit schönen newen außführlichen Land-Taffeln in Kupffer gestochen und an den Tag gegeben Durch Guil. und Iohannem Blaeu*. Vol. 2. Amsterdam: Iohannem Blaeu, 1647.

Blunt, Wilfrid. *Isfahan: Pearl of Persia*. London: Elek Books, 1966.

Bobzin, Hartmut. "Orientalisch-deutsche Literaturbeziehungen." In *Literatur Lexikon: Begriffe, Realien, Methoden*, edited by Volker Meid, 188–192. Berlin: Bertelsmann Lexikon Verlag, 1993.

Boemus, Joannis. *Omnium Gentium Mores, Leges & Ritus, ex multis clarissimis rerum scriptoribus, à Ioanne Boëmo Aubano Teutonico nupter collecti, & novissime recogniti. Tribus libris absolutum opus, Aphricam, Asiam, & Europam describentibus.*

Non sine Indice locupletissimo. Friburgi Brisgoiae, 1540.

Boissard, Jan Jacques. *Habitvs Variarum Orbis gentium. Habitz de Nations estra[n]ges. Trachten mancherley Völcker des Erdskreysz.* Mecheln: Caspar Rutz, 1581.

Botero, Giovanni. *Della ragion di Stato libri dieci.* Milano, 1589.

Botero, Giovanni. *Le relationi universali.* Venetia: Alessandro Vecchi, 1622.

Braider, Christopher. *Refiguring the Real: Picture and Modernity in Word and Image, 1400–1700.* Princeton: Princeton University Press, 1993.

Brancaforte, Elio. "Reading Word and Image: Representations of Safavid Persia in the Maps and Frontispieces of Adam Olearius (ca. 1650)." Dissertation. Harvard University, 2001.

Brandis, Lucas. *Rudimentum Novitiorum.* Lübeck, 1475.

Braun, Edmund W. "Cyrus." In *Reallexikon zur deutschen Kunstgeschichte,* edited by Hans Martin von Erffa, 899–912. Stuttgart: Alfred Druckenmüller, 1954.

Braun, Georg, and Franz Hogenberg. *Theatrum urbibus orbis terrarum.* Coloniae Agrippinae, 1606.

Brenner, Peter. *Der Reisebericht in der deutschen Literatur: Ein Forschungsüberblick als Vorstudie zu einer Gattungsgeschichte, 2. Sonderheft. Internationales Archiv für Sozialgeschichte der deutschen Literatur.* Tübingen: Max Niemeyer, 1990.

Broc, Numa. *La géographie de la Renaissance, 1420–1620.* Paris: Éditions du C.T.H.S., 1986.

Broecke, Marcel P. R. van den. *Ortelius Atlas Maps: An Illustrated Guide.* 'T Goy, Netherlands: HES, 1996.

Brotton, Jerry. *Trading Territories: Mapping the Early Modern World.* Ithaca, NY: Cornell University Press, 1998.

Bruyn, Abraham de. *Omnium pene Evropae, Asiae, Aphricae atque Americae Gentium Habitus.* Antwerp, 1610.

Canby, Sheila, "Farangi Saz: The Impact of Europe on Safavid Painting." In *Silk and Stone: The Art of Asia, Third Hali Annual,* 46–59. London, 1996.

Carter, Charles Howard, ed. *From the Renaissance to the Counter-Reformation; Essays in Honor of Garrett Mattingly.* New York: Random House, 1965.

Claussen, Nils. "Friedrichstadt—Friedrich III. und seine neue Stadt." In *Gottorf im Glanz des Barock. Kunst und Kultur am Schleswiger Hof, 1544–1713,* edited by Heinz Spielmann and Jan Drees, 107–109. Schleswig: Wachholtz, 1997.

Clifford, James. *The Predicament of Culture: Twentieth-Century Ethnography, Literature, and Art.* Cambridge, MA: Harvard University Press, 1988.

Clüver, Philipp. *Introductionis in Universam Geographiam, tam Veterem quam Novam, Libri VI.* Lugduni Batauorum, 1627.

Cole, Juan R. I. "Invisible Occidentalism: Eighteenth-Century Indo-Persian Constructions of the West." *Iranian Studies* 25, no. 3–4 (1992): 3–16.

Conley, Tom. *The Self-Made Map: Cartographic Writing in Early Modern France.* Minneapolis: University of Minnesota Press, 1996.

Corbett, Margery, and Ronald Lightbown. *The Comely Frontispiece: The Emblematic Title-Page in England, 1550–1660.* London: Routledge, 1979.

Cordier, Balthasar. *Catena Sexaginta Quinque Graecorum Patrum in S. Lucam*. Antwerp, 1628.

Curtius Rufus, Quintus, and Johann Freinsheim. *De rebus Alexandri regis Macedonum*. Argentorati: Dolhopff & Zetzner, 1670.

D'Agostini, Maria Enrica, ed. *La letteratura di viaggio: Storia e Prospettive di un Genere Letterario*. Milan: Angelo Guerini, 1987.

Daly, Peter. *Emblem Theory. Recent German Contributions to the Characterization of the Emblem Genre, Wolfenbütteler Forschungen 9*. Nendeln: KTO Press, 1979.

Daly, Peter. *Literature in Light of the Emblem: Structural Parallels between the Emblem and Literature in the Sixteenth and Seventeenth Centuries*. Toronto: University of Toronto Press, 1979.

Danckwerth, Caspar, and Johannes Mejer. *Newe Landesbeschreibung der zweij Hertzogthümer Schleswig und Holstein*. Husum, 1652.

Dannenfeldt, Karl H. *Leonhard Rauwolf*. Cambridge, MA: Harvard University Press, 1968.

Degenhard, Ursula. *Exotische Welten, Europäische Phantasien: Entdeckungs- und Forschungsreisen im Spiegel alter Bücher*. Stuttgart: Württembergische Landesbibliothek, 1987.

Degn, Christian. Introduction to the *Newe Landesbeschreibung der zweij Hertzogthümer Schleswig und Holstein*. Hamburg: Otto Heinevetter, 1963.

Des Prez, François. *Recueil de la diuersité des habits, qui sont de present en vsage, tant es pays d'Europe, Asie, Affrique & Iles sauuages, Le tout fait apres le naturel. A Paris. De L'imprimerie de Richard Breton, Rue S. Iaques, à l'Escreuisse d'argent. 1564* . Paris: Richard Breton, 1564.

Du Mans, Raphaël. *Estat de la Perse en 1660*. Edited by Charles Schefer. Paris: E. Leroux, 1890.

Du Ryer, André. *Gvlistan ov l'Empire des Roses Composé par Sa'di, Prince des Poëtes Turcs & Persans*. Paris, 1634.

Elsner, Jás, and Joan-Pau Rubiés, eds. *Voyages and Visions: Towards a Cultural History of Travel*. London: Reaktion, 1999.

Emerson, John. "Adam Olearius and the Literature of the Schleswig-Holstein Missions to Russia and Iran, 1633–1639." In *Études safavides*, edited by Jean Calmard. Paris: Institut français de recherche en Iran, 1993.

Emerson, John. "Ex Occidente Lux: Some European Sources on the Economic Structure of Persia between about 1630 and 1690." Dissertation. Cambridge University, 1971.

Ertzdorff, Xenja von, and Dieter Neukirch, eds. *Reisen und Reiseliteratur im Mittelalter und in der Frühen Neuzeit: Vorträge eines interdisziplinären Symposiums vom 3.-8. Juni 1991 an der Justus-Liebig-Universität Gießen*. Amsterdam: Rodopi, 1992.

Faugère, Annie. "L'Autre et l'Ailleurs dans quelques récits de voyage allemands." In *Les Récits de Voyage*. Paris: Éditions A.-G. Nizet, 1986.

Filip, V. "Löwe." In *Lexikon des Mittelalters*, edited by Norbert Angermann,

2141–2142. München und Zürich: Artemis Verlag, 1993.

Fleming, Paul. *Teütsche Poemata*. Lübeck: Jauch, 1646.

Floor, Willem M. "Dutch Painters in Iran During the First Half of the 17th Century." *Persica* 8 (1979): 145–161.

Floor, Willem. *The Economy of Safavid Persia*. Wiesbaden: Reichert, 2000.

Floor, Willem. "Fact or Fiction: The Most Perilous Journeys of Jan Jansz. Struys." In *Études Safavides*, edited by Jean Calmard, 57–68. Paris: Institut français de recherche en Iran, 1993.

Gabriel, Alfons. *Die Erforschung Persiens: Die Entwicklung der abendländischen Kenntnis der Geographie Persiens*. Wien: A. Holzhausen, 1952.

Gentius, Georg. *Gulistan—Mvsladini Sa'di Rosarium Politicvm, Sive amoenvm sortis hvmanae theatrvm, De Persico in Latinum versum, necessariisque Notis illustratum A Georgio Gentio*. Amsterdam, 1651.

Goethe, Johann Wolfgang von. "Noten und Abhandlungen zu besserem Verständnis des 'West-östlichen Divans.'" In *Werke, Hamburger Ausgabe in 14 Bänden*. München: DTV/Beck, 1988.

Goetz, Hermann. "The History of Persian Costume." In *A Survey of Persian Art: From Prehistoric Times to the Present*, edited by Arthur Upham Pope, 2227–2256. London: Oxford University Press, 1967.

Grafton, Anthony. *New Worlds, Ancient Texts: The Power of Tradition and the Shock of Discovery*. Cambridge, MA: Harvard University Press, 1995.

Greaves, John. *Binae tabulae geographicae, una Nassir Eddini Persae altera Vlug Beigi Tatari, operâ & studio Johannis Gravii*. Londini: Typis Jacobi Flesher, prostant apud Cornelium Bee, 1652.

Greenblatt, Stephen. *Marvelous Possessions: The Wonder of the New World*. Chicago: University of Chicago Press, 1991.

Gregorius de St. Vincent. *Opus Geometricum Quadraturae Circuli*. Antuerpiae, 1647.

Haase, Claus Peter. "Das Safawidenreich zur Zeit der Gottorfer Gesandtschaft." In *Gottorf im Glanz des Barock. Kunst und Kultur am Schleswiger Hof, 1544–1713*, edited by Heinz Spielmann and Jan Drees, 117–121. Schleswig: Wachholtz, 1997.

Hall, James. "Lion." In *The Illustrated Dictionary of Symbols in Eastern and Western Art*, 33–34. New York: HarperCollins, 1994.

Hall, Kim. *Things of Darkness: Economies of Race and Gender in Early Modern England*. Ithaca, NY: Cornell University Press, 1995.

Hanne, Michael, ed. *Literature and Travel*. Edited by David Bevan. Vol. 11, *Rodopi Perspectives on Modern Literature*. Amsterdam: Rodopi, 1993.

Harbsmeier, Michael. "Reisebeschreibungen als mentalitätsgeschichtliche Quellen: Überlegungen zu einer historisch-anthropologischen Untersuchung früh-neuzeitlicher deutscher Reisebeschreibungen." In *Reiseberichte als Quellen europäischer Kulturgeschichte*, 1–31. Wolfenbüttel: Heckners, 1982.

Harley, J. Brian. "Deconstructing the Map." In *Human Geography: An Essential Anthology*, edited by John Agnew, David Livingstone, and Alisdair Rogers,

422–443. London: Blackwell, 1989.

Harley, J. B. "The Map and the Development of the History of Cartography." In *The History of Cartography*, edited by J. B. Harley and David Woodward, 1–42. Chicago: University of Chicago Press, 1987.

Harley, J. B. "Maps, Knowledge, and Power." In *The Iconography of Landscape: Essays on the Symbolic Representation, Design and Use of Past Environments*, edited by Denis Cosgrove and Stephen Daniels, 277–312. Cambridge: Cambridge University Press, 1988.

Harley, J. B., and David Woodward, eds. *The History of Cartography: Cartography in the Traditional Islamic and South Asian Societies*. Vol. 2, Book 1. Chicago: University of Chicago Press, 1992.

Hendricks, Margo, and Patricia Parker, eds. *Women, "Race," and Writing in the Early Modern Period*. London: Routledge, 1994.

Henkel, Arthur, and Albrecht Schöne. *Emblemata: Handbuch zur Sinnbildkunst des XVI. und XVII. Jahrhunderts*. Ergänzte Neuausgabe, 2nd ed., [1st ed. 1967]. Stuttgart: J. B. Metzler, 1976.

Herbert, Thomas. *A Relation of Some Yeares Travaile*. London, 1634.

Herodotus. *The Histories*. Introduction and notes by Andrew Robert Burn. Hammondsworth, England: Penguin Books, 1972.

Hodgen, Margaret. *Early Anthropology in the Sixteenth and Seventeenth Centuries*. Philadelphia: University of Pennsylvania Press, 1964.

Hodgson, Marshall. *The Venture of Islam. Conscience and History in a World Civilization*. Vol. 3. Chicago: University of Chicago Press, 1974.

Hoffmeister, Gerhart. *Deutsche und europäische Barockliteratur*. Vol. 234, *Sammlung Metzler*. Stuttgart: Metzler, 1987.

Hollstein, F. *German Engravings, Etchings and Woodcuts, ca. 1400–1700*. Amsterdam: M. Hertzberger, 1954.

Homann, Johann Baptista. "Persia." Nürnberg: Io. Baptista Homann, 1723.

Homayoun, Gholamali. "Iran in europäischen Bildzeugnissen vom Ausgang des Mittelalters bis ins achtzehnte Jahrhundert." Dissertation. University of Cologne, 1967.

Hondius, Jodocus, and Jan Jansson. *Atlas minor, das ist: Eine kurtze, jedoch gründliche beschreibung der gantzen weldt*. Amstelodami, 1651.

Honour, Hugh. "Science and Exoticism: The European Artist and the Non-European World before Johan Maurits." In *Johan Maurits van Nassau-Siegen 1604–1679: A Humanist Prince in Europe and Brazil*, edited by E. van den Boogaart, 269-296. The Hague: Johan Maurits van Nassau Stichting, 1979.

Höpel, Ingrid. "Gottorfer Feste – Anlässe zur Repräsentation." In *Gottorf im Glanz des Barock: Kunst und Kultur am Schleswiger Hof, 1544–1713*, edited by Heinz Spielmann and Jan Drees, 237–244. Schleswig: Wachholtz, 1997.

Horapollo. *Hieroglihica*. Paris: P. Vidovaeus, 1521.

Horn, Georg. *Accuratissima orbis antiqui delineatio sive geographia vetus, sacra & profana*. Amstelodami: Joannem Janssonium, 1653.

Hourani, Albert. *A History of the Arab Peoples*. Cambridge, MA: Harvard University Press, 1991.

Itzkowitz, Norman. *Ottoman Empire and Islamic Tradition*. Chicago: University of Chicago Press, 1972.

Jardine, Lisa. *Wordly Goods: A New History of the Renaissance*. New York: Doubleday, 1996.

Judson, Jay Richard, and Carl van de Velde. *Book Illustrations and Title-Pages*. Vol. 2, *Corpus Rubenianum Ludwig Burchard*. London and Philadelphia: Miller & Heyden, 1978.

Kaempfer, Engelbert. *Am Hofe des persischen Grosskönigs, 1684–1685*. [Translation of *Amoenitates exoticae* (1712) by Walther Hinz]. Tübingen: H. Erdmann, 1977.

Karp, Ivan, and Steven D. Lavine, eds. *The Poetics and Politics of Museum Display*. Washington: Smithsonian Institution Press, 1991.

Karrow, Jr., Robert W. *Mapmakers of the Sixteenth Century and Their Maps: Bio-Bibliographies of the Cartographers of Abraham Ortelius, 1570*. Chicago: Speculum Orbis Press, 1993.

Kennedy, Edward S., and Mary Kennedy. *Geographical Coordinates of Localities from Islamic Sources*. Frankfurt am Main: Institut für Geschichte der Arabisch-Islamischen Wissenschaften an der J. W. Goethe-Universität, 1987.

Kiecksee, Ernst Markus. "Phantasie und Wagemut. Handelsprojekte in einer Zeit des Umbruchs." In *Gottorf im Glanz des Barock. Kunst und Kultur am Schleswiger Hof, 1544–1713*, edited by Heinz Spielmann and Jan Drees, 110–116. Schleswig: Wachholtz, 1997.

Kintzinger, Marion. *Chronos und Historia: Studien zur Titelblattikonographie*. Vol. 60, *Wolfenbütteler Forschungen*. Wiesbaden: Harrassowitz, 1995.

Kish, George. *La Carte: Image des Civilisations*. Paris: Seuil, 1980.

Koeman, Cornelis. *Joan Blaeu and his Grand Atlas*. Amsterdam: Theatrum Orbis Terrarum, 1970.

Krogt, Peter van der. *Koeman's Atlantes Neerlandici*. Vol. 1. Goy-Houten, The Netherlands: HES Publishers, 1997.

Larner, John. *Marco Polo and the Discovery of the World*. New Haven: Yale University Press, 1999.

Lewis, Bernard. *The Muslim Discovery of Europe*. New York: Norton, 1982.

Lewis, Reina. *Gendering Orientalism: Race, Femininity, and Representation*. London: Routledge, 1996.

Liszkowski, Uwe. "Der Rußlandbericht des Adam Olearius." In *Von allerhand Figuren und Abbildungen: Kupferstecher des 17. Jahrhunderts im Umkreis des Gottorfer Hofes*, edited by Holger Borzikowsky, 79–98. Husum: Husum Druck- und Verlagsgesellschaft, 1981.

Lockhart, Laurence. "European Contacts with Persia." In *The Cambridge History of Iran*, edited by Peter Jackson, 300–310. Cambridge: Cambridge University Press, 1986.

Lohmeier, Dieter. "Adam Olearius." In *Gottorf im Glanz des Barock. Kunst und*

Kultur am Schleswiger Hof, 1544–1713, edited by Heinz Spielmann and Jan Drees, 349–354. Schleswig: Wachholtz, 1997.

Lohmeier, Dieter. "Adam Olearius und die Gottorfer Kupferstecher." In *Von allerhand Figuren und Abbildungen: Kupferstecher des 17. Jahrhunderts im Umkreis des Gottorfer Hofes*, edited by Holger Borzikowsky, 59–78. Husum: Husum Druck- und Verlagsgesellschaft, 1981.

Lohmeier, Dieter. "Die Gottorfer Bibliothek." In *Gottorf im Glanz des Barock. Kunst und Kultur am Schleswiger Hof, 1544–1713*, edited by Heinz Spielmann and Jan Drees, 325–348. Schleswig: Wachholtz, 1997.

Lohmeier, Dieter. "Die Gründung der Universität Kiel." In *Gottorf im Glanz des Barock. Kunst und Kultur am Schleswiger Hof, 1544–1713*, edited by Heinz Spielmann and Jan Drees, 377–380. Schleswig: Wachholtz, 1997.

Lohmeier, Dieter. "Nachwort." In *Vermehrte Newe Beschreibung der Muscowitischen und Persischen Reyse (1656)*. Tübingen: Max Niemeyer, 1971.

Lühning, Felix. "Das Gottorfer Globenpaar." In *Gottorf im Glanz des Barock. Kunst und Kultur am Schleswiger Hof, 1544–1713*, edited by Heinz Spielmann and Jan Drees, 367–373. Schleswig: Wachholtz, 1997.

Lühning, Felix. *Der Gottorfer Globus und das Globushaus im "Newen Werck."* Vol. 4 of *Gottorf im Glanz des Barock: Kunst und Kultur am Schleswiger Hof, 1544–1713*, edited by Heinz Spielmann and Jan Drees. Schleswig: Norddruck, 1997.

Mandelsloh, Johann Albrecht von. *Des HochEdelgebornen Johan Albrechts von Mandelslo Morgenländische Reyse-Beschreibung*. Schleßwig: Johan Holwein, 1658.

Mandelsloh, Johann Albrecht von. *Journal und Observation: 1637–1640*. Edited by Margrete Refslund-Klemann. Kobenhavn: Andr. Fred. Host, 1942.

Mandelsloh, Johann Albrecht von. *Voyages Celebres & remarquables, Faits de Perse Aux Indes Orientales, Par le Sr. Jean-Albert De Mandelslo, Gentilhomme des Ambassadeurs du Duc de Holstein en Moscovie & Perse*. Edited by Adam Olearius and translated by A. De Wicquefort. Amsterdam: Michel Charles Le Ce'Ne, 1727.

Maravall, José Antonio. *Culture of the Baroque*. Translated by Terry Cochran. Vol. 25, *Theory and History of Literature*. Minneapolis: University of Minnesota Press, 1986.

Martels, Zweder von, ed. *Travel Fact and Travel Fiction: Studies on Fiction, Literary Tradition, Scholarly Discovery and Observation in Travel Writing*. Leiden: Brill, 1994.

Mason, Peter. *Infelicities: Representations of the Exotic*. Baltimore: The Johns Hopkins University Press, 1998.

Mas'udi. *Le livre de l'avertissement et de la revision*. Translated by B. Carra de Vaux. Paris: Société Asiatique, 1896.

Mas'udi. *The Meadows of Gold; The Abbasids*. Translated and edited by Paul Lunde and Caroline Stone. London: Kegan Paul, 1989.

Matthee, Rudi. "Between Aloofness and Fascination: Safavid Views of the West."

Iranian Studies 31, no. 2, Spring (1998): 219–246.

Matthee, Rudi. *The Politics of Trade in Safavid Iran: Silk for Silver, 1600-1730*. Cambridge, U.K.: Cambridge University Press, 1999.

Mejer, Johannes. *Die Landkarten von Johannes Mejer, Husum, aus der neuen Landesbeschreibung der zwei Herzogtümer Schleswig und Holstein von Caspar Danckwerth, 1652*. Edited by K. Domeier and M. Haack. Hamburg-Bergedorf: Heinevetter, 1982.

Mercator, Gerhard. *Atlas Minor, Das ist: Eine kurtze jedoch gründliche Beschreibung der gantzen Welt Das Ander Theil*. Vol. 2. Amstelodami: Ioannis Ianssonii, 1651.

Mercator, Gerard. *Atlas Sive Cosmographicae Meditationes de Fabrica Mundi et fabricati Figura* (Duisburg, 1595). Bruxelles: Culture et civilisation, 1963.

Mercator, Gerardi, and Iudoco Hondio. *Atlantis Novi: Pars Tertia, Italiam, Graeciam & maximias insulas Maris Mediterranei, nec non Asiam, Africam atque Americam continens*. Vol. 3. Amstelodami, 1638.

Mercator, Gerard, Jodocus Hondius, and Ioannis Janssonius. *Atlas or A Geographicke Description of the World*. Vol. 2. Amsterdam, 1636.

Merian, Matthaeus. *Theatrum Europaeum, oder Ausführliche und warhafftige beschreibung aller und jeder denckwürdiger geschichten* . . . Franckfurt am Mayn: W. Hoffmann, 1643-1738.

Mitchell, W. J. T. *The Language of Images*. Chicago: University of Chicago Press, 1980.

Mitrovich, Mirco. "Deutsche Reisende und Reiseberichte im 17. Jahrhundert. Ein kultur-historischer Beitrag." Dissertation. University of Illinois, 1963.

Montesinos, José. *Estudios sobre Lope de Vega*. Madrid: Anaya, 1969.

Morgan, David. *Medieval Persia 1040–1797*. London: Longman, 1988.

Müller, Wolfgang J. "Bildwelt und Weltbild im barocken Kupferstich." In *Von allerhand Figuren und Abbildungen: Kupferstecher des 17. Jahrhunderts im Umkreis des Gottorfer Hofes*, edited by Holger Borzikowsky, 113–126. Husum: Husum Druck- und Verlagsgesellschaft, 1981.

Münster, Sebastian. *Cosmographey: das ist Beschreibung Aller Länder Herrschafften und fürnemesten Stetten des gantzen Erdbodens sampt ihren Gelegenheiten Eygenschafften Religion Gebräuchen Geschichten und Handtierungen*. Basel, 1598.

Münster, Sebastian. *Cosmographiae universalis*. Basel: Henricus Petri, 1550.

Mustawfi, Hamd-Allah. *The Geographical Part of the Nuzhat-al-Qulub by Hamd-Allah Mustawfi of Qazwin in 740 (1340)*. Translated by Guy Le Strange. Leyden: E. J. Brill, 1919.

Necipoglu, Gülru. "Framing the Gaze in Ottoman, Safavid, and Mughal Palaces." *Ars Orientalis* 23: 303–342.

Obeyesekere, Gananath. *The Apotheosis of Captain Cook: European Mythmaking in the Pacific*. Princeton: Princeton University Press, 1992.

Ochsenbach, Johan. *Gvlistan. Das ist, Königlicher Rosengart: Des persischen Poeten Sa'di. Durch Johan Friderich Ochssenbach, aus dem Frantzösischen in das Teutsche gebracht*. Tübingen, 1636.

Olearius, Adam. *Adam Olearii Außführliche Beschreibung Der Kundbaren Reyse Nach Muscow und Persien* . . . Third ed. Schleswig: Johan Holwein, 1663.

Olearius, Adam. *Beschrijvingh Van de Nieuwe Parciaensche oste Orientaelsche Reyse, welck door gelegentheyt van een Holsteynische Ambassade, aen den Koningh in Persien gheschiet is. Waer Inne De ghelgentheyt der plaetsen en Landen, door welcke de reyse gegaen is, als voornamelijck Ruslant, Tartarien en Persien. Mitsgaders, Der selver in woonders nature, Leven, wesen en Religie, vlytigh beschreven is. Door Mr. Adamus Olearius, Van Aschersleben uyt Saxen, Mathematicus van 't Vorstelijk Holsteynsche Hof. Ende nu in onse Tael overgeset, Door Dirck Van Wageninge, Met een Register verbetert, en Kopere Platen verciert.* Translated by Dirck van Wageninge. Utrecht: Lambert Roeck, 1651.

Olearius, Adam. *Gottorffische Kunst-Cammer Worinnen Allerhand ungemeine Sachen So theils die Natur theils künstliche Hände hervor gebracht und bereitet. Von diesem Aus allen vier Theilen der Welt zusammen getragen. Jetzo beschrieben Durch Adam Olearium, Bibliothecarium und Antiquarium auff der Fürstl. Residentz Gottorf.* Schleswig: Holwein, 1666.

Olearius, Adam. *Kurtzer Begriff Einer Holsteinischen Chronic Oder Summarische Beschreibung der denckwürdigsten Geschichten so innerhalb 200. und mehr Jahren nemblich von Anno 1448 biß 1663 in den NordLanden sonderlich in Holstein sich begeben. Alles auß bekanten Geschicht=Schreibern so auff der andern Seiten nahmhafftig gemachet. Auffs kürzest zusammen getragen durch A. O.* Schleswig: Schultze, 1674.

Olearius, Adam. *Moskowitische und persische Reise: die holsteinische Gesandtschaft beim Schah, 1633-1639.* Edited by Detlef Haberland. Stuttgart: Thienemann, Edition Erdmann, 1986.

Olearius, Adam. *Offt begehrte Beschreibung Der Newen Orientalischen Rejse, So durch Gelegenheit einer Holstein Legation an den König in Persien geschehen* . . . Schleswig: zur Glocken, 1647.

Olearius, Adam. *Persianischer Rosenthal. In welchem viel lustige Historien scharffsinnige Reden und nützliche Regeln. Vor 400. Jahren von einem Sinnreichen Poeten Schich Saadi in Persischer Sprach beschrieben. Jetzo aber von Adamo Oleario, Mit zuziehung eines alten Persianers Namens Hakwirdi übersetzet in Hochdeutscher Sprache heraus gegeben und mit vielen Kupfferstücken gezieret. . . . Schleßwig In der Fürstl. Druckerey gedruckt durch Johann Holwein. Bey Johann Nauman Buchhändelern in Hamburg. Im Jahr 1654.* Schleswig: Johann Holwein, 1654.

Olearius, Adam. *The Travels of Olearius in seventeenth-century Russia.* Translated by Samuel Baron. Edited by Samuel Baron. Stanford: Stanford University Press, 1967.

Olearius, Adam. *Vermehrte Newe Beschreibung der Muscowitischen und Persischen Reyse.* Edited by Dieter Lohmeier. 1656 ed., *Deutsche Neudrucke 21.* Tübingen: Max Niemeyer, 1971.

Olearius, Adam. *Von Unbeständigkeit der Weltlichen Dinge und von Herrligkeit und Lobe der Tugend.* Schleswig, 1650.

Olearius, Adam. *Viaggi di Moscovia degli anni 1633 . . .* Viterbo, 1658.

Olearius, Adam. *The Voyages & Travels of the Ambassadors.* Translated by John Davies. London: Thomas Dring and John Starkey, 1662.

Olearius, Adam. *Voyages Très-curieux & très renommez faits en Moscovie, Tartarie et Perse, Par le Sr. Adam Olearius.* Translated by De Wicquefort. Amsterdam: Michel Charles Le Ce'Ne, 1727.

Opmeer, Petrus. *Opus Chronographicum.* Antverpiae,1611.

Ortelius, Abraham. *Theatrum Orbis Terrarum.* Antverpiae: Apud A. D. Diesth, 1570.

Osterhammel, Jürgen. "Reisen an die Grenzen der Alten Welt: Asien im Reisebericht des 17. und 18. Jahrhunderts." In *Der Reisebericht*, edited by Peter Brenner, 224–260. Frankfurt a. M.: Suhrkamp, 1989.

Planhol, Xavier de. "Caspian." In *Encylopaedia Iranica*, edited by Ehsan Yarshater, 48–61. Costa Mesa, CA: Mazda Publishers, 1992.

Pleithner, Regina, ed. *Reisen des Barock. Selbst- und Fremderfahrung und ihre Darstellung. Beiträge zum Kolloquium der Arbeitsgruppe Kulturgeschichte des Barockzeitalters an der Herzog-August-Bibliothek Wolfenbüttel vom 10. bis 12. Juni 1989.* Vol. 45, *Abhandlungen zur Sprache und Literatur.* Bonn: Romanistischer Verlag, 1991.

Porteman, Karel. *Inleiding tot de Nederlandse emblemataliteratuur.* Groningen: Wolters-Noordhoff, 1977.

Pratt, Mary Louise. "Fieldwork in Common Places." In *Writing Culture: The Poetics and Politics of Ethnography*, edited by James Clifford and George Marcus. Berkeley: University of California Press, 1986.

Pratt, Mary Louise. *Imperial Eyes: Travel Writing and Transculturation.* London: Routledge, 1992.

Ptolemy, Claudius. *Geographia.* Edited by Sebastian Münster. Introduction by Raleigh Skelton ed. Amsterdam (Basle, 1540): Theatrum Orbis Terrarum, 1966.

Ptolemy, Claudius. *La Geographia di Claudio Tolomeo Alessandrino, Nuovamente tradotta di Greco in Italiano.* Translated by Ieronimus Ruscelli. Venetia: Giordano Ziletti, 1564.

Ptolemy, Claudius, and Iacopo Gastaldi. *La Geografia di Claudio Ptolomeo Alessandrino.* Venetia: Giovanni Pederezano, 1548.

Pullapilly, Cyriac K., and Edwin J. Van Kley, eds. *Asia and the West: Encounters and Exchanges from the Age of Explorations. Essays in Honor of Donald F. Lach.* Notre Dame: Cross Cultural Publications, 1986.

Randow, Godela von. "Das Leichenbegängnis für Herzog Friedrich III. von Schleswig-Holstein-Gottorf." In *Gottorf im Glanz des Barock. Kunst und Kultur am Schleswiger Hof, 1544–1713*, edited by Heinz Spielmann and Jan Drees, 399–406. Schleswig: Wachholtz, 1997.

Rassem, Mohammed, and Justin Stagl, eds. *Geschichte der Staatsbeschreibung: ausgewählte Quellentexte 1456–1813.* Berlin: Akademie Verlag, 1994.

Robinson, Basil W. *Fifteenth-Century Persian Painting: Problems and Issues.* New

York: New York University Press, 1991.

Ruscelli, Girolamo. *Le Imprese Illvstri Con Espositioni, Et Discorsi* . . . Venetia, 1566.

Russell, Daniel S. *The Emblem and Device in France.* Lexington, KY: French Forum, 1985.

Saadi. *The Rose Garden (Gulistan).* Translated by Omar Ali-Shah. Reno, Nevada: Tractus, 1997.

Saavedra Fajardo, Diego de. *Idea de un príncipe político christiano.* Madrid, 1640.

Saba, M. *Bibliographie méthodique et raisonnée des ouvrages français parus depuis 1560 jusqu'à nos jours.* Paris: Editions Domat-Montchrestien, 1936.

Sadeler, Gilles. *Vestigi delle Antichità di Roma.* Prague, 1606.

Sa'di-ye Sirazi, Mosleho'd-Din. *The Gulistan or Rose Garden of Sa'di.* Translated by Edward Rehatsek. London: George Allen & Unwin, 1964.

Said, Edward. *Orientalism.* New York: Vintage, 1979.

Sánchez Pérez, Aquilino. *La literatura emblemática española: (siglos XVI y XVII).* Madrid: Sociedad General Española de Libreria, 1977.

Savory, Roger. *Iran under the Safavids.* Cambridge: Cambridge University Press, 1980.

Schedel, Hartmann. *Liber Chronicarum.* Nuremberg: Antonius Koberger, 1493.

Schlee, Ernst. "August John, ein Künstler in Gottorfer Diensten." *Nordelbingen: Beiträge zur Kunst- und Kulturgeschichte* 51 (1982): 77–125.

Schlee, Ernst. *Der Gottorfer Globus Herzog Friedrichs III.* Heide in Holstein: Westholsteinische Verlagsanstalt Boyens & Co., 1991.

Schlee, Ernst. "Kupferstecher im Umkreis des Gottorfer Hofes." In *Von allerhand Figuren und Abbildungen: Kupferstecher des 17. Jahrhunderts im Umkreis des Gottorfer Hofes,* edited by Holger Borzikowsky, 7-55. Husum: Husum Druck- und Verlagsgesellschaft, 1981.

Schmied–Kowarzik, Wolfdietrich, and Justin Stagl, eds. *Grundfragen der Ethnologie: Beiträge zur gegenwärtigen Theorie-Diskussion.* 2nd ed. Berlin: Reimer Verlag, 1993.

Schmidt, Harry. *Jürgen Ovens, Sein Leben und seine Werke. Ein Beitrag zur Geschichte der Niederländischen Malerei im XVII. Jahrhundert.* Kiel: Selbstverlag des Verfassers Dr. Harry Schmidt, 1922

Schöne, Albrecht. *Emblematik und Drama im Zeitalter des Barock.* München: Beck, 1964.

Schuster-Walser, Sibylla. *Das Safawidische Persien im Spiegel Europäischer Reiseberichte (1502–1722): Untersuchungen zur Wirtschafts- und Handelspolitik.* Baden-Baden: Bruno Grimm, 1970.

Shirley, Rodney. "The Decorative Cartographic Title-Page." *Map Collector,* no. 41, Winter (1987): 3-8.

Shirley, Rodney W. *The Mapping of the World: Early Printed World Maps, 1472–1700.* London: Holland Press, 1987.

Siebmacher, Johann. *New Wapenbuch.* Norimbergae, 1605.

Sluperius, Ioannis. *Omnium Fere Gentivm, nostraeq'; aetatis Nationum, Habitus &*

Effigies. In eosdem Ioannis Sluperij Herzelensis Epigrammata. Adiecta ad singulas Icones Gallica Tetrasticha. Antverpiae: Ioannes Bellerus, 1572.

Solis, Virgil. *Wappenbüchlein.* Nuremberg, 1556.

Spielmann, Heinz. "Die Persien-Mission Herzog Friedrichs III. und ihre Folgen." In *Gottorf im Glanz des Barock. Kunst und Kultur am Schleswiger Hof, 1544–1713,* edited by Heinz Spielmann and Jan Drees. Vol. 3: 53–58. Schleswig: Wachholtz, 1997.

Spivak, Gayatri Chakravorty. *In Other Worlds: Essays in Cultural Politics.* New York: Routledge, 1987.

Sprachman, Paul. "'Le beau garçon sans merci:' The Homoerotic Tale in Arabic and Persian." In *Homoeroticism in Classical Arabic Literature,* edited by J. W. Wright and Everett K. Rowson, 192–209. New York: Columbia Univesity Press, 1997.

Stagl, Justin. *Kulturanthropologie und Gesellschaft. Eine wissenschaftliche Darstellung der Kulturanthropologie und Ethnologie.* 2nd ed. Berlin: Reimer, 1981.

Strack, Thomas. *Exotische Erfahrung und Intersubjektivität. Reiseberichte im 17. und 18. Jahrhundert. Genregeschichtliche Untersuchung zu Adam Olearius — Hans Egede — Georg Forster.* Paderborn: Igel Verlag, 1994.

Straten, Roelof van. *An Introduction to Iconography.* Translated by Patricia de Man. Amsterdam: Gordon and Breach, 1994.

Strauss, Gerald. *Sixteenth-Century Germany: Its Topography and Topographers.* Madison: University of Wisconsin Press, 1959.

Strauss, Walter L. *The German Single-Leaf Woodcut, 1550–1600. A Pictorial Catalogue.* Vol. 2. New York: Abaris Books, 1975.

Struys, Jan. *Johann J. Straußens Reisen durch Griechenland, Moscau, Tarterey, Ostindien, und andere Theile der Welt.* Amsterdam, 1678.

Struys, Jan. *Les Voyages de Jean Struys en Moscovie, en Tartarie, aux Indes, et en d'autres pays etrangers.* Translated by Monsieur Glanius. Amstredam: La Veuve Iacob van Meurs, 1681.

Struys, Jean. *Les Voyages de Jean Struys en Moscovie, en Tartarie, en Perse . . .* Amsterdam, 1718.

Struys, John. *The Perillous and most Unhappy Voyages of John Struys . . .* Translated by John Morrison. London: Samuel Smith, 1683.

Szyrocki, Marian. *Die deutsche Literatur des Barock.* Stuttgart: Reclam, 1979.

Tanavoli, Parviz. *Lion Rugs: The Lion in the Art and Culture of Iran.* Basel: Werner Druck AG, 1985.

Tervarent, Guy de. "Lion." In *Attributs et symboles dans l'art profane: Dictionnaire d'un langage perdu (1450–1600),* 289–294. Genève: Librairie Droz, 1997.

Tibbets, Gerald R. "The Beginnings of a Cartographic Tradition." In *Cartography in the Traditional Islamic and South Asian Societies,* edited by J. Brian Harley and David Woodward, 90–107. Chicago: Chicago University Press, 1992.

Tibbets, Gerald R. "Later Cartographic Developments." In *Cartography in the Traditional Islamic and South Asian Societies,* edited by J. Brian Harley and David Woodward, 137–55. Chicago: University of Chicago Press, 1992.

Vogellehner, Dieter. Introduction to *Der Garten von Eichstätt: Das große Herbarium des Basilius Besler von 1613*. München: Schirmer/Mosel Verlag, 1988.

Wallis, Helen, and Arthur Robinson. *Cartographical Innovations: An International Handbook of Mapping Terms to 1900*. St. Albans, Herts: Map Collector Publications, 1987.

Weigel, Hans. *Habitus praecipuorum populorum, tam virorum quam foeminarum Singulari arte depicti. Trachtenbuch; darin fast allerley und der fürnembsten Nationen, die heutigs tags bekandt sein, Kleidungen beyde wie es bey Manns und Weibspersonen gebreuchlich, mit allem vleiss abgerissen sein, sehr lustig und kurtz-weilig zusehen*. Nürmberg, 1577.

Welu, James A. "The Sources and Development of Cartographic Ornamentation in the Netherlands." In *Art and Cartography: Six Historical Essays*, edited by David Woodward, 147–173. Chicago: University of Chicago Press, 1987.

White, Hayden. *Tropics of Discourse*. Baltimore: The Johns Hopkins Press, 1978.

Wilson, Arnold T. *A Bibliography of Persia*. Oxford: Clarendon Press, 1930.

Winter, H. J. J. "Persian Science in Safavid Times." In *The Cambridge History of Iran*. Cambridge: Cambridge University Press, 1986.

Witt, Reimer. *Die Anfänge von Kartographie und Topographie Schleswig-Holsteins, 1475–1652*. Heide in Holstein: Westholsteinische Verlagsanstalt Boyens & Co., 1982.

Woldan, Erich. "A Circular, Copper-Engraved, Medieval World Map." *Imago Mundi* 11 (1954): 12–16.

Yohannan, John. *The Poet Sa'di: A Persian Humanist*. Lanham, MD: University Press of America, 1987.

Young, Robert. *White Mythologies: Writing History and the West*. London: Routledge, 1990.

Zandvliet, Kees. *De Groote Waereld In't Kleen Geschildert: Nederlandse kartografie tussen de middeleeuwen en de industriële revolutie*. Alphen aan den Rijn: Canaletto, 1985.

Zincgref, Julius Wilhelm. *Teutscher Nation Klugaußgesprochene Weißheit Das ist: . . . Lehrreiche Sprüche geschwinde Anschläg artige Hoffreden denckwürdige Schertzfragen Antworten Gleichnüsse vnd was dem allen gleichförmig von Griechen Apophthegmata genandt ist . . . Auß allerhand Schrifften zusammen getragen . . .* Amsterdam, 1653.

Zöllner, Rudolf. "Zum Kartenschmuck der Mejer-Landkarten in Danckwerths Neue Landesbeschreibung von 1652." In *Von allerhand Figuren und Abbildungen: Kupferstecher des 17. Jahrhunderts im Umkreis des Gottorfer Hofes*, edited by Holger Borzikowsky, 99–112. Husum: Husum Druck- und Verlagsgesellschaft, 1981.

Zygulski, Zdzislaw. *Ottoman Art in the Service of the Empire*. New York: New York University Press, 1992.

Index